The Poetics of Enclosure

The Poetics of

//

Enclosure

American Women Poets
from Dickinson to Dove

Lesley Wheeler

///

The University of Tennessee Press • Knoxville

An earlier version of chapter 1 appeared as "What Death Will Buy: Escaping Gender in Emily Dickinson" in *Nature, Woman, and the Art of Politics,* ed. Eduardo A. Velásquez (2000). It is reprinted by permission of Rowman and Littlefield Publishers, Inc.

Selections from *The Collected Poems of Marianne Moore* by Marianne Moore. Copyright © 1941 by Marianne Moore, copyright renewed © 1969. Reprinted with the permission of Scribner, a Division of Simon & Schuster, Inc.

Selections from *The Collected Poems of Marianne Moore* by Marianne Moore. Copyright © 1935 by Marianne Moore, copyright renewed © 1963 by Marianne Moore and T. S. Eliot. Reprinted with the permission of Scribner, a Division of Simon & Schuster, Inc.

Selections from *The Poems of Emily Dickinson,* Ralph W. Franklin, ed., Cambridge, Mass.: The Belknap Press of Harvard University Press, copyright © 1998 by the President and Fellows of Harvard College. Copyright © 1951, 1955, 1979 by the President and Fellows of Harvard College. Reprinted by permission of the publishers and the Trustees of Amherst College.

"Insomnia" from *The Complete Poems 1927–1979* by Elizabeth Bishop. Copyright © 1979, 1983 by Alice Helen Methfessel. Reprinted by permission of Farrar, Straus and Giroux, LLC.

This book is printed on acid-free paper.

Library of Congress Cataloging-in-Publication Data

Wheeler, Lesley, 1967–
The poetics of enclosure: American women poets from Dickinson to Dove/Lesley Wheeler.—1st ed.
p. cm.
Includes bibliographical references and index.
ISBN 1-57233-197-6 (cl: alk. paper)
1. American poetry—Women authors—History and criticism. 2. Women and literature—United States. I. Title.
PS147 .W47 2002
811.009'9287—dc21   2002003608

for Chris
Gavaler

Contents

Acknowledgments

I've watched many houses rise from empty lots more nimbly than this one. I have many to recognize for their contributions to these seven rooms.

First, heartfelt thanks to A. Walton Litz and John Shoptaw for their crucial guidance in early construction.

I'm tremendously grateful for help from Cristanne Miller and Linda Kinnahan; they should receive much of the credit for what succeeds in this study. Joyce Harrison's encouragement and advice made this book possible. I also benefited from generous and intelligent readings by many others, including Edward Adams, Lisa Celovsky, Marc Conner, Suzanne Keen, Janet Gray, Kary Smout, Jim Warren, and Molly Weigel.

I received financial support at various stages of this project from the following sources: Washington and Lee University, through Glenn Grants, a Robert E. Lee Research Grant, and a Hewlett-Mellon/ Class of '62 Fellowship; the American Association of University Women for a Summer Faculty Fellowship; Princeton University for my graduate fellowship and a Robert H. Taylor Research Award; and the Garden State Fellowship program.

Thanks to the staff at Washington and Lee's Leyburn Library for all their labors on my behalf, especially the Inter-Library Loan Department.

Some of the text printed here appeared elsewhere in different versions. Part of chapter 1 was published as an essay entitled "What Death Will Buy: Escaping Gender in Emily Dickinson," in *Nature, Woman,*

x

and the Art of Politics, edited by Eduardo A. Velásquez (Lanham, Md.: Rowman & Littlefield, 2000), pp. 329–40, and is included here by permission of Rowman & Littlefield Publishers, Inc. A portion of chapter 4 appeared in *Callaloo* 24.1 (2001): 227–35 as "Heralding the Clear Obscure: Gwendolyn Brooks and Apostrophe." *Critical Matrix* 10.1–2 (1996) printed a review essay, "Attitudes of Mothering: Review of Rita Dove's *Mother Love*," which became part of my final chapter. I also acknowledge permission to reprint the following quotations: poems 605 and 644 reprinted by permission of the publishers and the Trustees of Amherst College from *The Poems of Emily Dickinson*, Ralph W. Franklin, ed., Cambridge, Mass.: The Belknap Press of Harvard University Press, Copyright © 1998 by the President and Fellows of Harvard College. Copyright © 1951, 1955, 1979 by the President and Fellows of Harvard College. "Insomnia" from *The Complete Poems 1927–1979* by Elizabeth Bishop. Copyright © 1979, 1983 by Alice Helen Methfessel. Reprinted by permission of Farrar, Straus and Giroux, LLC.

Last: my family furnished the toolbox. Madeleine and Cameron, wonderful and patient as they are, taught me sympathy for houses. Chris Gavaler helped provide land, materials, crew, architectural savvy, scaffolding, insurance, and may have performed an exorcism or two. I thank him most of all.

Introduction

Each poem has its house of sound, its own geo-
graphical reverberations. And we could analyze
poets for their preferences in domiciles, linguisti-
cally speaking: how, in her last poems, Anne Sexton
traded in her cellar, complete with its Freudian guilt
and the rat gnawing inside her, for . . . the yawning
depths of the sea (another kind of cellar). . . . Or
consider the extreme verticality of Sylvia Plath. . . .
Rather than say that Plath inhabited staircases, I
imagine her in a Manhattan elevator, with all the
thrilling dread of the attendant drops and lifts of the
stomach. Then there are Theodore Roethke's green-
houses, Lucille Clifton's kitchens, Richard Hugo's
Western roadside taverns, Elizabeth Bishop's inscrut-
able childhood houses or, later, her adult bedrooms,
snug and secure interiors in the face of Brazilian
electrical storms.

(Dove 1995a, 18)

In this study, I trace an idiom of enclosure employed by American
women poets from Emily Dickinson to Rita Dove. Each poet addressed
here connects her metaphors of shelter and constriction, noted above
by Dove herself, to the lyric as a genre, as well as to reserve as a poetic
strategy. Each treats the lyric, to some degree or for some part of her
career, as an enclosure, and together they express a variety of atti-
tudes towards its felicitous restrictions. My investigations, therefore,
touch on several large and controversial questions: What, if anything,

distinguishes women's approaches to the lyric from other work in the genre? How meaningfully do the terms "closed" and "open" pertain to the lyric? Is there such a thing as a "women's tradition" in American poetry, and if so, what is its relationship to the predominantly male canon? What would a women's tradition in poetry consist of, and, within it, how would influence operate? I focus all of these questions through a single figure, enclosure, as it functions in the works of six very different but strongly interconnected poets: Emily Dickinson, Marianne Moore, H.D., Gwendolyn Brooks, Elizabeth Bishop, and Rita Dove.

This introduction handles the intertwined questions I've posed in two sections. First, I sketch the implications of this study's central terms, "enclosure" and "lyric." Even as I sift definitions of "lyric" offered by various readers, I recognize that no one formulation successfully encompasses twentieth-century practice of the genre. However, although even the most dedicated lyricists challenge generic restrictions regularly enough to upset most critical assumptions, I argue for the continuing relevance of the category: certainly the women poets I read in the following pages work in reference to this traditional mode. Invoking twentieth-century debate about poetic closure and openness, I note the ambiguity of these terms as well, even as I set out the three meanings of enclosure upon which my analysis depends: formal confinement, reserve or privacy in both style and content, and a central dependence on imagery of narrow spaces. The first section also explains why lyrics by women especially feature such figures of enclosure and finds correspondences between this poetic and larger literary trends.

The introduction concludes by asking how a women's tradition might operate within and apart from other literary histories. Section two also addresses my principle of selection and summarizes the individual chapters. These capsule descriptions illustrate both the differences and the similarities among a range of writers divergent in period, experience, and temperament: Brooks does not exercise "privacy" in the same manner as Dickinson or H.D., and Moore's conception of poetic form contrasts dramatically with Bishop's and Dove's. Nevertheless, I show how these writers illustrate a common approach to the lyric that constitutes a crucial and overlooked mode of American poetry.

Gender and the Enclosed Lyric

The first question I pose—what, if anything, distinguishes women's approaches to the lyric from other work in the genre?—remains to me the most compelling and the most difficult to answer conclusively. It rests, first, on a generic category Marjorie Perloff and others have already declared extinct (1985, 176). Perloff's "Postmodernism and the Impasse of the Lyric" argues that the romantic/modernist lyric, that meditation out of time by "the enclosed self," has yielded to a Poundian esthetic: "in the poetry of the late twentieth century, the cry of the heart, as Yeats put it, is increasingly subjected to the play of the mind" (1985, 174, 197). I find her narrative reductive—modernism, and romanticism for that matter, produced many lyrics subjected to the play of the mind, even paradigmatic lyrics by Yeats or Frost—but also appreciate its provocative role in contemporary discussions of the genre.

In Northrop Frye's mid-century anatomy of literary genres, he emphasizes "the concealment of the poem's audience from the poet" in lyric, in which the poet "turns his back on his listeners" (1957, 249–50); this characterization codifies some of the assumptions behind Perloff's dismissal. His "oracular" lyric prioritizes rhythmic and pictorial structures over sense and to some extent constitutes a riddle or charm, a "curiously wrought object" (271, 280). Frye's definition highlights the relative solitude of the poet, who utters a specially patterned and powerful language overheard by the reader at the keyhole, as well as the lyric's complex relation to music. Jonathan Culler frames his own generic analysis in terms of readers' four basic expectations of pieces marked "lyric": impersonality created by the lyric's formal order and its distance from ordinary discourse, so that readers recognize "I" and "you" as formal constructs; unity or coherence; significance; and the poem's resistance to interpretation, its manner of mandating a changed attitude towards language from its readers (1975, 161–88). Both formulations suggest that the lyric may be enclosed, in the sense of private, contained, and/or difficult, by definition. Barbara Herrnstein Smith corroborates this when her treatment of poetic endings links closure with enclosure: the ordinary world, she argues, fuels our appetites for "structures that are highly organized, separated as if by an implicit frame from a background of relative disorder and randomness" (1968, 2).

Perloff and other recent scholars of the twentieth-century lyric, some of whom I discuss below, offer or imply a streamlined version of these definitions: in summary, the post-Romantic lyric prescribes a brief expression by a single speaker of a mental state or process of thought or feeling, especially such an expression that retains the structure of song. This generalization, like the more detailed and sympathetic analyses by Frye and Culler, presents a range of problems. "Brief" might encompass pieces from haiku to "The Waste Land," since, as Edgar Allan Poe famously requires, that modernist collage can indeed be read in half an hour's sitting.[1] The term "expression" generates its own discords at least since the confessional mode's decline in favor. The false binary of expressive (an authentic subject speaks through transparent language) versus experimental (the poem concerns itself with its own processes and the linguistic medium) profoundly inflects both twentieth-century poetry itself and the scholarship treating it. This apparent opposition of modes better describes strategies of interpretation—does a reader ignore or seek the smudges and reflections that render visible even transparent-seeming language? —than contemporary poetry itself, which at its most interesting interrogates categories including voice and self without wholly rejecting the continuing relevance of those tropes.[2] Linda Kinnahan's 1996 article on experimental British women writers, for instance, demonstrates how an apparent feminist mandate for an authentic lyric expression transforms, in the works of three British poets, into knowing investigations of the codes of sincerity "in poetries that necessarily put the authentic self under question" (621). As for the "single speaker," many contemporary critics assume that even short poems cannot be monologic, whether or not they cite Bakhtin. For instance, Sharon Cameron convincingly argues for a "choral voice" in Dickinson's poetry, which for many readers has so epitomized lyric privacy and interiority (1979, 207).[3] Further, any definition of lyric that mandates such interiority, that focuses on inward states and processes, excludes too much, especially in the twentieth century. Perloff, in the key essay cited earlier, observes how "the Romantic lyric, the poem as expression of a moment of absolute insight, of emotion crystallized into timeless patterns, gives way to a poetry that can, once again, accommodate narrative and didacticism, the serious and the comic, verse *and* prose" (1985, 181). While the definition of "Romantic lyric" that Perloff deploys retains some relevance as a starting point, many pieces prior to postwar experimentalism defy lyric's boundaries in multiple ways, and yet might be appropriately included under the label.

The significance of form to lyric definition similarly vexes analysis. The twentieth century witnessed a long and poetically productive debate about the relative merits of free verse and fixed measures. The terms "open" and "closed" forms sometimes indicate this distinction, especially since Charles Olson's 1950 manifesto "Projective Verse." However, as Alan Golding nicely demonstrates in his 1991 essay "'Openness,' 'Closure,' and Recent American Poetry," "open" and "closed" certainly indicated more than this to Olson and continue to slip and transform in their relative meanings. Openness, particularly, can signify a poetics of immediacy, presence, and performance to Olson (81), a "radically polysemantic" undecidability to the Language poets (82), and a "poetry of inclusion" (86) to the New Formalists. The virtue of openness (versus the failure of closure) remains clear to all parties, but openness designates conveniently shifting values.[4]

Conversely, I will sketch below why some poets of both sexes have appreciated the closed lyric as womb, as discipline, even as closet, and how the American women poets treated here conceive of lyric enclosure in a distinct way. This argument rests on my assumption that lyric remains a relevant category for American poets. However, many of the feminist critics on whose insight this study most relies exercise a profound suspicion of the genre and most value the women writers who challenge it. The anthology *Feminist Measures: Soundings in Poetry and Theory* (1994), edited by Lynn Keller and Cristanne Miller, presents the history of this perspective in its useful introduction, noting how the lyric has yielded prestige to narrative modes in the ascendance of recent critical theory (2). Within the collection, Susan Stanford Friedman's essay on women's long poems notes how those works rely on "lyric sequencing" to break narrative conventions, but also insists that the equation of poetry with lyric is an "ideological construct" (1994, 17) with negative consequences. Rachel Blau DuPlessis, in "'Corpses of Poesy': Some Modern Poets and Some Gender Ideologies of the Lyric," celebrates the "analytic lyric, or even the nonlyric" experiments of Marianne Moore and Mina Loy (1994, 77). She identifies "a cluster of foundational materials with a gender cast built into the heart of the lyric"; since, then, the genre is "fundamentally inflected with gender relations," meaning inherently sexist, a subversive woman poet must write against it, as Loy and Moore do with dazzling success (1994, 71). A yet more recent study—Lynn Keller's excellent *Forms of Expansion: Recent Long Poems by Women* (1997)—further shows how feminist critical energy now focuses on lyric resistance. Keller does demonstrate in her chapter on Marilyn Hacker that formal verse can display radical innovation, and questions feminist poets and critics who "remain wary of received poetic forms" and "tend to see in more 'open' or experimental forms greater possibility for subversion of the patriarchal and expression of the feminine" (157–58). She also justly resists "the notion that to be a major writer, one must work in the 'major' form," a prejudice that has shaped the careers of many writers and the critics who rest their own reputations upon them (5). Yet her study as a whole, of course, prioritizes nonlyric modes, and particularly celebrates how "many practitioners of the lyric have been pushing the boundaries and intellectual /cultural limitations of the genre" by, to use her title's term, expanding (opening) it (3).

While all the poets treated here do, in fact, mount challenges to familiar conceptions of lyric poetry—as, perhaps, most powerful practitioners do, if read closely enough—they also work in crucial relation to its traditions. All, for instance, conceive of the lyric in terms of rhythmic and/or visual patterns, although some manipulate inherited forms such as sonnets and hymns, while others invent original ordering devices. All, too, allude to the metaphor of the individual lyric voice, while they also demonstrate its fictional nature, and, sometimes, its ideological consequences, through various devices. In particular, they emphasize the boundaries between inside and outside, private and public that the printed lyric particularly highlights. The middle-class woman's special position in the American imagination undergirds this attention to enclosure, but, after Dickinson, the figure also signals successive poets' self-positioning in an accumulating tradition. Where figures of enclosure appear, American women poets are not only defining their lyric practice but also gesturing in shorthand to their female peers, predecessors, and even successors.

Many writers beyond those featured here render the lyric poem as a house, a kind of enclosure. However, as Dove's partial list suggests, and as I will argue, this conception of the lyric has been particularly evocative for women writers, because of the profound and often-remarked association between women and the domestic sphere. The American women poets featured here emphasize the lyric's character as a shelter and sometimes as a prison. The genre of the lyric obliges their "need for secrecy" as do Gaston Bachelard's enclosing drawers, chests, and wardrobes (1964, 81); paradoxically, it also can offer immense interiors, more free than exterior prisons. Dove acknowledges more directly than the others that she is "fascinated by occupied space" (1995a, 19), but the shared primacy of images of enclosure in the works of a string of outstanding American women poets inspired this effort.

Two related factors create metonymic and metaphoric associations between women themselves and the sheltering home. Women incubate all human life at its beginning; women's bodies themselves, therefore, have the potential to house and protect, and half of the writers I treat—H.D., Brooks, and Dove—are biological mothers, whether or not they perform this identity in poetic contexts. This linkage often under-lies figures of enclosure, although poets rarely invoke the actual space of the uterus until the work of two poets this study might have encom-passed, Anne Sexton and Sylvia Plath. Sandra Gilbert and Susan Gubar emphasize this point when they discuss the cave as an enclosure in *The Madwoman in the Attic:* each woman is "herself a kind of cave," they note, which partially explains why the image of the cave can represent both "enclosure without any possibility of escape" and also a "place of female power" (1979, 94–95).

The notion of separate spheres that influenced Dickinson's life so profoundly, segregating women to the private home-as-haven and assigning to them the domestic virtues, reinforces this equation: women constitute houses within houses, while men, by this scheme, possess the public world and the activity and aggression neces-sary to succeed in a marketplace. Daphne Spain treats the interaction between this ideology, gender roles, and actual American homes, schools, and workplaces in *Gendered Spaces*, arguing that spatial seg-regation "reduces women's access to knowledge and thereby rein-forces women's lower status relative to men's" (1992, 3). Spain traces the evolution of ideal houses in the United States, starting with the high level of gender specialization in Victorian homes ("a drawing room for ladies and smoking and billiard rooms for gentlemen" [12]), through to the open floor plans, great rooms, and large kitchens pop-ular in contemporary design. This decreasing segregation in the American homes reflects and influences increased social equality between the sexes, Spain asserts, and, in fact, parallels the reserva-tions about images of enclosure and challenges toward generic bound-aries raised by contemporary women writers.

Women poets employ images of enclosure in order to engage these powerful definitions of female identity. Sometimes, however, their houses and shells also figure the lyric convention of interiority in a manner that bridges content and style. All the poets treated here manipulate the paradox of privacy in a public form, inherent in the lyric but exaggerated in their individual variations upon the genre; all have been accused of, or celebrated for, restraint at various times in their careers. By linking these poets through their alleged reserve I don't mean to underplay the differences in their approaches, which this study attempts to elucidate in detail. Further, I mean reserve as a rhetorical strategy that does not suggest a true self concealed by a poetic mask. Instead, each poet suggests withheld information or attitudes just as, conversely, an apparently self-expressive poet conveys sincerity, through the performance of conventions. Frequently, a quality of reserve emerges from elaborate clues that the poem encodes a secret, as in some Dickinson, H.D., and Bishop pieces. Many of these poets, including Moore and Brooks, experiment with poetic voice to signal its constructed nature and hence the impossibility of revelation. Privacy operates differently for each poet—Dickinson and Moore, for instance, refuse or delay publication itself, while Brooks contradicts her notion of the socially useful lyric by employing astonishingly obscure imperatives—but each does undermine assumptions of authorial presence, challenging the very categories of private and public.

This property of reserve, further, possesses complex origins both in the situations of women writing and in the larger literary culture. Joanne Dobson's book-length study, for instance, convincingly yokes Dickinson's elliptical verse to "the nineteenth-century American ideology of female reticence" (1989, xii). Jeanne Kammer, whose early feminist essay "The Art of Silence and the Forms of Women's Poetry" charts these issues in a brief space, connects the compressions of Dickinson, Moore, and H.D. to the "diaphoric" mode of modernism, employing juxtaposition without explanation. Kammer cautions that "what has come to be called modern cannot be defined or defended as exclusively female in origin," yet notes that "the point at which diaphor takes hold in art is also the historical point at which female artists of major rank begin to emerge and receive recognition. . . . [W]omen artists in the early decades of this century found this new direction particularly well-suited to their experience and to their creative instincts" (1979, 163). Kammer theorizes that while male modernists use diaphor to respond in their art to the perceived fragmentation of the larger culture (158), women poets may practice the same mode for different reasons, such as the "habits of privacy, camouflage and indirection encouraged in the manner of the gently-bred female" (153). The elisions of modernism, in other words, bear a strong resemblance to proper feminine discretion.

Although this study does not propose an argument about modernism specifically, the innovations of the first part of the twentieth century merit a central place here. The poetic of enclosure this study defines arises from nineteenth- and early twentieth-century attitudes and strategies, although it maintains relevance to women writers long after mid-century poets and critics challenge modernist values.

Dickinson, partly through influence and partly through her own resistance to nineteenth-century lyric modes, initiates aspects of modernism even as she grounds the tradition of women poets I trace. For all her justly remarked connections to nineteenth-century sensibilities—I don't read Dickinson anachronistically as an innovative genius transcending her backward era—Dickinson's delayed publication dates her as an early modernist, as her distilled style anticipates twentieth-century taste; her poems exert a palpable influence on Robert Frost and William Carlos Williams as well as on Amy Lowell, H.D., Moore, Brooks, and later women writers. H.D. and Moore were celebrated poets at the centers of power in modernism for at least parts of their careers. Brooks, a writer working at the transition of modern into contemporary poetry, imbibed the imagist esthetic early, although she transforms it considerably in her attempt to reach a new audience; Bishop, who occupies a similar cusp position, uses Dickinsonian elision and modernist indirection as a mode suited to subjects too dangerous for open handling, and undermines her own rhetoric of sincerity even where she seems most personal. Dove's 1952 birthdate and substantive engagement with contemporary trends and issues place her well beyond modernism's scope, and yet she exhibits interesting affinities with modernism's impersonal mode and recourse to myth.

The modern lyric is renowned for its compression and difficulty; it shares these aspects, in fact, with the gendered lyric analyzed here. Suzanne Clark's *Sentimental Modernism* (1991) analyzes how gender functions in modernist self-definition; she notes that avant-garde intellectuals organized themselves through their "adversarial relationship to domestic culture," the feminine, nineteenth-century discourse of sentimentality in particular (1). "Modernism transferred the lover's discourse from an interior of persons to the interior of a text," she continues (6), highlighting the function of lyric space so crucial to this study: male and female modernists "recalled with disgust and longing, by an act like anamnesis, their estrangement from a maternal enclosure as from the vernacular, and their exile in a world of harsh divisions, borders, and separations" (8). The poets most identified with modernism value impersonality over sentimentality, telegraphic brevity over discursiveness, bare juxtaposition over explanation. T. S. Eliot, for instance, advocates objectivity in "Tradition and the Individual Talent" when he describes the poet's "extinction of" and "escape from" personality, and when he directs our attention "not upon the poet but upon the poetry" (1960, 3–11); Ezra Pound's articulations of imagist principles in *Poetry* magazine and in essays such as "A Retrospect" (1954, 3–14) give fuller, more insistent, and probably more influential voice to these values.

Dickinson and H.D. practice this poetic in its most extreme form, simultaneously influencing the literary mainstream towards concentration and offering an alternative modernism. If Pound, for instance, is responsible for articulating the imagist esthetic in *Poetry* in 1913, H.D. wrote the poetry that first crystallized these principles. T. S. Eliot's comments on Marianne Moore in a 1923 review might be made to stand in for the relationship between canonical modernism and these American women writers. On the one hand, he unreservedly praises her "laconic austerity," placing her in his international top five of favorite poets (1960, 48–49); on the other, he says of her poetry that "one never forgets that it is written by a woman; but . . . one never thinks of this particularly as anything but a positive virtue" (51). Moore profoundly influences the course of twentieth-century poetry away from lyric clichés of personal utterance, practicing a deflective and private style, but her power stems partly from her apparent compliance with norms of femininity.

These women poets' intensification of the lyric's inherent inwardness is motivated, as Clark observes, by a revulsion against the perceived effeminate excess of nineteenth-century popular poetry, a reaction shared by their male contemporaries. In *The War of the Words*, Gilbert and Gubar extensively catalog this reaction by male modern poets, finding that "the rise of the female imagination was a central problem for the twentieth-century male imagination" (1987, 156). Modern women poets, in fact, experience the same reaction: for Moore even more critically than for Eliot, positioning oneself as a strong poet means differentiating oneself from Hawthorne's infamous mob of scribbling women.

As women writing, however, Dickinson, Moore, H.D., Brooks, Bishop, and Dove approach their esthetics of reserve differently than their male contemporaries. This mode is protective, allowing them to downplay gender and avoid the stigma of the "poetess." Brooks's early work and some of Dove's similarly minimize the significance of race, while the white poets in this study may encode their varying degrees of sexual heterodoxy. Paradoxically, all recognize this narrowed lyric as the formal correlative of the restrictive stereotypes they encounter as women writing. Mimicry of their peers' expectations allows them to publish (or, in Dickinson's case, circulate her work among a limited community) with a degree of impunity.

The appeal of an enclosed mode to these poets lies in its ability to armor: it creates a walking shelter, enabling each woman to experiment with the voices, attitudes, and scenes the lyric might contain. Since reticence has been a womanly virtue, its practice can be a reassuring mask of femininity as well as an evasive one of androgyny. In such disguises, women may mimic stereotypical feminine behavior and yet compete with or critique the received canon. The poetics of enclosure these writers construct offers both a strategy and a critique —for some, a subversion of modernism and its ultimate expression, and for others, an alternative to and a dismantling of confessionalism's poetic of presence.

The History of a Strategy

This study benefits from more than twenty years of feminist speculation as to what might constitute a women's literary tradition. Gilbert and Gubar argue for a tradition of women writers who confront "central female experiences from a specifically female perspective" (1979, 72); Suzanne Juhasz describes a "new tradition" of poetry emerging from the "double bind" in artistic women's lives (1978, 1); Elaine Showalter observes "an imaginative continuum, the recurrence of certain patterns, themes, problems, and images from generation to generation" (1977, 11). While Showalter emphasizes social explanations for these recurrences, Alicia Ostriker highlights how many women poets "interpret external realities through the medium of the body" (1986a, 11). Ostriker also persuasively compares a women's tradition to less controversial canons of American, French, or Russian literature, insisting that "writers necessarily articulate gendered experience just as they necessarily articulate the spirit of a nationality, an age, a language" (9).

These theories are not without pitfalls; many subsequent theorists caution against reinforcing stereotypes of essential feminine identity and erasing the differences and dissensions among women writing. For instance, Jeredith Merrin's *An Enabling Humility* (1990) illustrates that a women's tradition cannot be neatly separated from all others, and Betsy Erkkila's *The Wicked Sisters* reclaims "women's literature and women's literary history as a site of dissension, contingency, and ongoing struggle" (1992, 4). Jan Montefiore's thoughtful *Feminism and Poetry* raises these problems and more, questioning the feasibility of constructing a "women's tradition" at all (1987). Sabine Sielke, focused on lyric projections of female subjectivity, declares that "neither the concept of a continuous female tradition nor that of a 'feminine discourse' could render the complex relations between Dickinson's, Moore's, and Rich's texts. Instead, their affiliation presents itself as an *intertextual network*" (1997, 6). This analysis concurs with many aspects of these revisionary arguments; I describe a poetic of enclosure marked by ambivalence, practiced with different emphases by dissimilar writers, and yet coherent enough in its strategies to constitute a distinct lyric mode.

Further, many studies have productively linked groups of women poets without discussing the notion of tradition so extensively. Generally, readers describe these traditions as alternatives to or critiques of male-dominated modes. For example, Joanne Feit Diehl posits "an American Counter-Sublime" practiced by Dickinson, Moore, Bishop, Plath, and Rich (1990, 25), emphasizing how women poets "perceive themselves as exceptions, as isolates, departing from, rather than building upon, a tradition" (2). Cynthia Hogue's *Scheming Women* links Dickinson, Moore, H.D., and Rich in their comparable means of opposition to "white male hegemony," describing their "destructuring of the very poetic power they assert" through their divided lyric subjects and resistance to unified meaning (1995, xvii–xix). I might similarly juxtapose this poetic of enclosure to paradigms of openness in Whitman, Olsen, Ginsberg, and others: in fact, Moore does resist what Diehl calls the "fundamentally rapine structure of Whitman's trope for creativity" (1990, 16); Bishop does deplore confessional indiscretion (exhibited, to Bishop's mind, by both male and female writers); Dove links the professed openness of the Black Arts movement to Don Lee's impotent masculinity in an early poem. However, this book charts an evolving and flexible practice that conveys richly various attitudes to the literary mainstream and to the concept of a women's tradition. Delineating a poetics of openness remains beyond its scope, and besides, the modes intersect frequently, since a preoccupation with closure in women's poetry often inspires counter-definitions of liberty and/or dangerous exposure within the poems themselves. Further, while I argue for this mode's special pertinence to women's poetry, men can and have created similarly enclosed lyrics reflecting a similar sense of marginalization, a related drive to protected subversion.[5]

However, many uses of enclosure in poetry by Anglo-American men reflect, rather than interrogate, received associations between women and enclosure. There exists a history of images of enclosure in the broader Anglo-American tradition, if simply in response to the defining characteristics of the lyric—its brevity and supposedly solitary voice. For instance, some British Romantic poetry withdraws into spatial solitude. From the "narrow room"s of Wordsworth's sonnets to Coleridge's lime-tree bower, the male poets immediately influencing Dickinson inhabit enclosures as womblike sanctuaries, from which they eventually emerge with literary offspring. The male Romantics occupy these narrow spaces only temporarily; for Dickinson and Moore they are permanent, sometimes involuntary shelters, and even H.D. and Brooks, depicting escape, cannot shed anatomical and cultural identity with these enclosures.

A brief example shows both how a women poet handles these associations differently, and the complex textual connections that often occur across sex lines in lyric poetry. Dickinson may resculpt Keats's vessel, for instance, into a sealed tomb in "I died for Beauty – but was scarce" (F 448, J 449).[6] According to Mitchell, Keats's "Ode on a Grecian Urn" "brings explicitly into play the multiplicity of roles played by literary space: as feminine object of desire and violence ('thou still unravish'd bride'), as rival and competitor with the poetic voice (the 'sylvan historian' can tell 'a flowery tale more sweetly than our rhyme'), as a 'cold pastoral' which 'teases us out of thought' with its ambiguous eternity of desolation, perfection, and frustration" (1989, 97). Keats's poem offers ravishment, or male penetration of cold female spaces, as a model for writing and reading. Dickinson not only partially reunites the sundered lovers in her rewriting, allowing them to "meet" by talking from room to room, but closes Keats's receptacle with a tomb door, even gradually gags the whispering lips with moss. By doing so, Dickinson mixes tribute with critique, as Brooks does with Wordsworth, Moore with Oliver Wendell Holmes, or H.D. with Swinburne. By recycling, repositioning, and often sealing these shapes, these women poets refuse to be exclusively muses, to belong to the passive and silent half of the binaries of public and private, inside and outside. Consequently, their various poetics of enclosure create poems that prove nearly impermeable, or that demand interpenetrating ways of reading.

Enclosure, further, is identified with maternity in poetry by men and women alike. For instance, Eliot, Pound, Williams, and Stevens take care to put epic distances between themselves and the suffocating lyric, which would forever keep a writer in his boyhood. Women poets, who may themselves be mothers but in any case share anatomical

identity with these enclosing creators, experience the insistent con-
nections between enclosure and maternity differently. Metaphors of
motherhood and daughterhood circulate in many of their efforts, as
each poet uses this relationship to figure the acts of reading and writ-
ing as nurturing and threatening, protective and smothering, but
above all as work that blurs the boundaries between writer and
audience. While I am careful not to conflate femininity and maternity
—these poets do not—I do find recurrent use of this tricky familial
model linked with enclosure and influence in many of the lyric poems
I treat.

The poetics of enclosure I describe does not account for all women
writing; I do not wish to underplay the diversity among even Ameri-
can women poets since Emily Dickinson, a narrow enough grouping.
Instead, this study outlines the history of a strategy, employed differ-
ently by individual writers. Nevertheless, the poetics of enclosure is
a fruitful means of discovering connections and understanding dif-
ferences between many poets. Exploring it means investigating a
"literary subculture" of the sort Showalter describes (11), even as it
suggests experience that is specifically female, such as pregnancy,
although not common to all women except insofar as they are daugh-
ters. Importantly, however, the relevance of female experience to fig-
ures of enclosure does not mandate an emphasis on "neo-confessional"
verse, as Merrin suggests, since the poetry I discuss often resists auto-
biography and remains intensely interested in the material aspects of
its own language (1990, 125). In fact, the poetics of enclosure traced
here links poetry's autobiographical elements with lyric experiment.

My study follows most American feminism in registering primarily
the cultural, as opposed to the biological, reasons for difference in
women's poetry; it also amplifies (and qualifies) discussions of enclosure
and reserve in women's poetry that have been put forward by other
critics. Gilbert and Gubar frequently note, as they do in *Madwoman,*
the likeness of "Emily Dickinson's haunted chambers . . . H.D.'s tightly
shut sea-shells and Sylvia Plath's grave-caves" (1979, 84). I have already
cited Jeanne Kammer's essay, which compares the first three poets I
treat in order to explore their respective "art(s) of silence," although it
does not connect these stylistic attributes with the enclosed images that
appear within the poetry. Terrence Diggory's "Armored Women, Naked
Men: Dickinson, Whitman, and Their Successors" draws this parallel,
briefly sketching a post-Dickinson "heritage" of armor images and a
female "anti-confessional" mode (1979, 135–50). Each poet has also
been discussed individually in terms of confined style and image by a

catalog of critics, as Thomas Travisano does with Bishop's "fables of enclosure" in *Elizabeth Bishop: Her Artistic Development* (1988); only a correlation of these readings, however, reveals the ways their figures of enclosure represent and realize influence and constitute a tradition. Inspired by such beginnings, this study describes an overarching poetic that illuminates similarities within this body of poetry.

This study cannot be encyclopedic; it does not attempt to cover every women poet who manipulates this idiom or even every woman poet who modifies this poetic through a deep engagement with its central figure. My chief principle in selection was the primacy of figures of enclosure to the poet's work. For instance, although Mina Loy's "The Effectual Marriage" and Adrienne Rich's "Diving into the Wreck" interact with the tropes I have identified, and the careers of both fall within the period I have defined, neither's body of work is, I feel, chiefly concerned with the enclosed lyric, and therefore I have reluctantly omitted both. Likewise, I wished to explore each poet's individual handling of the figure, alert to the way each does not fulfill my theories, and not to impose the grid of my expectations from above. For this reason, and as Sielke warns, I cannot forge a perfectly linear narrative for this tradition, although I must place the chapters in linear sequence: Bishop, after all, influences Moore as well as the other way around, and some of Brooks's poems predate H.D. pieces discussed earlier. My arrangement, particularly of these middle four chapters, must belie the complex interrelations of these bodies of poetry.

In "Emily Dickinson's Fairer Houses," I establish a poetic of enclosure operating on three levels. "Closed" has meant reserved or even inscrutable to many of Dickinson's critics, and, while qualifying the myth of Dickinson's mystery, I show how she does treat privacy as a subject and a strategy. I prioritize the house among Dickinson's metaphors for the lyric and note how often she compares domesticity to the grave's constriction: in many poems, she depicts death as a welcome escape from a culture that so persistently identified middle-class white women with the home sphere. The narrowness of the tomb yields a paradoxical freedom. Dickinson repeats this paradox in her formal practices, basing her experiments on traditional lyric forms to demonstrate how liberty inheres in containment. In the final section of chapter 1, my investigation of Fascicle 21 demonstrates how this poetic of enclosure, in all three senses, persists even when her lyrics participate in a sequence.

My second chapter explores this poetic of enclosure as a marker of influence through the genre-challenging lyrics of Marianne Moore.

First, I define what an "enclosed lyric" might mean in reference to Moore, famous for her images and strategies of armoring but also for her antipoetic attitudes; I find that she both echoes Dickinson's paradox of freedom through protection and undermines the implicit attitudes towards language and identity that enclosure suggests. Moore juxtaposes images of containment with descriptions of endless, impenetrable surfaces, fusing the categories of inside and outside. Second, I demonstrate how certain pieces employing formal, stylistic, and figurative enclosures show Moore's dialogue with other lyricists, especially Dickinson. Even by the early years of modernism, but certainly by World War II, enclosure signals poetic conversation between women writers.

Chapter 3 turns from this investigation of influence, sometimes marked in Moore's poetry by womblike shelters, to a more extended treatment of maternal enclosure in H.D.'s work. H.D. does employ enclosure as a stylistic strategy: I discuss both the dramatic compression and the impersonality of the imagist lyric, as well as the pertinence of the lyric genre even to H.D.'s long poems. However, I grant more space to H.D.'s manipulation of imagery of enclosure, through which she conveys her attitudes not only toward the lyric but toward female literary influence cast as maternal. Her early poetry rejects oppressive "sheltered gardens" and scatters the beaches with tellingly broken shells, while stylistically embracing an imagist reserve; later, formally expansive poems embrace enclosure for its implicitly temporary nurture. Instead of depicting emergence from these cocoons in her last poems, especially "Sagesse," H.D. balances depictions of imaginative escape with a humorous acceptance of her own confinement.

While Moore and H.D. engage maternal enclosure primarily, although not exclusively, as daughters, Gwendolyn Brooks joins her poetic of enclosure to a maternal voice often signaled by the definitively lyric device of apostrophe. Chapter 4 demonstrates how Gwendolyn Brooks challenges the post-Romantic lyric with different strategies than her precursors, especially through her increasing emphasis on the utility of poetry in social struggle, even as she also engages tensions between enclosure and openness in her work. Brooks moves from formal lyrics that employ negative images of confinement in her early work to the apparent openness of free verse and an insistence on accessibility in the late 1960s. However, even after she expresses allegiance to the Black Arts movement, Brooks continues not only to manipulate enclosure imagery, but to practice an esthetic of difficulty. Through the early 1970s, her union of these strategies marks her participation in the poetic of enclosure I've described. Eventually, however, her fusion of private lyric tradition with public forms, especially the sermon, suggests her rejection of this lyric mode.

Chapter 5 considers the enclosed lyric as closet. Elizabeth Bishop's poems, I argue, deflect attention from sexual definition even as her strategies signal the existence of a secret. According to Bishop, the very nature of language renders revelation impossible, even as the binary of enclosure and openness deeply informs her work; Bishop's complex position relative to the so-called confessional movement further charges her poetic of enclosure as she demonstrates the constructed nature of apparently personal utterance. While this mid-century poet, like Dickinson, works in close relation to fixed forms and frequently compares her lyrics to houses, she depicts homes as brittle, unstable, and even dangerous; only paradoxically open houses can balance the tension between private and public that inheres, for Bishop, in lyric practice. A similar ambivalence inflects her treatment of female poetic influence, as I suggest through tracing textual echoes of Dickinson and Moore in Bishop's work.

Through Rita Dove's exercise of the lyric, my conclusion weaves together two defining strands of the poetic of enclosure and suggests its persistent relevance to contemporary American poetry, despite pressures towards formal and personal openness. Both the mid-century poets, Brooks and Bishop, demonstrate considerable ambivalence about enclosure in its various aspects; Dove, similarly, finds form and privacy enabling yet insists on the permeability of the lyric to history and community. Therefore, like Bishop, Dove depicts her lyric as a series of unsettled houses, especially in her first volume, *The Yellow House on the Corner* (1980), reprinted in her *Selected Poems* (1993). *Mother Love,* her 1995 series exploring the myth of Demeter and Persephone, evokes two of Brooks's distinctive forms (the sonnet) and subjects (the mother's power and vulnerability), and yet omits Brooks from its roster of literary foremothers. Since Brooks, by far the most canonically secure African American woman poet, offers the most obvious model for Dove's success, Dove thereby identifies herself as an escaped and resistant daughter. "Rita Dove: The Expanded House" examines how two interrelated figures, domestic space and maternal enclosure, link a singular contemporary poet to female lyric tradition.

Emily Dickinson's Fairer Houses

In its spring/summer 2000 issue, *Fence* printed
statements on poetics by seven American women
writers. All had articulated versions of these
remarks at an April 1999 Barnard conference
entitled "Where Lyric Tradition Meets Language
Poetry: Innovation in Contemporary American
Poetry by Women," and the writers had been
chosen, according to the organizers, because
they "straddle poetic modes" (124). Three of
the seven women refer to Emily Dickinson's
poetry as an influence. One, Lucy Brock-Broido,
cites her own "agoraphobia" (120) in the face of Language Poetry's
openness; she alludes to herself as a lyric poet and asserts, "What I
want is a poem which – when all is said & done – acts as a *palpable
coffin*" (120). The others, however, mention Dickinson in describing
their own resistance to the lyric mode. Rae Armantrout, in particular,
describes how "I was drawn to poems that seemed as if they were
either going to vanish or explode – to extremes, in other words, to
radical poetries" (92). She appreciates the play of conflicting voices in
poetry and argues that Dickinson's poems "reveal the fissures in iden-
tity and ideology" (98).

Intriguingly, practitioners of both expressive and experimental
poetries, self-defined lyricists and critics of the lyric mode, admire and
identify with Dickinson's verse. This paradox raises a question central
to this chapter: Why does Dickinson appeal to such a range of writers,

and how does Dickinson's version of the lyric set such diverse practices into motion?

As I suggest in my introduction, poets and scholars of twentieth-century poetry both deploy the terms "openness" and "closure" to designate conflicts over style, form, and audience. Dickinson's critics, particularly when invoking the complexity and mysteriousness of her work, alternately describe it as hermetically closed and radically open. These terms obtain special meaning in recent Dickinson scholarship: insensitive critics have imposed closure on Dickinson by ignoring the indeterminacy generated by her manuscript practices; scholars who respect the undecidability of her calligraphic, variant-riddled "publi-cation" maintain the poetry's intrinsic and valuable openness. For instance, Martha Nell Smith persuasively theorizes how the original manuscripts should shape current Dickinson scholarship in her impor-tant study, *Rowing in Eden: Rereading Emily Dickinson* (1992). Smith raises crucial and provocative questions, and I agree with many of her conclusions; however, I also remark her frequent use of these loaded terms. She deplores treatment of the poems as "closed artifacts" (8), repeatedly refers to the risk of "closing off Dickinson's texts and life" (49), and characterizes print as "sealed" and "fetter[ed]" (53, 63). Smith, writing with Suzanne Juhasz and Cristanne Miller in *Comic Power* (1993), also notes how, "by asking readers to perform as co-authors, Dickinson creates what we might . . . call an 'open poetics'" (12). An earlier book, Susan Howe's *My Emily Dickinson* (1985), implicitly identifies Dickinson's poetic of openness by emphasizing the poet as pathfinder (11), the explorer of frontiers; however, Howe repeats that "the vital distinction between concealment and revela-tion is the essence of her work" (27). Sharon Cameron's *Lyric Time* (1979) juxtaposes the lyric's status as "pure unmediated speech" focused on the single moment (204–07) to the "problem of bound-aries" Dickinson's poetry persistently raises (91). In her more recent volume, *Choosing Not Choosing* (1992), Cameron's attention to the man-uscripts yields an account of Dickinson as yet more radically con-cerned with the status of the lyric. Cameron's term for enclosure here is "boundedness": for instance, she highlights the "discrepancy between the boundedness implied by the quatrain form and the apparent boundlessness implied by the variant" (28). Like Smith, she condemns "suppressing the context" the fascicles provide (19).

Far more commonly, however, critics have portrayed Dickinson as expressing herself through a closed, personal lyric. Scholars empha-sizing Dickinson's style often describe her verse as deeply formal;

in her 1968 study, for instance, Brita Lindberg-Seyersted cites one poem as possibly free verse, judges it a failure, and concludes that "Dickinson quite obviously felt that metrical, rhymed poetry was her appropriate medium" (155). Lindberg-Seyersted also applies the term "private" to Dickinson's invented diction (109) and unorthodox rhymes (156). Some critics identify enclosure as a key aspect of Dickinson's work even as they emphasize her poetic experiments. In *Dickinson: Strategies of Limitation* (1985), Janet Donahue Eberwein traces Dickinson's "pilgrimage from limitation to circumference" (47), connecting the poet's personal and poetic preference for constrictions; Eberwein simultaneously finds power arising from apparent renunciation. Cristanne Miller in *Emily Dickinson: A Poet's Grammar* (1987) stresses Dickinson's effects of multiplicity and indeterminacy and argues that they "provide the poet with the linguistic and psychological freedom she needs to express, or inscribe, herself" (18), the lyric's formal discipline enabling her "to articulate chaotic or rebellious feeling or thought" (12). This judgment modifies Karl Keller's earlier treatment of Dickinson as a rebel roughing up received patterns: he refers to her "Esthetic of Flawed Form" (1979, 326). Paula Bennett names Dickinson "a writer of personal lyrics" (1990, 154) even as she highlights her "process-poetic" (1990, 49). Judy Jo Small, in her 1990 study of Dickinson's rhyme, finds the poet rooted in lyric tradition (47) and yet resisting closure through her "aesthetic principles of instability and elusiveness" (174).

No consensus exists, then, on the extent to which Dickinson practices a formally closed or radically open version of the lyric, although all agree she at least alludes to traditional forms, especially hymnody, and also that she violates them by various means. The persistence of the terms, however, indicates their continuing relevance in reading Dickinson. Further, a few of the above quotes demonstrate how easily any account of formal characteristics slides into a discussion of expression versus reserve. Openness and closure can refer to the content of Dickinson's poetry as well: to what extent, many studies ask, is Dickinson's verse personal, variously suggesting and veiling autobiographical expression?

The preeminent study of Dickinson's reserve remains Joanne Dobson's *Strategies of Reticence* (1989). Like Miller and Bennett, Dobson characterizes Dickinson as a writer of "personal lyrics" (xiv); she contrasts "the reality of the individual female" to "stereotyped 'feminine' experience," signaling her assumption that a real self exists in need of translation (7). Dobson traces how Dickinson alternately rejects, modifies, and accommodates conventions of femininity in the context of a nineteenth-century "community of expression": "personal disclosure is screened through a series of fail-safe devices designed to allay anxiety about non-conforming speculation" (xii). Others have also noted this reticence as a kind of enclosure, and have described Dickinson's Yankee, phobic, or properly feminine reserve. Vivian Pollak paradoxically asserts both Dickinson's privacy and her "exhibitionistic art of insistent self-display" (1984, 19). Interestingly, Margaret Dickie shifts the public/private binary to an opposition between "the social and the intimate," while emphasizing the essential privacy or intimacy of Dickinson's lyric (1991, 31). Christopher Benfey treats Dickinson's "aesthetic of privacy" in a nuanced and extended fashion, noting that "Dickinson is fully aware of her poetry *as* an exploration of privacy" (1984, 34, 45).

Far earlier, poet Amy Lowell delivers a similar point, connecting Dickinson with the modernist strategies such as impersonality and juxtaposition. Lowell links Dickinson to the Imagists through her use of "the 'unrelated' method. That is, the describing of a thing by its appearance only, without regard to its entity in any other way" (1984, 81). Lowell's "unrelated method" is nothing but Dickinson's poetics of mystery, the frequent obscurity of referent that has so intrigued many readers and invited endless, controversial biographical speculation. Later readers often quote Jay Leyda's comment on the "omitted centers" of Dickinson's cryptic poems and letters: "so impenetrable is her reserve," he speculates, "that we may never be fully enlightened" (1960, xx–xxi). Robert Weisbuch addresses her "scenelessness" (1975, 16), David Porter stresses her "absences and omissions" (1981, 5), and Barbara Mossberg calls the poems "riddles or puzzles" containing a "secret" (1982, 7–8). Judith Farr characterizes Dickinson's art as "coded . . . because rich evidence indicates that much of the riddlesome poetry of the 1860s and 1870s was written for a married man and a married woman," Samuel Bowles and Susan Dickinson (1992, ix).

As many of Dickinson's explicators have tried to prove, such statements may exaggerate or mystify Dickinson's difficulty. However, the fraught terms of openness and enclosure do pertain strikingly to Dickinson's lyric practice. Despite the availability in facsimile since 1980 of somewhat clarifying primary contexts (the fascicle groupings), and notwithstanding invaluable studies exploring how Dickinson's cultural contexts do penetrate her work,[1] I agree with Eberwein and others that her "truest perspective remained more vertical than horizontal, more attuned to speculations on immortality (experienced even now and promised hereafter) than on Amherst, America, or the wider world opened by friendships and reading" (1998, 42). Enclosure more aptly describes the persistent interiority of her focus than openness.

Further, her poems epitomize lyric brevity and intensity because of the very strategies of compression, disjunction, and indirection Miller proves. Although Dickinson's lyric practice challenges traditional definitions of the genre, and close attention to the manuscripts betrays her experiments with lineation as well as long-noted deviations in capitalization, punctuation, meter, and rhyme, Dickinson does adhere to the ballad stanza as a reference point. Many have quoted her statement to Higginson in June 1862, explaining that she "could not drop the Bells whose jingling cooled my Tramp" (L 265):[2] although Dickinson never drafted a manifesto, such comments illustrate her reliance on the music of traditional measures. Dickinson remains a profoundly lyric poet even as she stretches lyric's boundaries.

Finally, in a significant analogy to her formal strategies, one of Dickinson's salient subjects remains constriction and, conversely, escape. Dickinson's poetry contrasts her freedom in eternity, where social constrictions no longer apply, to women's limited lives on earth, where they experience constraint through the doctrine of separate spheres. As Pollak puts it, Dickinson "reminds us of the advantages of death" (1984, 26). According to Dickinson, physical death offers women release from the constrictions of gender, extending significant advantages over figurative burial in domesticity.

The first half of this chapter seeks to prove how Dickinson critiques prevailing definitions of femininity not despite but through her treatment of the lyric as an enclosure. Dickinson uses the limited space of the lyric, which she often depicts as a kind of house, to mimic and subvert qualities of modesty and reserve typically associated with femininity. In the poems treated here, the presence of a third enclosure— namely the tomb, grave, or coffin to which Dickinson compares and contrasts the house—intensifies her critique: she compares the positions of women in houses, writers in the lyric genre, and corpses in graves to dramatize how women may suffer from and/or transcend conventions of femininity.

The second section of this chapter reads Fascicle 21, a group centrally concerning Dickinson's attitudes towards the lyric, in order to explore further the dynamic of openness and enclosure in Dickinson's work. Although throughout the chapter I do address fascicle contexts, this analysis particularly investigates the special status of Dickinson's lyrics when they participate in sequences. In fact, although this arrangement does deepen the meanings of individual poems, Fascicle 21 does not "open" pieces to interpretation so much as emphasize lyric containment.

Housebound

In *Emily Dickinson and the Image of Home* (1975), Jean McClure Mudge names the house Dickinson's most "penetrating and comprehensive figure" (1). According to her appendix, poems that mention "house," "home," or cognates of either word comprise about 12 percent of Dickinson's known verses (230). Suzanne Juhasz treats Dickinson's architectural diction differently in *The Undiscovered Continent* (1983), which concentrates on the mind as a space in Dickinson's lyric, but likewise explores the poet's "elaborate spatial vocabulary" (4). Helen McNeil characterizes Dickinson's house as an "uncanny container" (1986, 143), and in *Dickinson and the Boundaries of Feminist Theory* (1991), Mary Loeffelholz continues McNeil's emphasis on borders in this canon, while stressing their permeability and hence Dickinson's proposal of an "irremediably relational" definition of identity (111). Daneen Wardrop's study *Emily Dickinson's Gothic* (1996) grants centrality to the house as a gothic trope, going further than Mudge to suggest a correspondence between the house as an image and the lyric as a parallel enclosure.

Many American women poets of Dickinson's time reacted to the pressures of domesticity by reconstructing the lyric as yet another vehicle of womanly duty: in it they either pursued the charitable causes that were felt to be part of the feminine sphere, or consoled, moralized, or inspired their readers. While rejecting, even despising, this metaphor for her enterprise, domesticity and its defining structure, the private home, have powerful meanings for Dickinson as a nineteenth-century woman. In fact, the house, whose stability facilitates Dickinson's apparent retreat even as its associated cultural values seem to trap her, becomes the master enclosure of Dickinson's poetry.

Dickinson became housebound, although many scholars rightly stress her continuing engagement with friends and the worlds of writing and publishing, especially through letters. If contemporary feminist criticism of Dickinson possesses any common assumptions, one must be that Dickinson found career advantages in her voluntary, and significantly permeable, seclusion, although theories about anxiety disorders also retain persuasive force. Although this physical retreat resembles submission to cultural forces, Dobson proves that Dickinson's isolation constituted, in fact, a unique response among women writers, and thus must bear a complex relationship to nineteenth-century ideologies of femininity (1989, 46). Alternate models for feminine identity were available; Helen Hunt Jackson, a commercially successful writer and career-oriented woman, arose from a background nearly identical to Dickinson's.

Increasing industrialization in the nineteenth century strengthened Anglo-America's pairing of women with domestic and men with public spaces;[3] much of the literature Dickinson must have encountered, including works like Coventry Patmore's then popular, now notorious 1854 poem sequence *The Angel in the House* (1900, 1–153), reinforces these stereotypes. Dickinson's mother, the other Emily Dickinson and the most immediate model for feminine behavior in Dickinson's life, seemed to conform to the type of the quiet, nonintellectual domestic angel. Dickinson's ambivalence toward her mother, her occasional denial of her mother's very existence, correspond with the poet's distaste for many of the domestic activities expected of a woman.[4] She felt, correctly, that her main gifts were other than housewifely.

Although Dickinson dwelled in her family's two houses for nearly her entire life, eventually refusing to leave the grounds of the Homestead or, often, accept visitors, she was not always a dutiful daughter even in her behavior, much less in her writing. She baked bread for her father, in fact using his dependence on her skill as an excuse not to travel, and nursed her sick mother; on the other hand, she would not go to church, avoided chores in favor of reading and writing, kept an unorthodox late-night schedule, and neighbors believed that fights with her father had resulted in her voluntary seclusion.[5] Her poetic railings against a heavenly father reinforce an impression of intense feeling but less than perfect harmony between the imposing, successful public man Edward Dickinson and his eldest daughter. Her poetry and letters also document a feeling of alienation and difference, from her family, immediate society, larger culture, or all three. Dickinson represents herself alternately as an orphan, an outcast, or even a thief; very often, she is a prisoner, a potentially explosive "Vesuvius at Home" (F 1691, J 1705).

Paradoxically, many of the houses the poems describe do not constitute homes; Dickinson imagines herself exiled from the latter paradise. Imagining more satisfying companionship with a loved one, she writes, "This seems a Home – / And Home is not – " (F 891, J 944). In poems about houses that are not homes, in particular, Dickinson's critique of domesticity may possess an undertone of excluded anguish, even though her figure of homelessness may, as Paul Crumbley suggests, mark "an aesthetic coincident with thwarted expectations, a collapse of unity, and a wicked rejection of allegiances to identity, schools of thought, and historical tradition" (1997, 167). In other poems her female body constitutes another kind of house, unhappily, but temporarily, inhabited. In contrast stand eternity and freedom; for Dickinson the narrow "house" of the grave may be paradoxically roomier, even homier, than the above-ground kind. This condition can be especially the case for the wives in Dickinson's poems. Although Dickinson can declare her wifeliness with defiant exuberance, as in "Title divine – is mine!" (F 194, J 1072), even there she demonstrates ambivalence about the union she elsewhere expresses longing for. Wives are "Born – Bridalled – Shrouded – / In a Day – ," robbed of an old life, delivered into a new one that can be far more imprisoning.

Two wifely poems strike dark notes in Fascicle 9, an often playful sequence assuming a range of voices, also including a child's.[6] The variety of imaginative positions offered in this one grouping highlights the ambiguity of her bridal persona. Dickinson's own refusal of marriage does not cancel out biographical readings: Dickinson sometimes uses marriage as a metaphor for other transformations, particularly her commitment to poetry. Some housewife poems may also refer to a private compact of love made with another person, an alternative connection to the impossible legal one (impossible, for instance, if one posits Susan Dickinson or a married man as the lover, as various critics have done in regard to various poems). In any case, Dickinson generally constructs her housewifely speakers in a spirit of negativity about marriage. Whatever and whomever Dickinson desired, she criticized her culture's intimate association of married women with the houses they labored to maintain. "I'm wife – I've finished that – " (F 225, J 199), compares married life, which is supposed to be "comfort," to girlhood, which was supposed to be "pain," with a definite wistfulness. The speaker's decision to marry is "safer," conventional, and by the end of the poem she decides she dares not look back and make real comparisons. Further, Dickinson equates marriage with ascension into heaven, as if marrying is dying.

In the same grouping, "How many times these low feet / staggered – " (F 238, J 187) figures death as an escape from drudgery for the nineteenth-century woman, dying as somehow an "indolent" thing for a woman to do. The poem begins by trying to open the heavy lid of the housewife's coffin, to investigate the woman's situation:

"Try – can you stir the awful / rivet – / Try – can you lift the hasps of steel!" The sealed casket, this woman's new house, strongly resembles the sealed lips of the corpse, called a "soldered mouth." "Solder" explicitly links the metallic rivets and hasps with the dead body, as if the body itself serves as a sort of sarcophagus. The housewife is multiply enclosed: the first box the unspeaking corpse, the second the coffin, the third the chamber where the body is laid out, the last the poem itself.

Further, the poem operates in a housewifely manner. It tends the dead woman, strokes her forehead, arranges her hair and fingers the way the housewife may have laid out other corpses in her time. The word "feet" here, as always in Dickinson, possesses an extra resonance. Elsewhere she describes her metric as barefoot, deliberately at variance with the constricting "feet" of traditional stress patterns (L 265). Here "these low feet / stagger" the way the housewife's had under the burden of her chores, as if the subject burdens the prosody, or as if the speaker of the poem must shoulder the duties the deceased can no longer perform: as Wolff puts it, this piece deploys "the slow metric of unending domestic obligation" (1986, 206). This poem constructs no clearly defined speaker; instead, it employs the second person, directing its imperatives to the lyric's audience as Gwendolyn Brooks's poems so often do. Dickinson invites the reader to view the body in a strange but apt metaphor: readers of poetry do examine, in one sense, the remains of the dead. Further, while the poem raises the coffin lid successfully, the final enclosure of the dead body remains permanently incommunicado, lips sealed, the housewife refusing to make herself available for any more needy questions.

"How many times" identifies the living housewifely speaker with the actual dead housewife. It also comments upon the posthumousness-in-life of the Victorian lady. In *The Madwoman in the Attic* (1979), Sandra Gilbert and Susan Gubar suggest that the nineteenth-century "angel in the house," literature's ideal woman, "having died to her own desires, her own self, her own life, leads a posthumous existence in her own lifetime" (25). Nineteenth-century women were already profoundly linked with death through their roles as childbearers, midwives, nurses, and sitters of watches. For these angel-women, as Gilbert and Gubar write, this link became a lethal fusion: "For to be selfless is not only to be noble, it is to be dead" (25). Edgar Allan Poe's dubious theory that the death of a beautiful woman "is unquestionably the most poetical topic in the world" (1981, 982) offers only the logical extension of this association. Living female *objets d'art* are dangerously prone to moving, speaking, aging, and otherwise disrupting the male artist's adoration; the dead lady is the perfect blank page for imaginative projection. Dickinson's housewife poem parodies this esthetic: its object suggests a less romanticized literary fantasy than the funeral of a wasted maiden, both through the housewife's exhaustion and through insistently mundane references to thimbles, flies, and daisies. Further, for Dickinson's housewife death is not tragic or even particularly sentimental; instead, real death is preferable to the living death of faithful drudgery. Compared to the tedium of her life, "real" death offers a "Gay, Ghastly, Holiday" (F 341, J 281).

In "For Death – or rather" (F 644, J 382), a poem in this line of argument that comes much later in the fascicles (the thirty-first), Dickinson darkly advises that although "With Gifts of Life / How Death's Gifts may compare – / We know not – ," there is certainly good reason to consider putting away "Life's Opportunity."

> The Things that Death will
> buy
> Are Room –
> Escape from Circumstances –
> And a Name –

These amenities would not be inconsiderable to someone like Dickinson. She did indeed possess a room of her own, as Virginia Woolf famously requires, although many duties pressed upon her and she may often have craved real solitude; room in the sense of perceived freedom remained less available. The last valuable item death provides, according to the poem, "name," suggests, among other things, fame (posthumous, as Dickinson's was).

Cynthia Griffin Wolff writes about Dickinson's difficult relationship with her family name, her experiments with it, and her desire to claim it: "The entire Dickinson family was obsessed with the importance of 'name.' Edward hovered over his only son anxiously—eager that he marry, settle in Amherst, and produce a son of his own. This was not affection, but a strain of entrenched fanaticism concerning the 'House of Dickinson.' He expended no similar concern about his daughters' future: one or the other might marry and produce children, but if she did, these would carry their own father's name; the daughters might retain the Dickinson name and remain at home, but then they would be childless and be unable to perpetuate 'Dickinson'" (201). Edward considered his son Austin his only significant heir; ironically, only

Emily's literary productions continued the family name in Edward's line of descent (Austin's sons died before they produced children of their own). Wolff's explanation of the connotation of "name" for Dickinson also adds to the significance of the word "house" to the poet. "House" can mean family or line of descent, masculine power and its traditional transfer, something Emily Dickinson both designs to usurp and feels hopelessly excluded by.

"For Death – or rather" offers, ultimately, a hardheaded look at a woman writer's situation, based around an economic metaphor. The phrase "Life's Opportunity" here acquires a distinctly ironic ring. Perhaps death, offering seclusion in a tomb and one's name on a headstone, offers a proper lady's only chance of freedom, dignity, "escape." Once again, however, this poem's position within the fascicles suggests another reading: "circumstances" could mean Dickinson's distance from a beloved, and one of the things death might "buy" is a reunion. Interestingly, Franklin notes in his variorum edition that the first published version of this poem was probably based on a lost variant sent to Susan Dickinson in about 1863. This alternate version collapses the three stanzas into one and uses more conventional punctuation, perhaps increasing the effect of formal enclosure. More significantly, the alternate employs a more definite verb: "'twill" instead of "'twould" in line two. In the version sent to "Sister Sue," Dickinson sounds a degree less speculative about death's benefits.

Similar poems appear in Fascicle 26 (1863), which oscillates between elegy and impatience for death with its associated freedoms. One extraordinary lyric, "I watched the Moon around the House," observes the moonrise enviously; Dickinson compares it to a guillotined head "independent" of a lady's body, and regrets being unable to follow its intellectual vault (F 593, J 629). In the same vein (and fascicle), "I am alive – I guess – " (F 605, J 470) unfavorably compares the speaker's earthly home to entombment, her lifeless life to the advantages of death. Physical life, as elsewhere, stands in strong contrast to real "Life," which would entail ownership of her home and body and, possibly, reunion with God or the loved one addressed in the last line.

"I am alive – " gradually assembles evidence affirming the speaker's mortal state. She notes the warm color of her hands and fingertips, even holds a glass before her mouth to see if it will collect the moisture of breath. Still tentative, she notes optimistically that she does not occupy the parlor, where the dead would be laid out and also where the angel in the house, herself a kind of zombie, would dutifully receive her visitors. The best proof, the clincher, is

I am alive – because
I do not own a House
Entitled to myself – precise –
And fitting no one else –

And marked my Girlhood's name –
So Visitors may know
Which Door is mine – and not
mistake –
And try another Key –

The speaker finally knows that she remains a living woman because she does not possess property, privacy, or her born (not her married) name marking the (lockable) door as her own. The speaker's confusion about her own condition proposes a grim joke about the always posthumous nineteenth-century woman, who does not experience what a man would call "life," as well as about her own loneliness. The image of the parlor helps to blur the dead with the living lady, but the whole poem proves the near impossibility of telling them apart. The most significant difference, at least here, is that the dead woman acquires some rights.

Dickinson writes a great many poems imagining what happens after death, as her readers have frequently observed. Fascicle 16 (1862) also expresses a range of attitudes towards its chief subject, mortality, including grief, eagerness, fear, and defiance. Most strikingly, the presence of ghosts such as the "Mouldering Playmate" in "Of nearness to her sundered / Things" (F 337) clouds distinctions between death and life. Again, her lyrics about death often hover on the edge of metaphor. Dickinson writes so vividly from a corpse's perspective, as she does in the next poem, to suggest that many experience death-in-life, an existence apparently without the power to seize happiness.

"'Twas just this time, last / year, I died" (F 344, J 445) offers a first-person account of death in this sequence. Like the rest of the undead in Dickinson's poetry, this speaker experiences paralysis: she has "wanted to get / out, / But something held my will." She is able to hear and imagine what occurs in the outer world—for example, she heard the tasseled corn waving as she was carried to her grave, and remains able to follow the passing of the seasons—but cannot speak or move. Instead, she rehearses her memories of colors and textures, and imagines how her family spends the holidays without her.

An aspect of malevolence poisons these fantasies, apparently those of a child, dead prematurely, given the speculation about Santa Claus and her father's survival. "I wondered which would / miss me," she thinks, "least." She isn't sure her death will affect anyone's holiday cheer. In the last stanza, however, she brightens spookily; she turns from grieving that she may have been forgotten, to looking forward to when, "some / perfect year – / Themself, should come to me – ."

Dickinson's dead daughter, although as unspeaking as the housewife, implies her own hunger. This speaker died at harvest time and can't stop thinking about what she's missing. Corn, apples, and pumpkins occupy her mind; she wonders whether her father might accidentally set a plate for her on Thanksgiving. Her eagerness for her family to join her, somewhat insensitive to what their own wishes might be, also seems hungry, even greedy. This poem presents a dark version of the angel in the house who has become a ghost in a grave: her passivity becomes paralysis, renunciation becomes starvation, decorous silence and attention to male need become frustrated eavesdropping on father and brother, and of course the house becomes a tomb. Instead of devoting her labor and imagination to tending other people's lives, she wishes for their deaths. This extreme version of the domestic daughter is speechless and powerless, but thinking dangerous things. As the housewife parodies it, the daughter stands as the nightmare answer to Poe's idea that "a dead lady is the most poetical topic in the world."

This poem does treat space and time ambiguously, just as its manuscript version violates the traditional lineation and rhyme scheme of the implicit quatrains. "Out," for instance, escapes its place in the second stanza, dramatizing the speaker's desire to move; this stanza's account of paralysis parallels the poem's one perfect rhyme, "mill" and "will," linking formal regularity with actual enclosure in an encoffined rigor mortis. Paradoxically, this speaker later refers to her own "altitude," although her obsession with earth, family, and human ritual suggest she has not attained any version of paradise. The use of the past tense, too, competes with imagery of seasonal progression, as if the speaker has exited mortal time but remains focused on nature's clock. Dickinson's hungry ghost, adhering to a gendered role even in the manner of her murderous resentment, both maintains and unsettles lyric enclosure.

"'Twas just this time" portrays a daughter set apart from the rest of her family and from their sheltering house; it reverses Dickinson's claim in other lyrics to be an orphan, but creates the same effect of alienation. Dickinson repeats this motif elsewhere, as if to emphasize that while her life seems housebound, she remains in other ways a stranger to domesticity and all the values that would seem to be associated with her physical seclusion. In this Dickinson resembles the Romantics, identifying with isolate, defiant Promethean figures, marking her identity as an artist by her distance from the ordinary world.

Promethean moments proliferate in the thirteenth fascicle (also 1862). This sequence revolves around light and, in another sense, it catalogs the various "lights" in which to apprehend or cope with loss. Echoing the myth of the titan's theft of fire, the fascicle's first poem, "I know some lonely Houses / off the Road" (F 311, J 289), takes burglary as its subject. The speaker describes some likely looking houses in out-of-the-way places, and imagines two robbers looting one while its occupants, an elderly couple, sleep. By the end of the poem the robbers are "Trains away" (having escaped by locomotive) and the old couple awakens, supposing that the sunrise has left the door ajar. This poem suggests the relationship of adult children to their parents, figured here as one of plunder. The spoons and heirloom brooches even sound like wedding gifts to a young couple trying to make their own lives elsewhere, "gifts" that might have to be stolen if the "wedding" were disallowed. Dickinson submitted "I know some lonely Houses" to Susan Dickinson, perhaps suggesting a covert, rebellious sympathy between the sisters-in-law. Alternately, the robbers might resemble Susan and her husband. Wolff notes Dickinson's rage when her brother Austin and his fiancée Susan Gilbert contemplated a move to the Midwest in 1854; Dickinson's father's "solution" of building a house for the new couple to bribe them to stay in Amherst, while preventing the trauma of separation, aggravated the poet's feeling of rivalry with her brother (116–18). This episode, or any one of a number of times a marriage threatened or caused Dickinson's separation from a loved one, may provide background for this poem. Finally, "I know some lonely Houses" also implies the artist's antisocial function, since Dickinson identifies light itself as the thief. Dickinson's poems sneak into the domestic scene, critiquing domesticity by the act of shedding light on its valuables.

To the latter end, "I know some lonely Houses" mixes whimsy and violence. It provides playful particulars almost out of a nursery rhyme: barking mice, the moon sliding down the stair, the resident couple's own imaginative reading of the open door (they never, in the poem, realize that anything is gone). Here and there, however, again like some nursery rhymes, the language slips toward the murderous. After the robbers steal into the bedroom for the ancient brooch that matches the ancient grandmama, "Day – rattles – too – / Stealth's – slow – ." These two lines utter a "death rattle," a phrase submerged in the rearrangement of sounds.[7] Leaving home or loving illicitly or writing certain kinds of poems means killing one's parents and breaking up the household. This poem articulates a painful mix of loyalty to home and family, and resentment of this "orderly" world.

Breaking in, finally, links with Dickinson's broken language, or formal irregularities. The poem begins more or less in iambic pentameter, a pattern Dickinson disrupts even there by transcribing "off the Road" as a second line (suggesting her own departure as a poet from prescribed paths). Often when Dickinson's quatrains expand it turns out that the half lines could, in fact, be reassembled into more regular stanzas; this repair work is difficult to do here. Dickinson also uses a couple of unusual contractions, colloquial rather than metrical: "Robber'd" and "Kitchen'd." The word left out in both cases is "would"; this elision moves the theft away from fantasy, toward actuality.

Dickinson's houses can protect but often imprison; they exist as emblems of privacy and domesticity but become repositories of her culture's values. This doubleness produces Dickinson's mixed feelings, played out in such violent incursions.

Fascicle 21: Treason in the Pound

Any account of Dickinson's lyric practice must analyze the relation between individual poems and the fascicles. How do these stabbound booklets, arranged between 1858 and 1864, including over eight hundred lyrics, affect her poetic of enclosure? In this final section of the chapter, I treat this question through an examination of Fascicle 21.[8] This arrangement particularly addresses the lyric's enclosed nature, presenting reserve as a poetic value and finding paradoxical freedom through confinement. Like the individual pieces previously discussed, the fascicle often employs interior space as a metaphor for lyric containment.

Franklin, whose reassembly of the manuscripts into their original booklets enables any analysis of the fascicles, paradoxically grants little meaning to the groupings. Not finding unifying themes or narratives within them, he theorizes in his introduction to *The Manuscript Books of Emily Dickinson* (1981) that the fascicles might merely have served to "reduce disorder in her manuscripts" (ix), simultaneously providing "a record from which she made copies to friends" (x), and eventually becoming a "continuing workshop" (x) for revisions many years later. Finally, he posits, as others do later, that the fascicles might be a form of private publication, after Emerson's recommendation of publication through circulating portfolios in "New Poetry" of 1840 (1983, 1169–73).

The three book-length studies of the fascicles propose wildly various methods of reading them, although all presume an artistic meaning behind Dickinson's collections. Two follow Ruth Miller's argument that all these arrangements "have an intrinsic dramatic narrative as their central structure" (1968, 269). William Shurr theorizes that within the fascicles, a "unified persona" presents a recurring narrative of "the awakening of love, a moment of commitment and bliss in an anomalous marriage, a lifetime of separation and terrible emptiness conceived of as their 'Calvary,' and the hope for ecstatic reunion beyond the grave" (1983, 26, 22–23). In *Emily Dickinson's Fascicles: Method and Meaning* (1995), Dorothy Oberhaus reads fascicle 40 not only as "a carefully constructed poetic sequence" but as "the triumphant conclusion of a long single work, the account of a spiritual and poetic pilgrimage that begins with the first fascicle's first poem" (3). Oberhaus's theory that this coherent "magnum opus" (185), forty fascicles long, resembles a "conversion narrative" (87) could not contrast more starkly with Sharon Cameron's approach in *Choosing Not Choosing: Dickinson's Fascicles* (1992). "Unity is not produced by reading Dickinson's lyrics in the fascicle contexts," Cameron offers; "what is more radically revealed is a question about what constitutes the identity of the poem" (4). She resists the idea that the fascicles possess "a single discernable principle of order" (16), instead valuing the irresolvable "excess of meaning" Dickinson's poems yield in their manuscript contexts (43).

Although my reading of Fascicle 21 emphasizes different figures and ideas than do Cameron's treatments of other sequences, I share Cameron's assumption that the fascicles provide not unity but "multiple orders" (17). Where Cameron, however, finds openness and excess, I discover a persistent interest in enclosure. According to Cameron, Dickinson intended to call the bounded nature of the lyric into question by developing a "poetry that depends on variants which extend a single utterance, conceived as a unitary text, outward into the margins and downward through the fascicle sheet" (14), foregrounding her writing process and opening the narrow and ahistorical lyric to context and time. Rather than demonstrating a counterimpulse to the lyric, though, Fascicle 21 articulates her poetic of enclosure: within it, Dickinson dramatizes secrecy as a governing principle of lyric art.

Fascicle 21 offers not narrative—although it employs narrative elements—but clusters of poems around themes implicit between the texts, created by the juxtapositions. As do Dickinson's other arrangements, it treats subjects from several different perspectives and sometimes supplies opposed conclusions. Fascicle 21, often concerning deprivation and captivity and a corresponding release through poetry, demonstrates the complex organization of the fascicles in the specific thematic context of Dickinson's relation to the lyric. As Martha Nell Smith summarizes, "many of these lyrics are explicitly about poetry-making" (1992, 90). Fascicle 21 demonstrates how the lyric, even when benefiting from the extra information sequence provides, encloses as well as expresses; it also indicates how confinement may be positively transformed, as domestic enclosures yield to poetic escapes.

This particular collection, assembled in 1862, possesses a double structure, a lyric "wheel" and a narrative "journey," to use the fascicle's own metaphors. On the one hand, its construction is essentially lyric and associative. It employs many of Dickinson's favorite personae (child, thief, lover, artist) and enacts their relationships with various enclosures (confinement, exile, frustration, transcendence). Three clusters or plots occur within the larger grouping: one regards death, the speaker's own and/or a beloved's, literal or metaphorical; one concerns facing fear or meeting challenges; the third recounts a movement from a starved, imprisoned childhood into liberation through poetry. These clusters tangle so thoroughly that they cannot be completely separated, yet they fail to explain each other fully. The poems' meanings do not calcify through their positions in the fascicle; rather, the meanings of enclosure and the lyric as its formal counterpart multiply productively through the resulting intertextuality. Dickinson's lyric boxes, like her tombs that paradoxically contain eternity, remain larger inside than they appear from the outside.

Nevertheless, the fascicle suggests or evokes narrative, without ever naming the problem it seems to resolve. The three clusters contain mini-narratives of their own, especially the challenge group, which overlays the fascicle from beginning to end. Dickinson disperses at least six poems about obstacles throughout the fascicle. In the first two, the speaker fails to overcome her phobias: the thief or homecomer cannot open the dreaded door (F 440, J 609); another speaker fears to be "undone" by diving into the sea and a braver Malay beats her to the pearl (F 451, J 452). Later speakers can imagine, at least, how they might climb, cross, or behold Love (F 452, J 453), or they face crossroads with reluctance, but without turning back (F 453, J 615). The sequence's final two poems, however, suggest that whatever this challenge is, poetry empowers the speaker to conquer it. These six poems remain various, and hardly tell any story except in the most fragmentary and self-contradictory way, yet Dickinson orders them along a neat continuum of failure to success and confidence.

The connection between these two structures, these two ways of ordering, is poetry itself, circular in its rhythms, linear in its brief forward march. However, it is a half-truth to say that this fascicle ultimately concerns poetry. Dickinson's fascicle is no more content to be "about" a theme, except in the sense of "around" or "near," than her individual lyrics are. No one poem or plot provides the key; instead, Dickinson predicates this fascicle on a secret inside, an unnamed "central mood" (F 450, J 451) or protected pearl, that she defines as permanently inaccessible.

Dickinson evokes all three of the clusters I have located—death, facing obstacles, and escape through writing—in the first poem, although this lyric stubbornly inscribes its resistance to interpretation. "I – Years had been – from / Home – " (F 440, J 609) sets a scene in which the frightened speaker confronts some kind of a door—possibly to a previous home, as Mudge argues (1975, 50, 80), or a memory of past life, or her own or someone else's tomb. Although she never manages to open the door and face the dreaded interior, through the course of the poem the speaker comes to resemble the house: her laugh becomes "Wooden" ("crumbling" in a later version), her fingers like the "Glass" windows she peers into, emphasizing that she is performing a kind of fearful self-examination. Neither the contents of the "house" nor the motives of the speaker ever become clear, although Dickinson vividly records the details and feelings of both. Her subject is outsideness itself, fear, inaccessibility.

Only in revision does this piece begin to be explicitly self-referential. As Franklin explains, Dickinson prepared a second version ten years later, in 1872, "on notepaper as if for a recipient but retained it, unfolded, unaddressed, and unsigned" (Dickinson 1998, 462). Here another meaning suffuses this scene: it also represents the act of revision, returning to an edifice that houses an old life, long since left behind. To revise a poem means, for Dickinson, to reenter an abandoned house, to "linger with Before," and to risk encountering old ghosts.

Dickinson's houses are often interchangeable with graves; the fact that this poem immediately precedes a lyric about dying to be reunited with loved ones (F 441, J 610) and another that seems to actually enter a grave looking for that lost beloved (F 442, J 611) reinforces this reading. In this context, the house she returns to might indeed constitute a lover's burial place. Fascicle 21 repeatedly depicts separation from a loved one, through death or something resembling it. This separation plot abruptly dissolves, however, with a laying of flowers in the fourth poem, "Could – I do more – for Thee – " (F 443, J 447); it returns in later poems that explore romance and loss, but the fascicle deliberately disappoints any hopes its opening might raise toward a coherent plot of consolation or reunion. Instead, the fascicle suddenly shifts focus to poems more or less about poetry.

Modernist poets, among whom Dickinson has sometimes been ranked, often work with such unexplained juxtapositions; meanings lie in connections readers might infer between apparently unrelated segments, as in the associatively organized "The Waste Land." Dickinson makes clear her own metaphor for this kind of structure in "The Outer – from the Inner" (F 450, J 451). This poem sets out two models for how insides affect outsides (predictably, Dickinson doesn't provide nouns to anchor "inner" and "outer" to referents). In the first two stanzas, a "central mood" becomes the unobtrusive but controlling axis in a wheel whose "Spokes – spin – more conspicuous / And fling a dust – the while." Spokes, the spoken, the radial poems that comprise the fascicle, fling a dust that obscures a steady central purpose. The second half of the poem shifts to an image of painting, as a "Brush without the Hand" marks cheeks or brows with telltale color as if the face represents a canvas for feeling, and yet doesn't write out the "whole secret." Both metaphors demonstrate how a secret can be simultaneously exposed and enclosed through manner or art.

This poem about conspicuous discretion also restates Dickinson's usual priority of soul over body. Insides are always larger, more powerful than outsides in Dickinson's poetry, a paradox that conjures the physicallydiminutive woman with Miltonic ambitions, the recluse claiming a vast inner life. Her use of this binary is informed by Christianity's hierarchy of spirit over flesh; Dickinson looks toward eternity as a life of mind unfettered by gender, or love unfettered by culture, or both. For Dickinson, however, access to eternity and the power she will enjoy when disembodied exists in at least one earthly place: in poetry.

The fifth poem of the fascicle, like the first, explores an unhappy relationship to domesticity, although this time Dickinson performs a prisoner's, not an outsider's, role. Copied onto the same folded sheet in immediate sequence to "It would have starved a Gnat – " (F 444, J 612) is "They shut me up in Prose – " (F 445, J 613), a paired poem: both articulate a child's perspective, both concern confinement, but each represents an utterly different outlook on the experience. The transformative force is imagination, poetry, possibility: these constitute synonyms in Dickinson's work for the freedom that can be contained in the narrowest of closets.

In the first poem, Dickinson describes a childhood of clawing hungers. Unlike a gnat, this "living child" cannot fly and search for sustenance elsewhere, nor can she "gad [her] little Being out," exhausting herself at the window pane, without having to "begin – again – ." As in many other poems by Dickinson, the metaphorically starving child is trapped by unidentified forces in a house and remains too sturdy even to escape by exhausting herself to death as the gnat does.

Poetry opposes domestic captivity in the poem she pairs with "It would have starved a Gnat – ." The final terms of the mortality/eternity, circumscription/freedom binaries her poetry tends to construct are, as the next poem shows, prose and song. "They shut me up in Prose – " compares prose to punishing confinements in girlhood, "Because they liked me 'still' – ": that is, silent. Unlike in the first poem, however, this child feels free even in imprisonment because, like a bird, she can "laugh," a defiant kind of singing, and make the bars vanish. The poem following this one, "This was a Poet – " (F 446, J 448), as well as "I died for Beauty – but / was scarce" (F 448, J 449) and the closing poem, "It was given to me by / the Gods – " (F 455, J 454), reinforce Dickinson's meaning. Poetry, although always written by inmates, defeats prisons.

Dickinson's poetry is also "of" prisons, while defiant of them, in formal ways. Although these poems adhere relatively closely to traditional measures, as usual, her unorthodox use of capitalization and punctuation, her unstable syntax, and her deviations in rhyme push against the bars of regularity. "It would have starved a Gnat – ," a poem in which enclosure is apparently unescapable, slant rhymes "I" with "nescessity" *[sic]*, highlighting the gap between the speaker and her desire; the pairing of "remove" with "move" might suggest the child's blocked imagination or inability to devise her own flight. "They shut me up in Prose – " misrhymes "Girl" with "still" to demonstrate the incompatibility of these terms (despite their willful pairing in Dickinson's world, and many others). "Star" and "I" differ strikingly in sound, but the meaning-rhyme may indicate Dickinson's poetic ambition to stardom, or just her starlike immunity to capture: "Look down upon *[sic]*," the variant she offers for "Abolish," emphasizes her lofty superiority. These treasonous strategies constitute Dickinson's way of "laughing" within a jail cell of form.

The "they" whose tyranny motivates this poem, finally, remains deliberately unspecified. Her indefiniteness may well be purposeful, enabling Dickinson to link multiple authorities in oppression: teachers forcing a certain writing style on students, parents disciplining children, the government locking up "birds" for treason. The pronoun "themself" collapses all these authorities, combining the plural "them" with the singular "self," as if all these forces act identically, with the same goals, the same strategies. As this oppressive "they" heads the poem, the poem's only "I" ends it, in a symmetry that strengthens the rebellious opposition (and the poet's victory, her last laugh). The poet, as defined by this poem, defies, even laughs at authority, although often suffering its punishments—again, a marginalized Prometheus (himself a captive).

The small narrative in the juxtaposition of these two poems from domestic enclosure to poetic escape repeats through the fascicle's larger movement from fear and failure to success through poetry. In "I rose – because He sank – " (F 454, J 616), the speaker surprises herself with her own strength. Here the speaker nurses a lover back to health, spiritually but perhaps also physically, through the "Balm" of her powerful singing. Her "Hymn"'s possess "Thews" and "Sinews" and are muscular enough to lift someone out of a low faint. This power offers the only consolation available in the fascicle's love plot. The challenge of saving a fallen friend differs from other obstacle poems in this fascicle, but in this piece, the speaker finally manages to confront the problem victoriously.

"I rose – because He sank – " is also the poem in which the love plot concludes. The fascicle's last poem, "It was given to me by / the Gods – ," returns to childhood, the speaker remembering "hurrying to school" with a smile of secret knowledge that she possesses a divine gift. Dickinson never identifies this golden gift except by context, and by the pun on "solid Bars": the gold ingots resemble bars of melody, lines of poetry.

This child sharply contrasts the famished speaker of "It would have starved a Gnat – ." The speaker of the final poem feels empowered: "The Difference – ," she claims, "made me / bold." A building discovery of boldness, a confidence derived from poetry, offers the closest thing to a story in this fascicle, yet this development does not occur in a single speaker at a single point in time. Is it the nurturing lover or defiant schoolgirl who first fully realizes her gift? And what lack, precisely, does this talent stand in for? The fascicle suggests linearity, without ever reproducing an obvious plot curve. Dickinson is too much a poet of enclosure, constructing compressed and reserved lyrics, to resist flinging up a dust around the very shapes she creates.

Dickinson characterizes prose and narrative as prisons, but the lyric represented no place for unfettered self-expression for nineteenth-century women. As Dobson points out, Dickinson was socialized at a time when various kinds of women's writing were available and popular, but its content was extremely delimited by the code of reserve expected of all women, especially as far as personal details and "the presentation of a woman's passional life" (1989, xiv). It remained transgressive (even treasonous, in "They shut me up in Prose") to write on the subjects of erotic love and literary ambition as Dickinson did, or to write at all, unless, as Dobson points out, motivated by either "the desire to be 'an instrument of good'" or "a pressing need for money" (50). Dickinson, neither didactic nor destitute, fit neither excuse. Dickinson records her own frustration with these codes quietly, as in her slant rhyme of "girl" and "still," implying a forced but impossible semantic correspondence between femininity and obedient silence. Even the bird in that poem is gendered masculine, as if even in the act of breaking free Dickinson can't claim poetry as a woman's enterprise.

Nevertheless, Dickinson finds in the traditionally contained and containing lyric more room for dissent or subversion than she allows for in fiction. "Prose," in Dickinson, can be read broadly as a way of life that accepts social dicta: grammatical sequence, the marriage plot. Mossberg, who treats this poem as a touchstone, remarks that "prose becomes Dickinson's term for society's value and repressive enforcement of conformity" (1982, 108). Dickinson enacts her rejection of this not only by assuming the role of a social outcast, and, specifically, an outsider to conjugal bliss, but by frequent violations of grammar and form in both her poetry and her letters. "They shut me up in Prose," an example often invoked by feminist critics, introduces her hybrid pronoun "themself," misuses "himself," and confuses things further by suturing her phrases only with the ambiguous dash. As I've noted, she employs rhyme unpredictably, although meaningfully. Finally, the poem stands in a sequence that engages and disengages with at least three plots, as I have discussed.

"I dwell in Possibility – " (F 466, J 657), from the next fascicle, the twenty-second, also opposes itself to "prose" without using the word "poetry" to describe Dickinson's enterprise. Across the fascicles, it seems to continue or respond to "They shut me up in Prose – ." It duplicates the latter's structure, the middle of three stanzas providing regular rhyme, the first and third deviating. Both poems refer to prose as a confined space; here Dickinson compares prose to a smallish, or at least an ordinary, house. This time, however, the outer frame of the punishing authorities vanishes: this speaker chooses her own confinement, not in prose but in "Possibility," which is, I would argue, the lyric.

"Possibility" resembles a "fairer House," with its plentiful doors and windows, cedar-high chambers, and sky for a roof. The speaker's occupation in this felicitous space (to invoke Fryer's 1986 study of space in prose) is "The spreading wide my narrow Hands / To gather Paradise." Even generated by a small woman's hands, writing can cover a grand space. In poems, even eternity may be rendered. Juhasz remarks how the lady of this manor "makes not cakes but poetry . . . because of the power of the imagination, the 'housewife' can be a poet" (1983, 20). Possibility itself, nevertheless, seems finite; the speaker expresses paradise in a fallen language. Heaven too resembles a house, although so roomy the eye/I cannot "impregna[te]" it. There exist windows and doors and roofs in paradise, after a fashion. "Visitors" still come, although of the "fairest" variety, perhaps muses instead of the demanding interrupters a denizen of prose, a bourgeois lady, might expect in her drawing-room. As Mudge puts it, "the theme of limitlessness is ironically built on the details of the house which held her" (188). Narrow hands can only spread so wide, after all. Even the idea of possibility becomes an enclosure.

Dickinson, finally, insists on the lyric as an enclosure, constructed of sonic fences of rhyme, meter, and stanza, limited in length, often thematically concerned with boundaries. Her practice of it exaggerates these qualities: her cryptic language and grammatical strategies cocoon her referents, and mimic Dickinson's experience of confinement as a nineteenth-century American woman. Paradoxically, however, reticence liberates. By not publishing, at least in any traditional way, Dickinson gains space for experimentation and even, as Cameron and Smith argue, widens the ability of her poems to mean by avoiding the definiteness of typeset, authorized versions. And, under cover of mimicry, she critiques the ideology of domesticity in which she seems to be so thoroughly embedded. Her practice of this poetic of enclosure, simultaneously exaggerating and transgressing lyric boundaries, renders her a flexible model for subsequent poets of many temperaments.

Marianne Moore

Freedom and Protection

Marianne Moore employs a poetic of enclo-
sure in the same three ways as Emily Dickinson:
she invokes imagery of shelter, practices a strat-
egy of reserve, and creates formal enclosures,
primarily through rhymed and syllabically pat-
terned stanzas. Characteristically, however,
Moore qualifies this esthetic at every turn. Her
armored manner, so often remarked by readers,
coexists with a strong regard for plain speech
and candor; likewise, Moore challenges lyric
definition in multiple ways that work against
the formal enclosures of her poems. Moore famously rejects poetry as
a label for her work in "Poetry," elsewhere referring to herself as "an
interested hack rather than an author": "I can see no reason for call-
ing my work poetry," she remarked upon accepting the National Book
Award in 1952, "except that there is no other category in which to
put it" (*Prose* 648).[1] Her readers tend to disagree, but observe that
Moore's work does manifest a genre-breaking originality. While most
readily apply the term "poetry" to Moore's verses, far fewer scholars
treat this New York–based modernist as a writer of lyrics.

Marie Borroff renders a convincing case for the influence of "pro-
motional prose" on Moore's style (1979), and Moore herself accents
her admiration of prose stylists in interviews, reading lists, and ques-
tionnaires. However, Betsy Erkkila goes too far in asserting that Moore
"found her precursors among men rather than women, among prose

writers rather than poets" (1992, 102). In fact, while influence studies tend to focus on Moore's complex literary and personal relationship with Elizabeth Bishop (stressing, in fact, Moore as precursor), her prose, letters, and the poems themselves all confirm Moore's significant engagement not only with lyric poetry by her contemporaries (H.D., Wallace Stevens, William Carlos Williams, T. S. Eliot, and many others) but with the lyric poetry of nineteenth-century America as well.[2] Moore's poetic of enclosure, however qualified or partial, meditates upon literary influence and particularly marks her connections to other female lyricists. This chapter begins with an assessment of Moore's methods and figures of restriction, which posit a paradoxical freedom through limitation and blur the distinction between inside and outside. I then demonstrate how Moore negotiates poetic influence in three lyrics featuring such devices: "What Are Years?," "A Grave," and "The Paper Nautilus."

The Armored Lyric

This chapter describes Moore as a practitioner of lyric poetry but, as I've noted above, neither Moore herself nor the majority of her published readers endorse, or at least emphasize, this view of her work. T. S. Eliot's introduction to the 1935 *Selected Poems*, for example, flatly refutes it: he calls her poetry "'descriptive' rather than 'lyrical' or 'dramatic'" (x). While he distances her from some lyric qualities, however, Eliot highlights her formal patterns, noting that her "versification is anything but 'free,'" and declares that "of the *light* rhyme Miss Moore is the greatest living master" (xii–xiii).

Part of the problem remains the difficulty of defining "lyric," especially in twentieth-century contexts. If lyric means intrinsically musical, Moore's poetry employs lyric elements. To Eliot's ear, Moore's syllabic stanzas "move with the elegance of a minuet" (xii), and certainly Moore's unaccented rhymes contribute subtly to the distinctive cadences of her verse. John Hollander hears Moore's syllabics "tuning in and out of the accentual," and notes that she often uses "a pronounced accentual scheme for cadential closure" (1990, 86–87). Others, however, deny this music. Hugh Kenner declares that "her poems are not for the voice" (1975, 98), emphasizing the visual nature of her main ordering device: "if metric is a system of emphases, centered in human comfort, syllabic count is a system of zoning, implied by the *objectivity* of the words, which lie side by side for their syllables to be counted" (99–100). He concludes against her connectedness to previous work in the lyric, stating that her poetry "has no traffic— never had any at all—with the cadences of the Grand Style, with Tradition, but works by a principle exclusively its own" (114). While Kenner rightly observes how syllabic stanzas can resist lyric music, he overstates the visual element of her work; also, while he correctly remarks her originality, he misses the dialogue between her poems and the literary past.

Moore's syllabic stanzas do suggest a visual as well as an auditory orientation, as Linda Leavell observes in her excellent discussion of Moore's form, also pointing out that "Moore herself continually protested the term [syllabic verse]; insisting that she composed in 'rhymed stanzas' rather than lines, she used 'pattern,' 'mathematics,' 'symmetry,' 'arrangement,' and 'architecture' to describe these stanzas" (1995, 68). In fact, the lyric poem has been a visual as well as an auditory creature since the Renaissance. One might move on, then, to characterize Moore as a lyric poet by the brevity of her work: although she composed some medium-length poems ("Marriage" the longest, at almost three hundred lines) and published others in meaningful short groupings, and although Moore's poems rarely demonstrate Dickinson's extreme compression, most of them tally less than one hundred lines. Stylistic and thematic coherence, too, characterize Moore's work as much as any modernist's; thoughtful readers can recuperate her deliberate disorientations, such as the occasional continuity of title and first line or sudden shifts of tone and topic, into meaningful order.

The relatively complex issue of lyric voice, moreover, has rightly occupied many assessments of Moore's poetry. As this study's introduction states, convention prescribes a single speaker for the post-Romantic lyric utterance. As recent feminist critics suggest, Moore's poetry investigates and, to some extent, dismantles this notion, highlighting the illusion of unified voice that so much lyric poetry invents. Elizabeth Gregory, for instance, analyzes how Moore manipulates quotation from secondary sources to establish a feminine poetic voice resistant to traditional hierarchies (1996). Cynthia Hogue, referring to Moore's poems as "hybrid specimens," discusses their strategy of masquerade and asserts that Moore creates "a modern subject-in-process at once constituted by and dispersed into poetic language" (1995, 111, 73). Cristanne Miller finds that Moore "questions authority by exploring constructions of subjectivity, lyric agency and cultural empowerment" (1995, viii). According to Miller, Moore seeks a "shifting middle ground" amid limiting binaries such as personal (sentimental) versus impersonal (modernist) poetry (28); through devices such as quotation and direct address, Moore shows how "the fiction of [the lyric speaker's] presence is a fiction" (64) and creates dialogic, multivocal versions of the lyric (6). Although Miller sometimes refers to Moore's "lyrics," she seems to deploy this term as a synonym for "poems," and certainly highlights Moore as a subverter of the lyric mode who demonstrates a "remarkable openness to the non-poetic" (17).

While I agree that Moore's strategies particularly disturb notions of the solitary lyric speaker, I'd emphasize that her very preoccupation with voice shows Moore's urgent interest in the lyric genre. Further, her experiments with voice underscore the inadequacy of this lyric definition to much American lyric practice. Many American poets challenge the fiction of the single speaker and create lyrics that layer or channel multiple voices: examples might include Dickinson's "choral voice" (Cameron 1979, 207–08), Whitman's "translations" in "Out of the Cradle Endlessly Rocking," and James Merrill's séance poetry.

Jeanne Heuving also focuses on Moore's subversiveness, although demonstrating Moore's continuing allegiance to the lyric mode (1992, 14, 25); reading Moore through Irigaray, Heuving offers that one way to write as a woman is, in fact, by privileging "openness over closure" (24). Margaret Holley's *The Poetry of Marianne Moore: A Study in Voice and Value* (1987) remains the most extended discussion of Moore as a specifically lyric poet. While emphasizing the single speaker as a fiction created by the poem, Holley offers the following definition of the lyric: "to the extent that a poem yields this sense of a person speaking to us, we may say that it enters the lyric mode" (115). Holley tracks Moore's lyric experiments from the early pieces, in which "the second person is the perfect choice for the lyric that expresses the feelings and judgments of the self without spotlighting the self" (24–25), through the "nearly total eclipse of the personal voice in her poems" of the twenties and thirties (ix–x), to the "shared advocacy" of her communal lyric voice from World War II onwards (x). Holley also employs a vocabulary of openness and closure in characterizing Moore's productions. She refers to privacy as "closed circles of communication" in some poems (24), describes Moore's use of quotation as "open collaboration" (68–69), and mentions how the quoted first-person singulars of some mid-career poems "enclose the directly self-expressive voice within a limited portion of the poem rather than letting it be the voice of the whole poem" (81). Most significantly, Holley argues that "her work of the forties affirms not only poetic unity and closure but also concision," depending upon "a classical severity of form that is echoed in the poems' subject matters of exactitude and the virtues of enclosure" (113). According to Holley, Moore practices an impure lyric (123), "open" in some ways and "closed" in others, that yet retains profound affinities with the mode. I find Holley's analysis valuable here, confirming my sense of Moore's engagement with lyric tradition. Holley's vocabulary of enclosure, though, requires sharper definition: in what senses does Moore produce enclosed lyrics?

Although generic categories vex many Moore studies, scholars have far more easily identified stylistic reserve and imagery of enclosure throughout her work. An early study by Jean Garrigue finds compression, self-containment, and guardedness in Moore's style (1965). John Slatin emphasizes the difficulty and opacity of Moore's work (1986). Marilyn L. Brownstein observes that "Moore liked manners, decorum, reserve; 'reticence' and 'restraint' are part of a vocabulary of merit exercised throughout her assessments of artistic achievement" (1990, 327). Heuving qualifies the frequent yoking of the personality with the technique by arguing, "Moore herself isn't so simply reserved, reticent, or suppressed, but rather practices a reserve in her writing for the purpose of altering the very meanings she can make" (1992, 19). Elisabeth Joyce identifies Moore's compression and indeterminate meanings with abstraction in the visual arts (1998), as Leavell remarks the convergence of Moore's spatial form and spatial imagery in her study of Moore's relation to modern art (1995, 91).

Discussions of armor in Moore's work often encompass both style and theme. Some of these analyses fuse Moore's poetics with her personality to suggest a spinsterish revulsion from the world, or at least a submission to traditional stereotypes of femininity. "Some of her poems," Randall Jarrell charges in "Her Shield" after highlighting these images of armor, "have the manners or manner of ladies who learned a little before birth not to mention money, who neither point nor touch, and who scrupulously abstain from the mixed, live vulgarity of life" (1969, 122). Jarrell rightly links Moore's reserve with codes of ladylike behavior, but fails to understand the complexity of her pose, and is apparently blind to her many moments of pointing, touching, even barely veiled "vulgarity." He writes over instances that contradict his image of the relentlessly polite, asexual prodigy, sounding

remarkably like Higginson on Dickinson: "She is like one of those ear-
lier ages that dressed children as adults, and sent them off to college
at the age of eleven" (122). John Hollander theorizes that "a young
woman's vulnerable feelings hide behind the cleverness" of Moore's
polished surfaces (1990, 12), and memorably remarks, "Only the
wildest animals need cages so carefully made" (14). Helen Vendler
hears in Moore's poetry "the aggression of the silent, well-brought-up
girl who thinks up mute rejoinders during every parlor conversation"
(1980, 63). Suzanne Juhasz asks, "What sort of woman was she . . . ?"
(1978, 38), dismissing Moore's poetry as "limited" by a need to be
"'one of the boys'" demonstrated by an apparent "exclusion of femi-
nine experience from art" (1978, 35).

Other readers take umbrage at these criticisms. Laurence Stapleton
suggests that images of armor indicate "a preference for the incognito,
a way to see things in themselves, without modifying them by intru-
siveness" (1978, 19–20). Bonnie Costello argues that Moore's armor
represents not "a protective covering against the force and judg-
ment of the world" (1981, 108), but a figure for internalized combat
and also a challenge to "a political ethos that viewed material posses-
sion, mechanization, and material conquest as ultimate goals" (110).
For Costello, Moore's obsession with combat and armor represents
both "an intellectual and aesthetic principle" (8). Taffy Martin like-
wise insists that Moore's armor does not mark fearful withdrawal from
the world, nor are her formal difficulties "defensive, virginal attempts
to escape" the chaos of the twentieth century (1986, x); in biographer
Charles Molesworth's view these armors and impenetrabilities empower
Moore to venture into dangerous territories (1990). Even in her study
of Moore's prose, Celeste Goodridge cites this critical tradition and
construes Moore's "strategies of self-concealment—her 'hints and dis-
guises'—as integral to her critical stance" (1989, 11).

Many discussions of armoring in Moore's poetry center on a famous
1936 poem, invited to do so by its gently self-mocking opening words.
"Another armored animal," "The Pangolin" begins (CP 117), gesturing
both at Moore's frequent depictions of plated, scaled, quilled and
shelled creatures in her poetry, and at the way poets may proceed via
self-protective rhetorical strategies. According to Costello's extended
and insightful reading, Moore's task here is to unite armor and grace
(1981, 130), Moore shifting unpredictably between subjects to dram-
atize her own esthetic balancing act. "Privacy is the secret of equi-
librium," Martin adds, "and the pangolin is the very embodiment of

privacy" (1986, 16). Holley remarks that this is Moore's first explicit reference to armor, and stresses the poem's historical grounding in "the literal armaments of the 1930s" (1987, 102). Schulze builds on this observation by noting that "armor, then, serves the essential function of allowing the poet to face facts" (1995, 136), and emphasizing Moore's conviction that "verse must confront an ugly age . . . by pushing back against it with the imagination" (142).

Many of this poem's devices and concerns challenge lyric definition, from Moore's dry endnotes and extensive quotation to the absence of a controlling "I." Moore frequently shifts not only subject but tone, from journalistic description, for instance, to lyric exclamation, as at the end of "The Pangolin." Moore's rhetorical strategies often foreground language as a medium that complicates communication; this poem certainly does not, for instance, express personal feeling, although many have argued that it nonetheless conveys Moore's ethical and esthetic convictions.

"The Pangolin," with its nonlinear meander from subject to subject not unlike the peculiar walk of the armored anteater it describes, itself suggests resonances between the praised animal and Moore's own poetry: both are finely and fascinatingly made, armored and solitary, unpugnacious but with "power to defy," "made graceful by adversities," "unignorant, / modest and unemotional, and all emotion." Above all, for both creature and poem "armor seems extra": the pangolin's armor signifies not weakness or fear but efficiency and privacy, the ability to follow one's own "exhausting solitary" way without intruding or being intruded upon. Costello notes that despite the precision of the speaker's gaze, the "pangolin escapes both our physical and interpretive grasp" (124) by being unrollable, repelling the eager speaker's attention and sending the poem outward into other meditations, while remaining the poem's center of gravity. This image mirrors the deftness with which Moore simultaneously asserts and conceals her opinions. Moore follows emotionally charged phrases such as "If that which is at all were not forever" with complex syntax and a blizzard of detail and definition, inspiring descriptions of her poetry as difficult or even obscure.

Armor may be impenetrable, but as a surface it can be, to some extent, readable. "Black Earth" (later retitled "Melancthon"), first published in 1918 but eventually cut from what Parisi calls "the Incomplete Poems" (1990, xi), also casts its eye upon a surface, this time the mud-encrusted skin of an elephant (SP 43–45). This elephant-skin, a thick, armoring hide, represents both a "shell" to "inhabit" and the creature itself. Even the gray river sediment becomes part of the elephant's identity, suggesting the inseparability of self and context: "do away / with it and I am myself done away with." The poem deliberately confuses the world and the self, inside and outside, the looker and the looked at. It starts off in the first person and ends in the third, abstractly seeking the meaning of "elephant," and the lineation cracks open "submerged" to emphasize "merged," the intermixing of elephant and river-mud. The pangolin possesses a similarly shifting identity: he constitutes both a figure for the poet ("night miniature artist engineer") and an art object (compared to Westminster wrought iron, and further treasures), mimicking Moore's ambiguous position as a woman-yet-writer. Moore here layers the elephant's voice with the sensibility of a disembodied observer who doubts humanity's ability to value the creature.

Interestingly, critics have accounted for voice here in diametrically opposing manners. Vendler labels "Black Earth" Moore's "most personal and 'lyric' poem" (1980, 66), while Slatin opines that "of all her poems only this one purports to be spoken in its entirety by a voice other than the poet's" (1986, 77). I concur with Vendler that "Black Earth" fulfills lyric expectations more closely than "The Pangolin," another poem concerning enclosure and poetry. Further, in this poem Moore thinks about the complex relationship between form and content, implicitly rejecting as simplistic the notion that one can serve as the receptacle for the other. "Black Earth" conceives of the lyric as a continuous surface, for all its opposition of skin and soul, since, as Cristanne Miller observes in her discussion of this poem and race, stripping away apparently superficial identifiers "brings cultural as well as physical death" (1995, 146).

Sandra Gilbert argues that Moore characteristically sets up an "alternative," "natural" history in opposition to the "possessiveness and enslavement, arrogance and ignorance" of "'civilized' history" (1990, 40–41), suggesting that through animals, Moore imagines positions outside of human history from which to critique or appreciate it. This elephant-speaker describes human culture from a marginal perspective, a border-world of water and land, great age and indeterminate gender. The slippage between the first and third persons, however, indicates that categories of inside and outside don't hold for Moore. Her observers are always implicated in what is being observed. This poem, which begins uncharacteristically with the word "Openly," offers a coded revelation of Moore's situation as a woman practicing the modern lyric. She remains an insider and an outsider, enabled by the thick hide of her impersonal style to "do these / things which I do, which please / no one but myself."

The elephant's armor, rutted by experience, becomes, we are told, a manual of the "history of power": its markings resemble written language, readable at least by others of its kind, "the peanut-tongued and the / hairy-toed." Moore certainly has had readers of her own kind; H.D., for example, in the first printed review of Moore's work, finds in Moore's poetry a like-minded resistance to "squalor and commercialism" in their shared culture of "shrapnel and machine-guns."[3] Ultimately, the armor that protects the speaker/elephant from violent attack, or dangerous misreading, is not her physical strength and toughness but the impregnability of her "soul" to earthly assailants. Inside the marred surface exists a "beautiful element of unreason," something impenetrable by ordinary means of assault, and perhaps irreducible to verbal translation.[4]

Moore's poetry tells this story again and again: would-be students gaze at surfaces, trying to decipher the codes of form and syntax, while the inside remains inaccessible. "Black Earth," itself a sort of secret by its omission from the collected works, exists, like "The Pangolin," at the center of Moore's poetic of armoring. "Black Earth" advances an esthetic of impenetrability related to, but ultimately substantially different from, Dickinson's, largely because Moore's figures for the enclosed lyric are living rather than humanly constructed. Moore's lyric suggests not a permeable house of possibility but a Möbius strip of continuous surface: an eloquent hide contains but also defines the mysterious animal, so that readerly penetration constitutes a bloody safari. This poem directs its audience to sub-merge, to see unreason, to participate in a different model of reading.[5]

"Black Earth" and "The Pangolin," unlike most of Dickinson's poems, completely collapse enclosure with the body. While I agree with Miller that "Black Earth" constitutes a not-so-oblique treatment of racial identity, I'd suggest that it also implies female embodiment, the cultural equation of woman and body Cixous has traced.[6] The identity of outside and inside not only critiques the gendered hierarchy of soul and body but hints at the peculiar fusion of pregnancy. Although Darlene Erickson wrongly suggests, I think, a simple binary between poet and persona in this piece, she does nicely play out the enclosures of earth, seed, and trunk-tendril this poem invokes in botanical parallel with animal gestation in the mother's nourishing body (1992, 155–56). Maternity, in fact, constitutes a key aspect of Moore's poetic of enclosure.

Enclosure and Poetic Influence

My discussion of influence in Moore's work begins with her elusive connections to Emily Dickinson. Many have noted Moore's one published treatment of Dickinson's work, a 1933 review appearing in *Poetry* of *Letters of Emily Dickinson,* edited by Mabel Loomis Todd. Since this lone assessment appeared in the middle of Moore's career, some have doubted whether Dickinson exercised significant influence on Moore's poetry.

Joanne Feit Diehl maps out many similarities between Dickinson and Moore, both in style and in their relations to the American Sublime (1990). Further, two recent publications reflect on the connections between these American women. Sabine Sielke's *Fashioning the Female Subject: The Intertextual Networking of Dickinson, Moore, and Rich* (1997) also devotes a chapter, "Select Defects—Disrupted Discourse and the Body," to the pair. Sielke traces their "reluctant radicalism" (20), finding likenesses in the divided and multiple subjects they fashion, their use of form, and their ambivalent representations of the female body. Although, interestingly, she employs the same phrase from Moore's review in her title, Cynthia Hogue's 1998 essay approaches the issue very differently, tracing Moore's allusions to Dickinson through the vast Rosenbach archive. In "'The Plucked String': Emily Dickinson, Marianne Moore and the Poetics of Select Defects," Hogue amplifies the significance of the single essay by showing that Moore only reviewed work of "essential poetic interest" and by examining the substantial notes Moore prepared perhaps prior to writing, perhaps working towards a lecture on Dickinson she never actually delivered (94). According to Hogue, Moore's reading diaries also demonstrate her close attention to the arc of Dickinson's reputation from 1912 to 1937 (91). As far as possible, Hogue proves Moore's thoughtful engagement with a key female predecessor, throughout her early career but especially around Dickinson's centenary. My comments build on this work, beginning with the famous review then turning to an even better-known lyric of World War II, "What Are Years?", to express the relative poetics of enclosure of these writers. This chapter will conclude with a return to Dickinson in "The Paper Nautilus," where, I believe, Moore both acknowledges and qualifies Dickinson's influence.

Of course, as Hogue observes, Moore's essay not only sketches an insightful image of Dickinson but tells us a great deal about the critic's predilections. As competing versions of Dickinson's substantive, if bowdlerized, body of work came to publication in the early part of the twentieth century, many opportunities arose for her successors to produce reviews and overviews of her poetry. As I noted in my first chapter, Amy Lowell and other modernist-identified critics described an affinity between Dickinson and the Imagists. Dickinson would surely have rejected this label for her work, as Moore did for her own, despite historical, personal, and esthetic conjunctions between the latter poet and the Imagist movement.[7] Moore, in fact, uses her review to situate herself and her own choices among her contemporaries and within American literary history.

Moore's description of Dickinson's poetic, while smart and plausible, also encapsulates her own. She praises Dickinson's "select defect[s]" of startling juxtapositions, innovative rhyme, and "the self-concealing pronoun" by arguing that "Emily Dickinson was a person of power and could have overcome, had she wished to, any less than satisfactory feature of her lines" (*Prose* 292). These characterizations happen also to defend Moore's own unique work against accusations of antipoetic eccentricity. Interpreting Dickinson's refusal to publish as "deferred publication," Moore theorizes that "she valued her work too much to hurt it if greater stature for it could be ensured by delay" (291). Moore's own correspondence with literary friends including T. S. Eliot, William Carlos Williams, H.D., Bryher, and Ezra Pound, collected in the Rosenbach Museum and Library and now partially published in *The Selected Letters* (1997), shows how often these friends urged her to publish and how repeatedly she delayed, reluctant to part with work she would revise and reconsider almost endlessly. In fact, Moore's first book was published without her participation through the machinations of H.D. and her companion Bryher, who became Moore's friend and benefactor. Moore describes her own publishing strategy here by translating Dickinson's avoidance of publication into a deferral of publication; the Amherst poet, Moore suggests, was as ambitious for her work as anyone, her very delay a sign of that seriousness. Moore tells us that modesty, a value very much associated with Moore's own persona and poetry, does not contradict with high poetic goals.

For Moore, Dickinson's was a "seclusive, wholly non-notorious personality" (290): "she was not a recluse, nor was her work, in her thought of it, something eternally sealed" (291). Moore, anticipating contemporary feminist interpretations of Dickinson's biography, sees in Dickinson not a frightened agoraphobe but a private person, making deliberate choices about how best to present her work—a description that, again, fits Moore herself. The most provocative quote for this study, however, occurs after Moore admires Dickinson's treatments of "death in its several forms": "To free or to protect was her necessity, and not to be able to break the fetters mental or actual that are too strong for mortality was her discipline" (291). Moore's summary, typically, begins by uniting two impulses many would find antithetical, as if in anticipation of that later poem, "The Paper Nautilus." It closes by asserting the salutary effects of constraint, referring both to Dickinson's human inability to control real separations and failures in her life, and to the formal and metaphorical fetters that shape Dickinson's lyric practice.

To free or to protect: this is the double function of enclosures, evoked by Moore's images of enabling armor. Not to be able to break the fetters: Dickinson certainly writes about the impossibility of escaping from mortal chains, but just as often fantasizes the soul's bolt into eternity. In fact, Moore's own review, while celebrating Dickinson's concision and indirection ("splendor of implication"), also contrasts Dickinson's "openness" and "frankness" with modernism's "mock-modest impersonalism" (293). Moore, however, clearly does make a discipline of containment. Further, since her enclosures emphasize the fettering and freeing materiality of language by blurring the distinction between inside and outside, Dickinson's escapes remain impossible, or unrepresentable, in Moore's poetic.

Moore and Dickinson share many likenesses, in temperament and in poetry: reserve, fierce originality, ambivalence about publication, a relative solitariness. Their differences, however, remain radical: Moore, unlike Dickinson, published and was greatly respected in her time; she employed naturalistic particularity in her work, in contrast to Dickinson's stretch for the universal; she often wrote poems in moderate lengths Dickinson doesn't ever to seem to have attempted. Moore clearly knew Dickinson's work and found much to admire in it, but Dickinson's influence was certainly not the only great drive behind Moore's poetic choices.

Yet, for reasons in addition to direct influence, profound affinities exist between the two American poets. The cocoons, houses, graves and other figures of enclosure so prevalent in Dickinson's poetry recur in Moore's, especially in images of armor. Structurally, Moore's stanzas are as enclosed as Dickinson's, her syntax nearly as obstructive, her pronouns as "self-concealing." Each constructs a poetics of closed spaces because each responds to related cultural pressures, especially the identification of women with private virtues such as domesticity, modesty, and chastity. Even in Moore's time, to pursue aggressively a career, as Moore's contemporary Amy Lowell did in her appropriation of Imagism and production of anthologies, could be to risk ridicule or worse. Each disguises her transgression by various postures of modesty, antiliterariness, or, in Moore's case, an apparent concern with "minor" subjects and secondary sources.

Yet, partly because of her powerful relationship with her own mother and partly because, as a modernist, Moore followed a more substantial line of female literary precursors including Dickinson herself, Moore's strategies of enclosure assume a resonance that Dickinson's possessed barely, if at all. For Dickinson, the body's femininity imprisons it in preset cultural roles; death means escape from gender. Moore's poetry, while hardly a naked reflection of the human female's physical glory, does register the female body as a potentially maternal enclosure, able to protect and nurture.[8] I don't mean that Moore defines femaleness by reproductive capacity: like Dickinson, Moore in fact chose against marriage and motherhood, and famously criticizes the former institution in her poem of the same name. Whether she "mothered" as a mentor to other poets, especially Bishop, remains arguable: after Bloom, feminist revisions of Bloom, and challenges to those feminist revisions, influence seems impossible to characterize by any single familial model.[9] Nonetheless, Moore sometimes codes her close, collaborative relationship with her own mother into her images of enclosure. Likewise, these enclosures can express her complicated relationships to literary forbears, including Dickinson.

"What Are Years?" (CP 95), the title poem of Moore's 1941 volume, illustrates both what Dickinson and Moore have in common and where they diverge. The poem represents a call to courage that severs its connections to its context; it may have been written as a response to the death of a child (Stapleton 1978, 114), a subject that motivated many of Dickinson's contemplations. Finally revised and published about ten years after its initial drafting, it also evokes but does not name its second context, World War II. It employs masculine pronouns, as if the poet's gender does not bear on the experience the poem describes. These evasions, and the poem's subject of imprisonment and resistance, suggest Dickinson. However, Moore's poem advocates a paradoxical freedom through accession to limitation, innovating within strict stanzas, the way the bird it describes sings within a cage. "Not to be able to break the fetters mental or actual . . . was her discipline": success through surrender is not Dickinson's objective, but Moore's.

In this poem, imprisonment figures mortality; while dwelling inescapably in a mortal body, one's responsibility is to persist like "the sea in a chasm, struggling to be / free and unable to be," or to make art within constricted circumstances. Moore's captive bird resembles the bird in Dickinson's "They shut me up in Prose—" (F 445, J 613), an 1862 poem about incarceration, in which the variant "Abolish" may also suggest a wartime context, referring implicitly to the American Civil War and Dickinson's identification with the experience of slavery. Dickinson's poem was first printed in 1935 in *Unpublished Poems of Emily Dickinson*, so while it may have played a role in Moore's completion of "What Are Years?", it could not have inspired her initial attempts at this lyric; both pieces, after all, employ a familiar trope, the bird as lyric poet. Nevertheless, these poems possess telling correspondences and discords.

While Dickinson's bird laughs and abolishes his captivity "easy as a Star," Moore's bird

>   grown taller as he sings, steels
>   his form straight up. Though he is captive,
>   his mighty singing
>   says, satisfaction is a lowly
>   thing, how pure a thing is joy.
>   This is mortality,
>   this is eternity.

Both remain imprisoned; both sing despite their condition; both are even male. Dickinson, however, practices an irreligious defiance of teacher, father, state; laughing at authority makes the bars vanish (this laugh resembles, in fact, Ireland's quieter smile in Moore's "Sojourn in the Whale"). Culture restricts Dickinson's lyricist, who resists human, though generalized, forces. Moore, however, does not consider our caged condition alterable, although one can resist its effects—not its perpetrator, mortality itself—within given limits. The sea "in its surrendering / finds its continuing"; falling back into itself gives it the energy to surge forward and upward again. Surrender enables combat. The poem admires not wild defiance but a straightening of the spine, dignity, courage in the sense of stoicism.

"What Are Years?" diverges stylistically from Moore's earlier poetry, expanding her preexisting tendency toward aphorism while maintaining a rhymed, syllabic structure. It speaks unusually plainly, and so omits syntactic dodges that can reinforce her ethic of reserved resistance, although Hollander rightly observes this poem's ambiguities, especially regarding the title (1990, 98). Further, it uses general images far removed from her frequent preference for the exotic: she offers us a mere bird, not a pelican or an ibis. "What Are Years?" connects with Moore's other works, however, in its faint evocation of armor, in the metallic "steels / his form straight up." The armor is actually inner here, an attitude of the spine; the steel also suggests the bars of the cage, linking prisons and armor, limitation and protection. As in other poems, this armor invokes the poem's structural design by the word "form." Also, the sea in the chasm calls back to the relentless wave in her early poem "The Fish," locked in its relation to the scarred but enduring cliffside. Again, Moore's fusion of outside and inside marks her particular poetic of enclosure, which eschews escape as an option.

Finally, whether or not Moore means to revise Dickinson here, "What Are Years?" does collaborate with Mary Warner Moore. Merrin quotes an unpublished 1941 letter of the poet's ascribing the key lines, "satisfaction is a lowly / thing, how pure a thing is joy," to her mother (1990, 135). Moore's very paraphrase of the bird's "mighty singing," her translation of the lyric utterance, unobtrusively quotes the older woman who most influenced Moore's writing. Moore's image of isolated captivity nevertheless chimes meaningfully with other women's voices.

Moore engages many influences in her poetic conversations, sometimes simultaneously. Merrin's argument against "neatly separated patriarchal and matriarchal traditions" (1990, 1) corresponds well not only with various studies I have cited that link Moore to diverse precursors and contemporaries, but with Moore's own rebuttals to questions about her influences.[10] However, Moore does employ enclosure as a metaphor for literary connections between women, especially enclosures that enable even as they confine. Sometimes enclosure also signals significant engagements with male literary precursors, as in "A Grave." In this case, however, Moore's disapproval of the man dominating this American seascape generates a threatening central image: her gravelike Atlantic meets his "rapacious look" with a deep and ominous appetite (CP 49–50).

Armor represents "that weapon, self-protectiveness" for Moore (CP 34), oxymoronically potent through containment. Similarly, water's shapelessness yields many of Moore's forms, and she seems to see in that element the latent power of passivity: fluid, its movement determined by external forces like the pull of the moon, lacking the firm separate identity of a solid thing, its very "weaknesses" give it awesome abilities. As Taffy Martin suggests, "water, particularly, and other images of docility or calm become Moore's codes for subversive discourse" (as they do in Bishop's poetry) (1986, 123). Several of her poems gaze at the sea, and in these the ocean often suggests armoring, enclosure, and the connected subject of surfaces. For example, in "Sojourn in the Whale," a poem occasioned by the 1916 Easter Rebellion in Dublin (Molesworth 141), Moore indicates her awareness that such images of power in passivity also resemble traditional images of femininity. She identifies the subordination of Ireland to England with the subordination of the feminine to the masculine. Moore describes Ireland's resistance obliquely as an automatic rising of water over obstacles. The sea, as in "The Fish," pushes tirelessly forward; it flexibly adapts to contingencies. These are the responses to oppression that Moore admires, in Ireland and generally. The title, "Sojourn in the Whale," links this wateriness with enclosure. Ireland, by implication, is subsumed into Britain as an alien into a larger animal, for a limited amount of time; Ireland even resembles Jonah, learning the hard way about the punishing force belonging to greater powers.

"A Grave" was published a little later, in 1921, but concerns the same war, evoked in diction like "phalanx," and the same ocean. The sea itself becomes an enclosure in "A Grave," its deep cradle serving as a giant tomb. "A Grave" was first published under the title "A Graveyard"; an even earlier title on a draft in the Rosenbach archive is "A Graveyard in the Middle of the Sea."[11] These revisions suggest a narrowing of focus, gradually eliminating clues to location, and finally identifying the sea as a grave, instead of a place for graves. This poem represents Moore's most frightening take on water, very different from "Sojourn in the Whale" and "The Fish" in its meditativeness and unbroken flow of free verse lines (although Moore originally drafted the piece in syllabic stanzas [Holley 1987, 47–48]), but carrying further many of the same themes. As in those other early successes, masculinity and possessiveness connect negatively, poetic form derives from the water's movement, and the poem focuses on the relation between surface and depth.

The poem begins with a "Man looking into the sea"; according to anecdote, Moore and her mother were standing on some rocks on Monhegan Island taking in the view when a man came and stood directly in their line of vision. Moore was irritated, but her mother's response, quoted in the poem, was that "it is human nature to stand in the middle of a thing" (Friar and Brinnin 1951, 62). The speaker notes, however, that "you cannot stand in the middle of this," and that the sea is "quick to return a rapacious look," as a swallower of all manner of "dropped things." In fact, another identity for this man blocking Moore's view might be Whitman: as a previous writer of the sea and this scene, specifically in "Out of the Cradle Endlessly Rocking," he stands permanently within her perspective.[12]

I'm not the first reader to suggest that "A Grave" offers a response to male literary precursors. Schulze briefly but intriguingly links this bully with Stevens (1995, 30); much earlier, Stapleton suggests Poe's influence on the original drafts (1978, 20). In the most extended discussion, Merrin disputes Stapleton and reads Moore here as "a critical observer and wily respondent to the male-dominated poetic tradition, Romantic and post-Romantic as well" (1990, 67), creating an arrogant male figure whose imagination fails to circumscribe the ocean as femme fatale. Whitman, however, dominates the candidate pool for romantic precursors just as central figure in "The Grave" attempts to dominate this northeastern seascape.

"A Grave" is written not in repeating, syllabically structured stanzas, but in long lines that become more flowing and sibilant towards the end of the poem. Jerrald Ranta suggests that the poem divides in halves begun by lines 1 and 12, the poem's two short lines; the first half demonstrates stasis, the second motion (1988, 252). Whether or not this constituted Moore's structuring principle, the poem does become almost carried away by the wash of the long last sentence. The long lines and sibilance evoke Whitman and his great poem about becoming a poet. Whitman's "twining and twisting" perhaps become Moore's "turn and twist," his bird singing to a lost mate transforming into her much less translatable birds "emitting cat-calls." Both poets concentrate in these poems on identifying the ocean with death, although Moore stands with her "fierce old mother" beside her, rather than rocking the cradle-sea. This demonstrates the greatest difference in how Whitman and Moore treat the sea: Moore takes the mother out of it, her ocean completely dispassionate, possessing neither "volition nor consciousness." If "A Grave" answers "Out of the Cradle," it says "you cannot stand in the middle of this": there can be no pathetic fallacy; even when human beings raid nature for metaphors, the world itself remains terrifyingly indifferent. Costello says of this poem that "what is at stake is our tendency, in finding metaphors for death, to think that we have comprehended it" (1981, 63). Moore observes with precision but she does not translate; her world is more chaotic and incomprehensible, more unpossessible, than Whitman's.

In this poem outsides do possess insides, but Moore's surfaces enclose death, something uncontainable, unimaginable, calling back to Dickinson's many poems about the tomb enclosing eternity. Even the procession of pine trees is "reserved," keeping its secrets. "The wrinkles progress among themselves in a phalanx—beautiful under networks of foam": the sea resembles once again a set of repeating patterns, the waves, the circling birds, the lighthouse beam. These represent reassuring and beautiful surfaces, but the interior is menacing, if mysterious, the opposite of the shell in "The Paper Nautilus" with its dull outside and glossy inside.

At the end of her 1935 *Selected Poems,* Moore adds a postscript that she carefully differentiates from a dedication: "Dedications imply giving, and we [note the "self-concealing pronoun"] do not care to make a gift of what is insufficient; but in my immediate family there is one 'who thinks in a particular way;' and I should like to add that where there is an effect of thought or pith in these pages, the thinking and often the actual phrases are hers." The pithy woman to whom Moore refers, to whom Moore, in fact, seems to grant the status of collaborator, is her mother, Mary Warner Moore, with whom Marianne Moore lived for most of her life. Mary Warner Moore left her unhappy marriage before Marianne was born; Marianne's father was shortly institutionalized, and the poet reportedly never met him. After several years living with relatives in St. Louis, Marianne, her elder brother, and her mother moved gradually eastward, Mary Warner Moore supporting the three through her teaching. Mary Warner Moore offered a model of strength and self-sufficiency to her daughter; many scholars have remarked on their unique collaborations.

Unsurprisingly, Moore records this primary relationship of her life, again in a veiled way, in her poetry; in fact, maternal protection in its positive and negative aspects informs some of Moore's use of enclosure. The poet's friends often imply their own ambivalence about Mary's power in Marianne's life. Elizabeth Bishop's fascinating memoir of Moore, "Efforts of Affection," portrays Mary Warner Moore as a rather daunting eccentric with whom even the aging poet was locked into relation as the wayward daughter: "Her manner toward

Marianne was that of a kindly, self-controlled parent who felt that she had to take a firm line, that her daughter might be given to flightiness or—an equal sin in her eyes—mistakes in grammar" (1984, 129). Moore's expatriate colleagues, especially H.D. and Bryher, gently tried to extricate Moore from her mother through pressuring her to travel abroad; Moore may have aggravated perceptions that her mother impeded her social life by using her mother's indispositions as excuses not to receive visitors (Bar-yaacov 1988, 517–19). Moore, however, did not leave direct record of any ambivalence in her poetry. Instead, her poems of tribute barely articulate the implicit threat of maternal power. This threat, in fact, pervades Moore's own metaphors not only of identity but of reading and writing.

"The Paper Nautilus," like "Bird-Witted" in the same collection, enacts a balance between tribute to and fear of a watchful maternal figure (CP 121–22).[13] This poem, which holds the final position in *What Are Years*, focuses on a sea animal who vigilantly guards her young until they are hatched. It defines motherhood partly through fierceness and strength. The "devil-fish" of the poem "constructs her thin glass shell" to protect her eggs until they are hatched. Parenting requires more than gentle nurturance; the language is tense with the mother's restrained power. The nautilus's freight is "hid but is not crushed," the very possibility of crushing emphasizing the mother's Herculean strength: in fact, one phrase Moore scribbled down on a draft of this poem as a possible title was "A Second Hercules."[14] Maternal enclosure strongly relates to Moore's other images of armor and the possibility of combat, although the prospect of battle in this poem published during World War II never materializes.

Not only the topic of protective motherhood, but the odd details of the first stanza, invoke Mary Warner Moore as a specific referent of this poem. The poem begins:

> For authorities whose hopes
> are shaped by mercenaries?
> Writers entrapped by
> teatime fame and by
> commuters' comforts? Not for these
> the paper nautilus
> constructs her thin glass shell.

Moore had one brother, a navy chaplain; presumably the authority whose hopes are shaped by mercenaries and writer entrapped by teatime fame are negative versions of Moore's brother and herself, futures both are exhorted to avoid, with their mother's previous efforts in mind.

"The Paper Nautilus" particularly reflects upon the moment of separation, of leaving the nest. "The intensively / watched eggs coming from / the shell free it when they are freed," in a mutually beneficial gesture. The speaker depicts a mother-child separation in which both sides feel freed by the outward movement. The last lines harmonize with Bonnie Costello's argument that combat suggests humility and love, not possessiveness and aggression, in Moore's work. Moore's image of the nautilus embracing the imperiled shell is a potent one, reversing the usual connotations of armor.

The mother nautilus in this poem not only protects but creates; maternity becomes a model for literary creativity. As the nautilus encloses the developing eggs in a shell, a poet hides but does not crush her new poems, much as Moore sought to protect her works from "premature" publication (Hall 1969, 27). Or, to carry forward my readings of "The Pangolin" and "Black Earth," the shell and the young together represent Moore's metaphor for poetry, the flawed artifact of shell standing in for Moore's detailed linguistic surfaces, veiling her purposes. This shell of form may be dull on the outside, yet the inside—or "inner surface," as if there exists no real inside or outside but one smoothly connected whole—is "glossy as the sea." Once again, we are trapped on the Möbius strip of Moore's surfaces; although here the protected objects seem to have the chance to free themselves, the poem does not finally bring itself to describe such an exposure.

Moore's identity as poet blurs with her mother's in this poem as inside blurs with outside, the presence of the ocean emphasizing the fluidity of these identities and categories. "The Paper Nautilus" suggests a metaphor for literary influence that evokes but crucially alters Harold Bloom's model, outlined in *The Map of Misreading*, of poets wrestling for voice at the side of the ocean. Bloom suggests that poets including Dickinson, Whitman, and Stevens attain poetic strength through an oedipal wrestling with literary forefathers at a watery scene, as if regressing to an "improved infancy" (1975, 15). "The Paper Nautilus" may indeed represent an idealization of Moore's relationship with her biological mother, but it does not depict an isolated striving; her metaphor for influence is a mutually beneficial collaboration, although one fraught with tension and even danger of being overwhelmed by predators.

Further, "The Paper Nautilus" takes part in at least four other collaborations. First, Elizabeth Bishop reports having given Moore the shell that inspired the poem (1984, 134). Upon reading Moore's literary transformation of the gift, Bishop wrote to her mentor of its own galvanizing effect on her writing: "There are so many things in it I'd like to thank and praise you for. I admire especially from 'wasp-nest flaws / of white on white,' to the end. The whole poem is like a rebuke to me, it suggests so many of the plans for things I want to say about Key West" (1994, 90). Kalstone and Diehl find allusions to "The Paper Nautilus" in subsequent poems by Bishop, "Jerónimo's House" and "Santarém," respectively (1989, 69; 1993, 27).

According to Diehl, Bishop imagines Moore as a "mother-child" (1993, 37), although the circumstances of the relationship mainly suggest Moore as a maternal surrogate to Bishop. Moore herself aligns in this sense with the powerful nautilus. However, Moore also invokes Dickinson as a poetic mother. Moore's naturalistic details and prosaic rhythms are alien to Dickinson's poetic, but her habit of close observation, her omission of the poem's real referents, and her concern with literal and poetic narrow spaces are not. Moore imagines the emergence of the nautilus's young, but, as in Dickinson's poems, the prisoners never quite make a living escape. Moore's key revision of Dickinson is to see the positive, protective value of enclosure, as well as the heroic intentions of the encloser. A corroborating detail may exist in Moore's notes for the Dickinson review: according to Hogue, Moore transcribed "The Soul selects her own Society – " (F 409, J 303) on the reverse of a typescript, indicating her interest in at least one of the Dickinson poems that parallels house and body in an image of contained life. Handwritten notes reveal that Moore read the valve imagery of that piece as suggesting a mollusc, so Moore may be developing a long-standing association of Dickinson with shell imagery (Hogue 1998, 99).

Third, this poem takes place in a two-way dialogue with H.D.'s poetry. H.D.'s early lyrics, which Moore read and reviewed, were typically full of broken shells at stormy shore scenes, reflecting H.D.'s urgent need to separate from the United States and from her own family, as well as from an American literary tradition many modernists perceived as stunted and secondary. Moore offers in "The Paper Nautilus" a different model for how a woman and a poet might respect yet differentiate herself from these oppressive sources. H.D. takes her up on this new model for influence a few years later in "The Walls Do Not Fall," the first section of *Trilogy*, H.D.'s long poem interweaving psychoanalysis, religion, and the London Blitz of World War II. Here H.D. is finally able to recuperate images of enclosure for their strategic value even as she finally comes to terms with her memories of her own mother. In a draft of this poem, H.D. penciled in Marianne Moore's initials next to a lyric about a pearl-creating mollusc, H.D.'s new model for literary production (Ostriker 1986b, 485).

If there is any particular poem, however, that "The Paper Nautilus" reads or misreads, it must be "The Chambered Nautilus" by Oliver Wendell Holmes, written over eighty years earlier. Both poems are structured into five stanzas of seven lines each, and both use the shell as a metaphor for the poem, although there the resemblance seems to end. Moore revises this poem, which she would have known since her school days as a great American poetic achievement, in order to position herself as an American poet, building on without deposing that tradition. She redraws Holmes partly by choosing a slightly different animal: Holmes describes the true nautilus, found in deep water in the Pacific and Indian Oceans, and emphasizes its character as a wanderer. Moore's paper nautilus is in fact related to the octopus, and, significantly, only the female of the species builds the shell, a kind of egg-case, in which she, her young, and sometimes the male live. Nor is her poem about movement; her creature protects far more than explores, focused inward on her young rather than outward, as Holmes's nautilus is, on sirens and coral reefs. Finally, Moore remains as interested in the life within the carapace as on the relic of shell; where Holmes meditates on death and spiritual growth, Moore reflects on motherhood, responsibility, and identity both nurtured and imperiled by the powerful forces around them.

In "The Paper Nautilus," several aspects of Moore's poetics of enclosure converge. The poem remains firmly planted in an American poetic tradition, manifesting a collaborative notion of influence in which the poet is protected by but needs to free herself from her precursors. "The Paper Nautilus" blurs Moore's project and her very identity with those collaborators, especially with her mother, in a fluidity that the poem values for its literary productivity but also for its properties of camouflage. The poem also demonstrates the necessity of armor in such efforts by reminding us of the presence of predators, who would attack anything important that is carelessly exposed. Finally and miraculously, Moore's scientific particularity and obscuring syntax, all of her reserve and caution, culminate in an emotional closure: "love is the only fortress strong enough to trust to." Moore rarely employs the rhetoric of personal sincerity; as both partisans and critics have observed, her lyrics do not pretend to express a unified, authentic self, and her imagery of continuous insides and outsides suggests, in fact, that a true, concealed self does not exist apart from linguistic surfaces.[15] Occasionally, however, Moore in armor is empowered to approach sentiment, that greatest taboo and most dangerous temptation of modernist poetry. Such evocations of the personal lyric in the context of her disruptive strategies create a poetry of tremendous and complex appeal.

H.D.

Smothered in Wool

Although H.D. began her career as a lyric poet, and her engagement with the lyric as enclosure is central even to her late poetry, her reputation, unlike Dickinson's or Moore's, increasingly rests on her achievement in other genres. In *H.D. and Hellenism,* for instance, Eileen Gregory rightly observes that "the energetic and revisionary critical climate allowing the recovery of H.D.'s published and unpublished writing is also one remarkably skeptical of, if not hostile to, the lyric—the genre wherein H.D. first made her mark, wherein her achievement is as remarkable and durable as any other aspect of her career" (1997a, 131). Recent critics emphasize H.D.'s accomplishments in prose for a variety of purposes. Appropriately, they call attention to an underrated and fascinating body of writing: H.D. found many of her essays and narratives difficult to publish for a range of reasons Susan Stanford Friedman illuminates, including the sexual transgressions they sometimes depict, their experimentality, and the ambivalence H.D. and others felt about violating the successful persona of "H.D., Imagiste" (1990, 18–32). Further, as Gregory demonstrates, some critics focus on H.D.'s prose out of a postmodern preference for narrative's personal and historical revelations over the lyric's apparent timelessness.

Friedman, whose two valuable book-length studies devoted to H.D. (*Penelope's Web* [1990] and the groundbreaking *Psyche Reborn* [1981]) place her at the forefront of H.D. scholarship, discusses H.D.'s lyric

3

poetry in a sophisticated and thorough manner; she is far from dismissive of this segment of H.D.'s oeuvre. However, her more recent study, which analyzes the "double discourse" of H.D.'s poetry and prose, clearly prizes the accessibility of the prose over the obscurities of the poetry. Initially, Friedman argues, H.D.'s poetry "was lyric, impersonal, and clairvoyant while her prose was narrative, personal, and 'ordinary'. Of course, her novels were, like Woolf's, lyric and increasingly hermetic; her poetry, in turn, became increasingly narrative, even personal" (1990, 5). Early in H.D.'s career, then, the prose supplemented a lack her poetry suffered, until H.D. evolved sufficiently as a poet to incorporate the relative openness of her prose into the actual verse.

The openness of the later poetry, however, remains only relative, as does the closure of her early verse. Like Dickinson and Moore, H.D. rewards the diligent with sunbreaks of directness, but her lyric practice does engage with a poetic of enclosure as I've previously defined it for the full arc of her career: to varying degrees in different stages, she conceives a formally enclosed lyric, conveys reserve through various stylistic strategies, and creates multiple images of enclosure that figure her poetic aims and methods. Friedman's reading of H.D.'s shift away from the "crystalline" (1990, 54) towards self-exposure dovetails with the writer's own statements about her fruitful analysis with Freud (during 1933 and 1934). In fact, H.D.'s use of stylistic and thematic figures of enclosure undergoes a dramatic metamorphosis in the thirties. Her poetry of the teens and early twenties fervently desires a breaking of boundaries; it disparages "sheltered gardens" and is littered with broken shells. At the same time, these first works employ not traditional forms but a comparably restrictive Imagist brevity and compression. This Imagist reserve renders the poems oblique about their connections to H.D.'s personal life—"circumspect," she calls them in "A Dead Priestess Speaks" (CP 369–77).[1] In contrast, while a poem like *Trilogy*, written during World War II, formally expands and overtly refers to the conditions of its making, it embraces images of enclosure for their nurturing, sheltering capacities. The reasons for this change are complex, but at least partly concern a changed attitude towards mothers—H.D.'s own mother Helen Wolle Doolittle, but also literary and mythical foremothers, metamorphosed into what Susan Stanford Friedman calls in *Psyche Reborn* a "mother-symbol" (1981, 231). The molluscs and cocoons of *Trilogy* strongly evoke maternal nurture, and her feelings about such protectiveness alter in the thirties: what seems real and oppressive to the young poet becomes metaphoric and empowering for the older one.

Although I begin with a description of the imagist lyric and note H.D.'s allusions to this mode even in her long poems, this chapter focuses on such transformations in her rich imagery of enclosure. H.D. reassembles the fragments of shells from her early poetry into jars, boxes, whole feminine enclosures in *The Gift, Tribute to Freud,* and *Trilogy* particularly. As in her psychoanalysis with Freud H.D. sought to repair her fractured self, in her poetry she transforms scattered shards of lyric into a larger narrative. All *Trilogy*'s enclosures, after all, yield metamorphoses: crucibles heat bitter words into fragrance, gardens protect impossible flowerings, cocoons resemble tombs from which there will be resurrection. H.D.'s last long poems—here represented by *Helen in Egypt* and "Sagesse"—do not, however, depict the full emergence from enclosure *Trilogy* seems to prepare. Instead, they portray only brief or imaginative rebirth or escape: H.D. remains as reluctant to shed the chrysalis of the lyric as she is to abandon her aging body. Through the lyric sequences of World War II and beyond, H.D. has not only found a way to value mothering, but has renegotiated her position within a tradition of women writing.

This chapter, therefore, posits a revisionary poetics for H.D. Although she declares in *Tribute to Freud* that "I am no longer interested in a poem once it is written" (1974, 149)—Marianne Moore and, to a lesser extent, Emily Dickinson redrafted old poems frequently, unlike H.D.—the expatriate poet nevertheless revisits her early accomplishments in later work. Her career-long manipulation of enclosure imagery reveals her shifting approaches to poetry generally and to an emerging tradition she casts in familial terms. Since H.D., again unlike Moore and Dickinson, wrote multiple works that verged on or included autobiography, my analysis incorporates more biographical detail than other chapters, particularly focusing on H.D.'s attitudes towards her own mother as expressed in various literary forms. My approach to this issue relies not only on H.D.'s writings but on extended treatments of H.D.'s biography and experiences with psychoanalysis provided by Friedman (1981, 1990), Guest (1984), Kloepfer (1989), Hollenberg (1991), Chisholm (1992), Edmunds (1994), and others. However, like Claire Buck (1991), I emphasize the complex relation between her poetic speakers and the "authorial self" I and others construct from nonpoetic sources. Buck observes that lyric voice constitutes one of H.D.'s chief subjects (1991, 35), just as voice intrigues Moore: even where H.D. employs conventions of personal expressivity, any careful reading will register her deliberate constructions of a

poetic self. The mothers and maternal enclosures in H.D.'s poetry sug-
gest many referents: H.D.'s versions of her actual mother, H.D. herself
as mother, religious icons, lost goddesses, and a network of women
poets from Sappho to H.D.'s own literary descendants.

H.D.'s Imagist Lyric

Imagism itself prescribes a closed poetics, as Pound's "don'ts" pub-
lished in *Poetry* in 1913 illustrate even through their exclusionary
framing language.[2] Since the middle of the twentieth century, how-
ever, scholars have struggled to define the imagist lyric with mixed
success. In 1951, for instance, Stanley K. Coffman Jr. characterizes
H.D.'s imagism as intensely personal, "rigidly limited," isolated from
the world, and economical in language (146). Demonstrating the
movement's ambiguities, A. R. Jones identifies imagism as impersonal
and avoiding "direct lyricism" (1965, 120); he also observes a dedica-
tion to "restraint and decorum" in the original group and repeatedly
mandates the hardness and dryness of the image (1965, 121–26). All of
imagism's historians agree that these writers compose primarily,
although not entirely, in free verse and, therefore, that imagist poems
cannot be described in terms of any stable patterns of rhythm or
rhyme. John T. Gage, however, finds an imagist dependence on "accu-
mulative structure": the poems do not develop since "the order of the
parts is not itself meaningful, and the reader's attention is therefore
drawn to the parts themselves, and to the accumulated effect of the
whole" (1981, 109). According to Gage, H.D.'s use of repetition con-
tributes to this effect, in its recurrences "reducing the reader's sense
of a developing process" (1981, 123).

Gage also notes the manifestos' limited use in predicting how the
poems actually operate. In one sense, the imagist lyric offers openness,
free verse in opposition to received forms: H.D. does not shape her
verse into predictable, repeating stanzas, as do Moore and Dickinson
to a large extent. Nevertheless, readers have responded to H.D.'s para-
digmatic version of this mode as closed partly because of stylistic
qualities and partly because of the pressures style places on content.
In an analysis of H.D.'s "lyric impersonalism," for instance, Friedman
writes that "like Dickinson, H.D. intensified the tendencies in the lyric
for a discourse that privileges vision over action in a landscape of the
imagination seemingly constituted outside the social order" (1990, 52).
Dodd ascribes the "reticence" of the early poems to the very vividness
of the images, which "retain an integrity independent of the speaker,

and so the level of emotional projection is diminished" (1992, 41). Buck calls imagism a "straitjacket" (1991, 1).

Imagist poems do tend toward brevity, and H.D. composes in short lines that intensify the effect of constriction. H.D. herself emphasizes their abbreviated quality when she describes them as "finished fragments" in a 1937 letter to Norman Pearson (Hollenberg 1997, 10). Imagism's extreme compression and "direct treatment of the 'thing'" prescribe a sort of hieroglyphic lyric,[3] producing what Gage calls the "illusion of instantaneity" (1981, 107); imagist poems can seem, if only at a superficial level, contextless, hermetically sealed boxes that discourage extrapolative readings. Buck points out how frequently H.D.'s critics speak of "encoding" to express the relationship between the urgent lyric "I" in some of these poems and the apparently neutral scenes and objects they depict (1991, 15). Only this seeming impersonalism separates the imagist poem from the conventional post-Romantic lyric: otherwise, imagism exaggerates lyric brevity, solitude, and timelessness, as Friedman suggests. Imagism even retains lyric music while it departs from song-based measures, sensitive as it must be to the rhythm of "the musical phrase," to quote the original tenets.

Michael Kaufmann characterizes imagism as a temporary reevaluation of the importance of the lyric genre: "Imagism, the first modernist poetry, inverted completely the usual poetic hierarchy that estimates the value of a work 'by its acreage'" (1997, 60). He also notes how H.D.'s poetry precedes and shapes Pound's public pronouncements about the movement, as does Cyrena Pondrom in an earlier piece (1990b), and correlates negative assessments of H.D.'s work with "critical suspicions towards lyric as a minor and 'feminine' form" (Kaufmann 1997, 67). Even or perhaps especially to her detractors, H.D. embodied imagism; she condensed her Victorian-sounding name, Hilda Doolittle, with Pound's approval, into brief, identity-blurring initials. However, she quickly felt trapped in this poetic, berated by her husband Richard Aldington for experimenting in prose (Zilboorg 1992, 89), dismissed by others for apparently getting stuck in imagism's frigid zone.[4] For Ezra Pound and others, H.D.'s androgynous beauty incarnated this static, Greek, cool marble ideal. Her 1924 poem "Helen" evokes an unspeaking, statuelike muse, only lovable when dead, and while this piece almost certainly refers back to her artistically silenced mother Helen, it probably also reflects H.D.'s experience as the exemplar and muse of imagism. Her own later criticism of this movement cues later scholars who formulate her project "in terms of an escape narrative from the constraints of imagism" (Buck 1991, 15).

Pound deployed the term "imagism" at least partly to label and promote Hilda Doolittle's lyric innovations, but his prescriptions, not coincidentally, also describe other, earlier poetries, including Emily Dickinson's. Jeanne Kammer, comparing Dickinson, Moore, and H.D., proposes that "the woman poet may have come to the 'modern' style of the early decades of the twentieth century by a very different route than her male counterparts," writing in compressed, ambiguous forms "in part from habits of privacy, camouflage and indirection encouraged in the manner of the gently-bred female" (1979, 156). An additional motive for terseness may have been to avoid the stereotypically sweet (and trivial) effusiveness of the "poetess." In this Kammer's poets may have shared ground with male modernists; Gilbert and Gubar suggest in *No Man's Land* that male poets like Pound and Eliot could have been making a similar repudiation of the "aesthetic of soft, effusive, personal verse supposedly written by women and romantics" (1987, 154). As Betsy Erkkila reminds us in *The Wicked Sisters*, the male moderns were not the only ones with an anxious need to distinguish themselves from "the tradition of female lyricism" (103).[5] Suzanne Clark further sophisticates this point when she observes how modernism uses antisentimentality, and thereby a resistance to mass culture, to establish its own authority: modernists did not only assert themselves against established male powers but "also recalled with disgust and longing, by an act like anamnesis, their estrangement from a maternal enclosure as from the vernacular, and their exile in a world of harsh divisions, borders, and separations" (1991, 8).

Hogue observes parallel strategies of "equivocation" in Dickinson, Moore, and H.D., a resistance to the traditionally unified lyric subject through "maintaining a (non)commitment" to multiple meanings (1995, 29). Many readers, then, identify lyric ambiguity not only with modernism but especially with the strategies of female poets. Dickinson, Moore and H.D., at least, not only needed to negotiate poetic authority but may also have wished to conceal or at least defuse aspects of their personal lives beyond sex itself, including sexualities that may have diverged from the expected course. For H.D., whose bisexuality is certain, the ambiguity of imagism may have even served as a kind of "closet." In fact, H.D. displays reticence on multiple registers, as do Dickinson and Moore: not only do readers remark the play between authorial presence and absence in her early work, but H.D. displays a related ambivalence about publication. Limited fine-press releases narrowed her audience, and H.D. even wrote to Bryher, "Dickinson is really very nice crystalline stuff. I am tempted after reading her to do her own str[?] and publish 20 years post mortem" (qtd. in Friedman 1983, 47, n.7). The imagist poetic as employed by H.D. fuses a female esthetic of reserve *and* a modern, "masculinist" revulsion against the feminized nineteenth century.

Wind-Tortured Places

While H.D. wrote short lyrics under the imagist banner and adhered to its strict esthetic, her poetry thematically dissolved prisons. The very title of H.D.'s first book, *Sea Garden*, oxymoronically links a vast openness with an image of containment (DuPlessis 1986, 12). The book situates itself, as many of her works do, at the clashing of land and sea; this conflict echoes not only the Great War but the struggle of H.D. herself against what she regarded as the oppressions of family and her native culture. *Sea Garden* celebrates the "marred" (CP 5) flowers that thrive in this difficult environment, like the "Sea Violet" that grows among "torn shells."[6] Most tellingly, a "sea garden" seems to possess no walls, but allows its species to face the elements unprotected. This anti-enclosure poetry allegorizes H.D.'s escape not only from the perceived proprieties of nineteenth-century poetry, but from the United States, and metonymically her Victorian girlhood, her parents, and the conventions that stifled both a young woman's worldly ambitions and sexual life. The expatriate poet has become a "marred" (married) woman, hymen broken.

"Sheltered Garden" (CP 19), in this first volume, describes the opposite of the wild sea garden, a contrast meant to invoke the difference between the kind of poetry eschewed by Pound and the supposedly swifter, fresher work of the moderns. This poem speaks from the perspective of the sheltered garden, articulating a desire for change that has not yet occurred. Its melons and pears, the poet warns, will be bitter, will taste of dead grass and wadding, if "smothered," or mothered, from the frost. Better, she advises, to knock down the walls, let in the wind—the impatiently short lines of the penultimate stanza begin with the same gesture, snap / fling / scatter / hurl / break. This poetry defies the sheltered gardens of poetesses, but it addresses most directly H.D.'s mother, as overprotective gardener. Further, as Cassandra Laity remarks in *H.D. and the Victorian Fin de Siècle*, H.D. alludes with this closed, sterile garden to the "Venusbergs" of Decadents like Swinburne: "Usually overripe, overflowered, and located in an enclosed space—a garden, bower, or glade—the Venusberg conceals a deadly trap behind its apparently safe, sensuous refuge. Its dense, enclosed atmosphere proves stifling rather than protective" (1996, 44). H.D. rejects the sheltered garden as a dangerous snare of indoor femininity, presided over by a malevolent maternal angel (who will murder if she is not murdered, as Woolf warns in "Professions for Women").

Other poems from the 1916 book seek alternative guidance. "The Shrine," for example, addresses the spirit of a rocky coast, identified as female only in the parenthetical, unattributed epigraph, "'She watches over the sea'" (CP 7). In four sections, it first echoes men's condemnation of this half-shelter of curved beach because it is "useless" as a port (CP 7–9), then speaks for an elite group that admires its dangerous, jagged splendor without reference to the coast's pragmatic value to men. H.D. prefers, here, the hazards of openness to those of enclosure. "We sing to you," the poet declares, locating her inspiration at this dangerous shoreline, erotically evoked as the female body: "honey is not more sweet / than the salt stretch of your beach" (CP 8). "Your hands have touched us," she recognizes, offering perilous nurture at least to female speaker and her fellow initiates, if not to male sailors (CP 10).

"The Shrine" addresses an unnamed goddess, as many poems in the volume do: as Morris argues in "The Concept of Projection," "the speaker in *Sea Garden* is a supplicant in search of deities that are everywhere immanent in the landscape," and the poems themselves "are thrown out as bridges to the sacred" (1990b, 277). H.D. here seeks the ethereal embrace, and implicitly the approbation of, such a mother-muse as she will find in the Lady of *Trilogy*; however, her early poetry depicts the search as potentially lethal. The spirit of the shrine, perhaps like Emily Dickinson in her darkest and most fragmentary lyrics, repels visitors even as she "touches" them with her sublime beauty. Eileen Gregory detects H.D.'s engagement with Sappho in *Sea Garden* and elsewhere, and her comment that the modern poet's "relation to Sappho would seem to be implicated in an ominous sense of taboo" may illuminate the intermingled fear of and attraction to the female power here (1997a, 151). "The Shrine" enacts the conflicting desire for and fear of enclosure—the curve of the coast potentially represents both harbor and grave—that mark many of H.D.'s early works. Her ambivalence in this poem emphasizes wariness of female lyric tradition, but the volume as a whole both invokes and refutes American predecessors generally, who become entangled with the forces toward conformity in H.D.'s own family.

This ambivalence toward enclosure becomes even more complex given that, unlike Moore or Dickinson, H.D. was not only a daughter but a mother. Donna Krolik Hollenberg, in her book-length study of the links between childbirth and creativity in H.D., points out that during the period in which *Sea Garden* was probably composed (1913–16), H.D.'s first daughter was stillborn (May 1915). The "shrivelled seeds" of the poem "Mid-Day" (CP 10) seem to predict this first, devastating experience of maternity, an apparent failure of H.D.'s own body to shelter, as well as signaling an early frustration with this limited kind of lyric that cannot seem to take root. The very broken shells of "Sea Violet," "Sea Poppies," and "The Wind Sleepers" might be read doubly, indicating H.D.'s desired and feared break from a feminine American tradition, but also encoding the broken pregnancy. H.D. blamed the war and especially the sinking of the *Lusitania* for her miscarriage: meanings for the sea in H.D. multiply alarmingly, identified with death and drowning, and uncertain uterine waters (in an anxiety about fertility resembling the water imagery of "The Waste Land"). The ocean these poems edge along constitutes an attractive and dangerous site. It supplies an imaginative source but also places identity in peril, in both its aspects strongly associated with the pre-oedipal mother.

In her later work H.D. not only needs to reclaim relationships with her biological and literary mothers, but to reconcile tensions between the two kinds of mothering she herself undertakes. The metaphoric equivalence of creation and procreation, as Hollenberg points out, remains a fairly loaded one for women writers generally, because it "perpetuates both the split between mind and body and women's confinement to the domestic sphere" (1991, 10), and "because it is based on a harmony that has been disallowed in women's lives" (1991, 7). H.D. herself chose against traditional motherhood after the birth of Frances Perdita in 1919, opting for travel and writing time; much later her daughter recalls that H.D. "was hardly an archetypal mother. . . . She venerated the concept of motherhood, but was unprepared for its disruptions" (Schaffner 1990, 4).[7] Enclosures in H.D.'s later writing represent not only shelters H.D. seeks as daughter, but harbors she offers as mother, giving birth not only to a biological daughter and a new self, but making new spaces in poetry for and dispensing advice to literary children, advice most obviously taken up in Adrienne Rich's "Diving into the Wreck."

(S)mothered in Wolle

H.D.'s lyric begins to expand in voice and length, and her figures of enclosure to grow paradoxically more positive, almost immediately after the publication of *Sea Garden*. For example, in "Eurydice," written in 1917, the title character openly articulates her resentment against careless Orpheus, even as she adopts Hades, depicted as a fringed, vaginal fissure in the earth (CP 52), as a positive enclosure. As DuPlessis states in "Romantic Thralldom in H.D.," "Locked in that space, defined within it, she declares it to be not the space of rejection, negation, and loss, but the splendor of her essential life" (1990, 411). Eurydice's fierce self-assertion, "At least I have the flowers of myself," offers a not wholly convincing consolation, given the intensity of loss she expresses, but the poem nevertheless represents a crucial recognition of the positive potentials of narrowed spaces (CP 55).

However, the length and repetition of "Eurydice" distance it from H.D.'s imagist lyrics. H.D. works increasingly within prose and verse narrative from the twenties onward, blurring genres in such hard-to-define works as *The Gift, Tribute to Freud*, and *Trilogy* itself. However, the best of her mature writings remain in dialogue with lyric poetry: H.D. divides long poems into "lyric units," as Friedman terms them (1990, 352), and even prose works resonate with images of enclosure inherited from Dickinson and shared with Moore. For instance, even in an essay tellingly entitled "No Rule of Procedure: The Open Poetics of H.D.," Alicia Ostriker observes the aural play "between the closed and the open" in *Trilogy* (1990b, 339). For Ostriker, the very openness characterizing the long poem derives from "that astonishing sequence of enclosure images which turn out to be generative opening wombs" (346). Indeed, as writers including Friedman and Chisholm prove, H.D.'s continued engagement with figures of enclosure has everything to do with a desired return to the maternal world she repudiates in *Sea Garden*.

H.D.'s roman à clef *Paint It Today*, composed in 1921–22 although not published until 1992, gives us some idea of the young Hilda Doolittle's struggle to escape from her mother's world. The short, apparently unfinished novel moves from a literary transformation of H.D.'s affair with Frances Gregg, through her failed marriage to Aldington, and into her early relationship with Bryher—the period that frames and infuses the composition of her first two books of poetry, *Sea Garden* (1916) and *Hymen* (1921). *Paint It Today* depicts its Helen Doolittle character as a petty, conventional woman, disapproving of her daughter's choices and unable to understand why H.D. might want to stay in Europe: "We only just had your bedroom repapered," she complains (41). Hilda Doolittle's representative, the improbably named Midget Defreddie, sympathizes with mythical Orestes, telling herself: "'Your mother, your mother, your mother . . . has betrayed, or would betray, through the clutch and the tyranny of the emotion, your father, the mind in you'" (43). Midget does not actually slaughter

Clytemnaestra, even figuratively, instead marrying Basil (Aldington) to enact her escape.[8]

H.D. wrote *Paint It Today,* one of her many apparently unpublishable works, in the early twenties, towards the end of her imagist period and the beginning of the second phase of her career, in which she felt so blocked. Friedman describes how some of H.D.'s other early autobiographical novels, especially *Asphodel* and *Her,* paint Helen bitterly as "the embodiment of Victorian social convention," while in *Trilogy*-era prose, especially *The Gift* and *Tribute to Freud,* her "recollections of her mother have lost their ironic cast and taken on a tone of compassion, even reverence" (1981, 139). I don't agree with Friedman's early assessment that these works revere the poet's actual mother, but a shift does occur: H.D. knows that her mother failed to support her daughter's talents, but begins to see why, to recognize the forces that beset her mother and may have helped to frustrate her happiness. She learns to retrieve an idea of Helen Doolittle that focuses on her gifts to H.D. In the same way, enclosed spaces that negatively confine in the early poetry—sheltered gardens that spoil the fruit—become nurturing of creativity in the molluscs of *Trilogy.*

H.D.'s changed feelings toward her mother connect to her analysis with Freud. The analysis focused on this mother-daughter relationship and H.D.'s unresolved feelings about her mother's favoritism of Hilda's brother Gilbert. "Freud concluded," as did H.D. herself, "that H.D. longed to fuse with her mother, to recreate the early period in infancy when the ego is as yet undifferentiated and cannot distinguish itself from the mother" (Friedman 1981, 131). In the Scilly Islands in 1918, for example, H.D. underwent an emotional experience she compared to being cupped in two bell jars; both analyst and analysand read this memory as a prenatal fantasy (*Tribute to Freud* 168). H.D. herself commented to Bryher, "'back to the womb' seems to be my only solution. Hence islands, sea, Greek primitives and so on" (qtd. in Friedman 1981, 132), implying that all her images of the sea connect to this bell jar and other images of enclosure, and a desire to be protected and nurtured by her mother in a way she felt she was not as a child.

H.D. strongly links images of enclosure with maternal shelter, oppressive in her adolescence but revealed as a continuing longing in her later work with Freud. This insight allowed her to achieve a spiritual reunion with her mother (who died six years before the analysis), and begin to trace her own creativity back through her maternal ancestry, especially in *The Gift.* Although she did not recognize or encourage H.D.'s talent, Helen Doolittle was not only a musician but a painter, whose example, however muted, inspired H.D. "The mother is the Muse, the Creator, and in my case especially, as my mother's name was Helen," H.D. declares in *End to Torment* (41). H.D. found a way to resolve the contradiction between the mother who inspired and the mother who discouraged: she transformed her real mother into an approving, unnameable Lady. This mother-muse appears in *Trilogy* as a source of inspiration to write, symbolizing values of love in a world at war, and releasing H.D.'s right to identify herself as a poet. Not coincidentally, with the recovery of this maternal source of strength, H.D. discovers the strategic value of enclosure, as it appears in the poetries of women before and after her.

Crucially, however, while H.D.'s work of the forties and beyond recuperates a relationship with Helen Doolittle that suggests neither a pre-oedipal merge destroying individual identity, nor an oedipal revulsion, it also erases H.D.'s actual mother. In *The Unspeakable Mother,* Deborah Kelly Kloepfer emphasizes that "the mother" in H.D.'s work, though in many ways central and magnetic, is crucially "censored, repressed, or absent" (1989, 2); for Kloepfer the mother returns only textually, her "voice and rhythm" invoked as "a grotto in language (the semiotic), which is the mother's space" (131). Helen herself is certainly impossibly lost in H.D.'s revisions. H.D.'s return also constitutes an escape; the "mother" of *Trilogy* remains very much an idealized construct, a revision not only of one human being (or, to emphasize the distance, H.D.'s memories of one human being), but of a cluster of myths and stereotypes. "Our Lady" has everything and nothing to do with Helen Wolle: she exists as a possibility, a fantasy.

Trilogy, like T. S. Eliot's *Four Quartets,* is a war poem, written in London during the Blitz; it uses the crumbling city as the explicit setting for its explorations. H.D. had the resources to return to America or relocate to the English countryside during this dangerous time, but she found living through the air raids paradoxically exciting and stimulating, proof of her ability to endure. The worm in the storm in the first third of the poem, "The Walls Do Not Fall," declares, "I profit / by every calamity; / I eat my way out of it" (CP 516); adversity similarly enables H.D. She invents a long form, three separate poems in forty-three sections each, written in couplets and triplets, and attempts an ambitious archaeology of language.

The very title "The Walls Do Not Fall," as Susan Gubar observes, "reveals the primacy of spatial imagery" in the work (1979, 202). The enclosures in this first section of the poem offer shelter from hostile environments, including the cocoon the worm eventually spins, but most especially the shell and its inhabitant of part 4. Perhaps like H.D. writing feverishly in her cramped London apartment, this "flabby, amorphous hermit . . . opens to the tide-flow" only occasionally, out of hunger, otherwise needing to fend off "invasion of the limitless ocean-weight" (CP 513). Although lowly, this animal is "closed in, complete, immortal" (CP 513) in its sealed shell—the shell itself an emblem of art since Hermes transformed one into a lyre. In this section, H.D. first uses the pronoun "I," and when she gives a directive at the end of the section, she instructs her readers not only how to survive but how to write poetry (here not the literary daughter, but herself the experienced and advising mother):

> be firm in your own small, static, limited
>
> orbit and the shark-jaws
> of outer circumstance
>
> will spit you forth:
> be indigestible, hard, ungiving
>
> so that, living within,
> you beget, self-out-of-self,
>
> selfless,
> that pearl-of-great-price. (CP 514)

The sea (*mer, mère*) must be shut out for the poet to survive (even here, an indictment of the unsupportive mother threatening to overwhelm the daughter's art), yet the sea always echoes inside the shell's chambers. Susan Gubar argues *Trilogy* improves upon this shell in the next two poems, first in the crucible/grave/womb of "Tribute to the Angels," then in the jar of "Flowering of the Rod," "a symbol of aesthetic shape" that "can contain without confining" (it is sealed, but fragrance escapes) (1979, 211). The mollusc, she believes, represents for H.D. her outgrown imagism, "a beautiful but nevertheless inescapable tomb of form" that "will not be cracked open or digested" (1979, 204).

Gubar's reading may underestimate the centrality of the shell image to H.D.'s body of work. Back at her poetic beginnings, even the poems of *Sea Garden* tell us that they are fragments of shells, reflecting a split sexuality and endangered identity. Linking sea and land, art and sexuality, enclosure and transformation, the shell over and over again provides a site for H.D.'s exploration of the tensions inherent in enclosures, whether they can "contain without confining." In "The Fortune Teller," a chapter of *The Gift* recounting Helen Wolle's girlhood visit to a gypsy, the sea shell speaks a language of identity-melting joy (1998, 78); H.D. has shared her mother's fear of listening to it.

The storm the mollusc-poet shelters herself from is the Blitz. However, as in *The Gift,* she links this war metonymically (or palimpsestically) with many other wars and finds it symptomatic of a larger crisis —a crisis caused by materialism, intolerance, the denigration of spirituality, and a related devaluation of the work that poets do. She acknowledges the immediacy of physical human needs, especially hunger; food represents a kind of nurture profoundly associated with mothers, and the poem is full of eating. (Rationing may have offered one of the more trying aspects of the war for H.D.) However, H.D. insists on the simultaneous necessity for what she calls "spiritual realism." She attempts a kind of research into hidden meanings, a reading of external symbols akin to Freud's translations of dreams or neurotic symptoms.

To describe this research, H.D. extends a metaphor that appears in Freud's language. The analyst, according to Freud, tries to bring to the surface memories or feelings long "submerged" (1953, 291) or "buried in oblivion" (211). He or she therefore becomes a sort of archaeologist, sorting "through the patient's dreams and fragmentary memories to re-create some forgotten or repressed event" (Friedman 1981, 51). Further, for Freud human psychology serves as a repository for "prehistoric experiences" (1953, 380). An understanding of history could illuminate an understanding of the self, and vice versa, interweaving the patterns of personal and mythological or historical events in a manner H.D. clearly appreciated. H.D. applies this archaeological metaphor in *Trilogy*: "the rubble contains, she believes, a coded message whose interpretation can reveal an order underlying the surface reality of chaos" (Friedman 1981, 104). If she decodes well, she will not only understand herself but understand what events in history led to this terrible war.

H.D. does excavate a symbolic framework for her own and human history. Just as she blames her personal crises on a lack of maternal nurture, she attributes the present destruction to the forsaking of old fertility goddesses in obedience to the Judeo-Christian tradition demand, "Thou shalt have none other gods but me" (CP 538). The values associated with "Isis, Aset or Astarte" were broken and buried under a new unbalanced militarism, and she as poet must "recover old values" (CP 511), "steal" and "plunder" the fragments of what the "new-church" shattered, reforging them into wholeness in the crucible of "Tribute to the Angels" (CP 547).

Without *The Gift,* American colonial history would not be especially implicated in H.D.'s "healing-of-the-nations" (CP 530). H.D.'s memoir, whose writing overlapped with the construction of *Trilogy,* embroils her maternal grandmother Mamalie in a betrayal that prefigures the present crisis. The broken promise of a spiritual union between Moravians and Native Americans, in *The Gift* set to occur at a site named Wunden Eiland, leads, H.D. suggests, to sickness and massacre.[9] Associated images of shooting stars link to the bombings of World War II on the Wunden Eiland, or wounded island, of Britain. Mamalie murmurs about "Great Wars and the curse on the land, if we did not keep the Promise" (1998, 173); she seems to feel partly responsible for the failure of the pact and all the apparent consequences. H.D. refers obliquely to the Nazis, the swastika, and the Second World War as results of the curse, pleading, "Mamalie, there will be savages and they will have ugly symbols like some of the bad Indians, to bring ugly and horrible things back to the world and the *Storm of Death* is storming in my ears now" (1998, 178).

In *The Gift,* H.D. seems to assume of the role of healer: immediately, she tends her wounded father, but implicitly she fulfills in her writing of the broken promise of Wunden Eiland. *The Gift* indicates that this may be one of the central aims of *Trilogy*—to reunify the myths of the world, to bring all gods together, and to recover the gift for words and rhythms that had been thwarted in all the women of her family. However, American history, highlighted in the prose, remains submerged in the verse. Her lists of gods in the long poem do not include Native American names, instead following the Bible back through its Greek, Egyptian, and Sumerian roots. *Trilogy's* first triplet calls back to H.D.'s "old town square," "rails gone (for guns)," indicating her awareness of Bethlehem's role in the war effort as a steel manufacturer (CP 509), and she later renounces steel altogether (CP 584); one dream takes her back to a "colonial interior" (CP 525); she remembers (without naming them) the Lehigh and canals of Bethlehem and "home" (CP 528).

H.D. does not explicitly frame her long poem as the fulfillment of promises broken at Wunden Eiland. Instead, *Trilogy* follows the spirit of *The Gift,* continuing Mamalie's translations of ancient documents, emphasizing the points of connection between religions and, unlike Mamalie, not betraying the vision she has received.

H.D.'s mothering use of the second person throughout *Trilogy* (which resembles Gwendolyn Brooks's favored mode of address) reflects this sense of obligation to her gift and its continuing transmission. Having labored to uncover and reassemble old idols, she insists that they not be lost again.

H.D. takes this archaeology further, excavating language itself. This is a technique that, in *The Gift,* originates in childhood games of anagrams initiated by Helen Doolittle (1998, 41). In *Trilogy,* H.D. unlocks "the meaning that words hide" (CP 540) through associative etymologies, what DuPlessis calls "phonemic punning" (1986, 92) and Charlotte Mandel calls "word-dissolves," linking the technique to film (1983, 39). "Gods have been smashed before," she writes, "and idols and their secret is stored / in man's very speech" (CP 517). This poetry describes words as sealed containers: "they are anagrams, cryptograms, / little boxes, conditioned // to hatch butterflies" (CP 540). H.D. "hatches" "Osiris" in "The Walls Do Not Fall" into the star "Sirius" (CP 540) or even the "zrr-hiss" of falling bombs (CP 43). In the second poem of the series, "Tribute to the Angels," the poet fuses in a crucible (London in flames) the metonymic chain "marah-mar" with "mer, mere, mere, mater, Maia, Mary, // Star of the Sea, / Mother" (CP 552). In a related sequence she notes that "Venus" has been corrupted to "venery . . . while the very root of the word shrieks / like a mandrake"; she reclaims it in "venerate" (CP 553–54).

H.D.'s vision of the Lady in "Tribute" enacts her reclaiming and mythologizing of the mother as symbol.[10] Tellingly, this time, "the [male] Child was not with her" (CP 567), "her attention is undivided" (CP 571): H.D. doesn't have to compete with brother Gilbert for this idealized mother. Moreover, she carries "the unwritten volume of the new" (CP 570). H.D. has distilled a version of Helen Doolittle as an artist and/or a muse for artists (in a doubleness that must derive from H.D.'s own ambiguous position as poet/object of beauty). This mother does not disapprove of H.D.'s ambitions; "she must have been pleased with us" (CP 568), *Trilogy*'s speaker divines. Importantly, she is not "shut up in a cave like a Sibyl" or imprisoned in a stained glass window, her reality lost or dimmed to her daughters; "she is Psyche, the butterfly, / out of the cocoon" (CP 570). This idealized, abstracted mother-muse remains always available to H.D., a supporter with whom the daughter need never have conflict. This figure materializes again in the third poem. The manger scene at the end of "Flowering of the Rod" depicts a Mary again without Christ, this time the infant displaced not by a book but by a "bundle of myrrh": as Susan Schweik points out, the aphrodisiac myrrh is a sign of war-disrupting desire (1991, 284–89). Further, "Mary holds nothing but a sign of herself" in an image of "fertility without maternity," since Mary herself *is* myrrh, according to H.D.'s word-dissolves (Schweik 1991, 269).

Through these versions of a mother who embodies and nurtures her daughter's creativity, H.D. provides herself with an archetype for the woman poet, using maternity as a metaphor but displacing the child in favor of the poem, complicating the Madonna with the Magdalen. This complication pertains to her own identity: unlike a great many women artists of the nineteenth century to whom H.D. might have turned for inspiration (Elizabeth Barrett Browning offers the major exception among poets), she *was* both mother and writer, enabled in large part by Bryher's wealth to combine these long-contradictory roles.

One of these inspiring nineteenth-century women behind H.D.'s mother-symbol is Emily Dickinson. Like Dickinson, H.D. uses images of enclosure and metamorphosis to evoke her poetic processes; the expatriate especially borrows the Amherst poet's cocoons and bulbs, or at least they share them as images of the Christian resurrection each rereads. Dickinson's recurrent volcano, the exploding enclosure, also appears in the beginning of *Trilogy* with Pompeii's "slow flow of terrible lava" (CP 510). References in H.D.'s poems and letters suggest H.D.'s careful reading of Dickinson at various stages of her career; Eileen Gregory's notes on H.D.'s 1924 collection of Dickinson's poems corroborate this impression (1997b). H.D. marked "Candor – my tepid friend – " (F 1608, J 1577), as if to signal the poetics of reserve she shares with Dickinson. Interestingly, the same lyric excludes candor in favor of "The Myrrhs, and Mochas, of the Mind," providing a further source for *Trilogy*'s myrrh imagery.

Marianne Moore is another mother to this poem; her then-recent "The Paper Nautilus," a poem H.D. certainly would have read, makes the same links between mother, shel(l)ter, and daughter's literary production that H.D.'s longer poem elaborates. Alicia Ostriker tells us that "in the copy of 'The Walls Do Not Fall' in which H.D. initialed specific lyrics to specific friends, the mollusk lyric is of course Moore's" (1986b, 485). Similarly, as Pondrom suggests, *Trilogy*'s use of worm and butterfly imagery reworks Moore's poem "Half-Deity" (1990a, 398–99). H.D.'s vatic pose differentiates her from both Moore and Dickinson, but her recycling of their figures links the three in a literary community, the textual counterpart of her personal relationships with other women writers including Moore and Bryher.

Not only do enclosure and a transformed, symbolic maternity obtain new value in this long poem, but H.D. particularly reworks *Sea Garden*, with its resistance to mothering and sheltering. H.D. reencloses the torn, twisted, exposed trees she desires to see in "Sheltered Garden" so that they blossom again in the London walled garden of "Tribute to the Angels" (CP 558–60); the vision of the revered Lady of "Tribute" resembles a cluster of the previously despised "gardenpinks" (CP 574); even the word "mothered," previously concealed in a negative image, emerges positively from "smothered," when in "Walls" the cocoon is protectively "smothered in wool" (or Wolle, in a lightly coded reference to her mother's maiden name) (CP 527). "Mar" from "Sea Rose," the opening poem, is one of the very words that gets cooked in the crucible. Both on the level of language and the level of image, H.D. picks up the pieces of this World War I book and imagines how they might be assembled into something more powerful.

H.D. qualifies her figures of enclosure: they must not be "closets" for illicit desires, nor restrictions on a woman's right to invent her own life, nor back-to-the-womb retreats from stress. However, an expatriate bisexual woman poet, multiply outsider, requires some shelter in a still-hostile world, if only to create her pearl-of-great-price. Moreover, through these images H.D. converses with a tradition of women's poetry, accessing some positive mothering that enriches her own work.

Psyche, with Half-Dried Wings

The poetry written between H.D.'s great, interconnected texts of World War II and her death in 1961 demonstrate continued engagement with such figures of enclosure. *Helen in Egypt*, her epic poem written in the early fifties and published in 1961, remains the most famous and ambitious of these works. It deploys an alternative version of the Helen of Troy story, in which the real Helen stayed in Egypt while armies battled over her illusionary double, to look back over H.D.'s own traumatic, war-related experiences and her return to maternal shelter, and hints at what may be an emergence from the regenerative shell. For Moore, enclosures and surfaces remain fused and by definition inescapable; for Dickinson, the rebirth that enclosures promise can only be death; H.D., while continuing to link metamorphosis with death, does suggest that this awakening might be carried back productively into the world of the living. Much of H.D.'s later work hints at this goal of hatching: enclosures, she sometimes implies, serve a crucial but finite function.

Book II of *Helen in Egypt,* "Leuké," supplies yet another version of H.D.'s analysis; this time, Freud becomes Theseus. He cares for Helen's wounded feet by producing fleece-lined shoes from a cedar chest (151), and wraps her in a wool shawl to heal her: "my butterfly, / my Psyche, disappear into the web, / the shell, reintegrate" (170). This healing wool continues to encode H.D.'s mother's maiden name; DuPlessis reads the shawl as "woven for her out of the 'bright thread' of his own accomplished quest—the invention of psychoanalysis" (1985, 80). "Return to the shell, your mother," Theseus tells Helen; you are "a Psyche / with half-dried wings" (165–66). Leuké, the island to which Helen has retired with these meditations, itself represents the "hollow shell" of retreat (193).

This middle book is itself enclosed between the first and third sections of *Helen in Egypt,* "Pallinode" and "Eidolon." Unlike in the major works of the forties, H.D. creates a formal space to describe emergence from enclosure. Helen has a chance to evaluate what has been gained—"a rhythm as yet unheard" (229), perhaps the sea-rhythm echoing in the shell. Her arrival at Leuké from the falling walls of Troy suggests a death, figured as a butterfly slipping from a husk (141); in the last book, "Helen seems to start awake" and considers returning to Egypt (220). Crucially, however, she never quite issues from the "closed circuit of mother-child-mother" this book depicts, existing simultaneously as Helen and Helen's daughter, the "complete family . . . but most particularly 'the child in the mother'" (1985, 82). H.D. ends at the sea where she began, her Helen locked in a study of memory, still enclosed.

In fact, the late poems don't entirely aspire to emergence, unless they invoke a brief and imaginative escape from enclosure. H.D. explicitly depicts herself trapped in an aging and ailing body, a condition that she can only abandon through death. Enclosure, then, becomes a fact of existence treated with more humor than in her earlier work. This is particularly true in the poem "Sagesse," written from a sanatorium in 1957. DuPlessis insightfully observes that "as *Helen in Egypt* will have a 'coda' in 'Winter Love,' so *Trilogy* has a coda in 'Sagesse'": both of the latter poems "counter the scepticism of a psychoanalyst" (in this case Erich Heydt, coded as Germain) and depend on "the thematic and structural use of angels" (1986a, 99–100). "Sagesse," like *Trilogy* and to a greater extent than her epic revision of the Helen myth, centers on a series of enclosures. Combining the attitudes of *Sea Garden* and *Trilogy,* it analyzes not only the satisfactions but the frustrations of confinement.

Although parts of "Sagesse" were published shortly after their composition, the entire piece was only collected posthumously in *Hermetic Definition* (1972). In his introduction to that volume, Norman Holmes Pearson writes that H.D. herself, like the caged owl at the beginning of the sequence, "felt captive and imprisoned at Kusnacht, on Lake Zurich," and was perhaps also considering the confinements "of Pound in Pisa and at St. Elizabeth's Hospital" (introduction unnumbered). H.D. infuses the poem with her own bedridden presence, gazing at periodicals, consulting references on the angels who preside over each hour, listening to the noises of the outside world without possessing the mobility to encounter them physically. However, the poem also slides into the perspective of a girl in London who has survived the Blitz, and who, like H.D., feels disturbed by imprisoned divinity on display at a zoo.

The caged owl who initiates "Sagesse" materializes, H.D. tells us, in a picture printed in *The Listener*. This startling image connects to a memory discussed at length in her memoirs "Writing on the Wall" but also in "Advent" (collected in *Tribute to Freud,* 1974) of a white owl under a bell jar in her father's study. "The wretched and fascinating creature" (1974, 125) seems to stare at H.D. with its large gold eyes as she, a child, plays quietly in her father's room. Eventually she asks her father if she might have it, and her father mock-agrees, "on the condition it stayed where it was" (1974, 125). H.D. identifies her father's study with Freud's office; her father, like Freud, possesses "sacred symbols" (1974, 25); further, both men seem owl-like and scholarly. Further, H.D.'s father, an astronomer, worked nocturnally. H.D. even refers to Freud as an owl watching her quietly a few pages after she recounts this memory of her father's owl, although she imagines Freud not under glass, but "in a tree" (1974, 22).

The real owl under glass, the silenced scholar, is the young H.D. In the sentence immediately after the first mention of the stuffed bird, H.D. writes of her permitted role, "I could sit on the floor with a doll or a folder of paper dolls, but I must not speak to him when he was writing" (1974, 19). She can play at being a (silent) mother, but she may not speak, and certainly cannot understand her father's strange writing. H.D. identifies with Mamalie as a translator of ancient secrets in *The Gift*; however, H.D. also wishes to claim her paternal heritage as a scholar of classical language and literature, a translator of difficult symbols, and reader of the stars (H.D.'s interest in astrology repeats her father's skyward gaze). This man-made bell jar encloses in a negative sense, evoking the confining cultural roles enforced by both her

parents, not in the natural, protective manner H.D. begins to recuper-
ate in her works of the forties.

The "'white-faced Scops owl from Sierra Leone'" in "Sagesse,"
with whom the elder poet certainly identifies, echoes and modifies this
image from *Tribute to Freud*. Both birds inhabit real cages, while H.D.
suffers figurative ones. However, unlike her father's stuffed bird, the
Scops owl yet lives, and more explicitly possesses divine qualities:
"Sagesse" compares him to a "God . . . kept / within the narrow con-
fines of a cage, a pen" (1972, 59). Also, H.D. addresses the owl directly
in "Sagesse" as "my friend," asking him to "'stare out, glare out, live
on'" (58). She remarks the daylight comedy of the predator's "'baggy
trousers / and his spindly legs'" (60). Although the unnamed London
girl thinks, "I wish they wouldn't laugh, it isn't funny," her older
double understands and perhaps enjoys the occasionally ridiculous
manifestations of divinity (60).

Trilogy balances its celebration of poetry's importance with
extremely humble, even comic images of the actual poet as worm and
flabby mollusc. In "Sagesse," one of H.D.'s very last works, the pathetic
and sublime also intermingle, although the poem ultimately empha-
sizes humor as the best way to defy enclosure. Certainly, the poem's
mysticism is utterly serious, as are many of its poignant transforma-
tions. For example, a real owl hooting outdoors initiates momentary
transcendence of a limiting body: "my bones melted and my heart was
flame, / and all I wished was freedom and to follow / the voice" (61);
later in the poem, a mother-goddess gives the speaker a shell, which,
like the jars of myrrh in *Trilogy*, paradoxically contains the infinite:
"the echo of the sea, our secret / and our simple mystery" (75).

However, as in *Trilogy*, H.D. repeatedly describes her own frail-
ness, referring to "this small ark, this little body" (70) and contrasting
her insignificance to the might of angels supposed to protect her (66).
Finally, the best way for a weak mortal to abolish captivity is, like
Dickinson's caged bird, to laugh (F 445, J 613). As Moore does in
"What Are Years?", H.D. may allude to Dickinson's instruction man-
ual for the imprisoned writer with her own impounded owl in
"Sagesse." She echoes Dickinson's strategy, at least, in the last lyric of
the sequence, when she commands in a broad apostrophe (to other
initiates, to the owl), "laugh the world away" (24).

Laughter, in both Dickinson and H.D.'s poems, represents a lyric
speech that recognizes poetry's containments—and "Sagesse" formally
suggests containment, moving freely over wide associative terrain but
within the strictures of *Trilogy*'s slim couplets—even as it eludes

them. For both poets, the lyric and language unfold beyond themselves, paradoxically large. H.D.'s poetry speaks more openly than Dickinson's, and her increasing use of narrative and the scaffolding of sequence render her enclosures more accessible than Dickinson's, even when contextualized in the fascicles. I also must agree with Ostriker that H.D. bequeaths to successors, male and female, a more open, tentative, experimental voice, whose mystical correlations precede the radically open poetics of the Beats by a decade. However, figures of enclosure remain intrinsic even to H.D.'s long poems, even as those expansive sequences open the lyric to larger meditations.

Gwendolyn Brooks

Heralding the Clear Obscure

Dickinson, Moore, and H.D., as this study demonstrates, show persistent interest in the relationship of private to public, inside to outside, closure to openness. Gwendolyn Brooks differs markedly from this triad in many ways: a black midwesterner a generation removed from the modernists, committed to urban life differently than the cosmopolitan Moore and H.D., she began her career under much tighter financial constraints than any of these white poets. Further, although the young Moore campaigned actively for women's suffrage, Brooks renders her commitment to civil rights far more visible in her writing, eventually conceiving of poetry as a potential spur to social change. I seek to honor these distinctions while arguing that Brooks does, in fact, construct a poetic of enclosure with strong resemblances to the esthetic I identify in previous chapters. Dickinson exerts some influence here; imagism also affects Brooks, although to a lesser degree. However, while influence profoundly shapes how Moore and H.D. deploy these figures, it plays a reduced role in how Brooks manipulates enclosure. Instead, Brooks associates the lyric's potential confinements with domesticity and maternity for broader cultural reasons; enclosure in style and image also mark the effects of race and class on her speakers and characters.

Brooks fashions a considerable portion of her early work, represented here by *A Street in Bronzeville* (1945) and *Annie Allen* (1949), in

fixed forms; even her free verse displays an intense formal conscious-
ness. (I give original publication dates for Brooks's volumes, but all the
collections I discuss are reprinted in *Blacks*.) Echoing this stylistic clo-
sure in content, Brooks concentrates on urban constrictions, depict-
ing worlds narrowed by race, class, and sex. She ostensibly abandons
the lyric as a framework in later verse, although her long poem "In
the Mecca" includes some fragments of received forms and conjures
the architectural enclosure of the Mecca building. However, even her
three subsequent "Sermons on the Warpland," alluding as they do to
the public voice of the sermon rather than the relatively intimate
scene of the lyric, not only employ imagery of enclosure but indicate
an esthetic of difficulty. Brooks may advocate accessibility, but the
radical ambiguity of her directives suggest, if not Dickinsonian reti-
cence, at least a commitment to indirection.

Brooks depends on a specific strategy as she fuses the privacy of
the post-Romantic lyric with public aims and contexts: apostrophe.
This quintessentially lyric device, ironically, grants her a powerful
public authority to advise, which she construes alternately as mater-
nal and ministerial. As Brooks herself insists, the question of audience
vitally concerns her, and not only after her famous change of heart at
the 1967 Fisk University Black Writers' Conference. She wrote of her
new aims after this apparent conversion: ". . . NOW the address must
be to blacks; that shrieking into the steady and organized deafness of
the white ear was frivolous—perilously innocent; was 'no 'count.'
There were things to be said to black brothers and sisters and these
things—annunciatory, curative, and inspiriting—were to be said
forthwith, without frill, and without fear of the white presence"
(Brooks 1975a, 4). However, from *A Street in Bronzeville* through the
more deliberately instrumental work of her maturity, Brooks's poetry
often enacts a tension between the lyric convention of isolate interi-
ority and the poem's status as public speech. Brooks extends her lyric
voice to animate and address an absent other, characterized variously
in different poems and at different stages of her career. She uti-
lizes many speakers, from the experienced mother of *Annie Allen* to
the enigmatic proselytizers of her later "sermons," but whether she
announces as a leader, cures as a mother, or inspirits as a preacher,
apostrophe defines her poetic mode. She uses that most lyric of devices
to undermine one of the most pervasive, though arguable, assump-
tions about the post-Romantic lyric: its removal from politics. Brooks
forces her version of the lyric to become a public forum, to sustain the
marks of and even participate in political struggle. Paradoxically,

though, from her earliest volumes onward but especially in her "Sermons on the Warpland," which purport to advise from a position of authority in the explicit context of race riots, her imperatives perplex as much as illuminate.

In "Apostrophe, Animation, and Abortion," Barbara Johnson begins discussing Brooks in relation to the figure of apostrophe, which she defines as "the direct address of an absent, dead, or inanimate being by a first person speaker," specifically in terms of one of Brooks's early and most famous poems, "the mother" (Brooks 1987, 185).[1] The "mother" of this piece addresses aborted children; Johnson reads this situation as a reversal of the "primal apostrophe" that informs the entire history of the lyric, a demand addressed to a mother by an infant, "which assures life even as it inaugurates alienation" (198). Johnson notes that the Brooks poem exists "*because* a child does not" (195), reminding us of the competition for some women writers between poetry and motherhood. "The attempt to achieve a full elaboration of any other discursive position than that of a child" in poetry, psychoanalysis, or politics is fraught with difficulties, but, Johnson theorizes, might have enormous impact in all three arenas (199).

In fact, Gwendolyn Brooks's lyrics often wield apostrophes; specifically, they most frequently apostrophize children or adults who, childlike, need care, advice, or motivation. More than H.D., who does experiment with a similar voice in the mollusc section of *Trilogy*, Brooks repeatedly writes as a mother, addressing her readers as children in imperatives that reach out of the private world of the lyric long before she asserts this expansion as a political goal of her poetry. Although Brooks has been criticized for apparently abandoning her compelling depictions of women's lives in her early poetry, this rhetorical innovation remains as important (and perhaps as feminist) as Johnson suggests. Brooks creates a powerful kind of mother, a public actor, fusing her speech with that of a preacher or prophet, articulating an unusually authoritative, distinctly female voice.

Further, Brooks's invocations are not apostrophes in the usual sense of a speaker's deflection of address away from her readers. A poetic opening like "Stand off, daughter of the dusk" (1987, 137) surpasses overheard imperative; it also names her intended readers. In fact, in a 1949 review, J. Saunders Redding chastises Brooks for this same poem, which, he argues, excludes white audiences by its overly "special and particularized" subject (1996, 6). While the apostrophes Brooks employs inevitably circle back to constitute her identity as a poet, mother, and/or preacher, she primarily intends to influence her real audience.[2] Through so vividly imagining and animating her readers, Brooks gradually constructs a poetic that demands active, collaborative audiences: her work challenges the binary of private and public that has so deeply shaped the lyric poem.

Brooks's critics increasingly argue for such continuity in her work. Gwendolyn Brooks's own autobiographies, tellingly entitled *Report from Part One* and *Report from Part Two*, divide her career into two sections, a sort of Before and After separated by the Black Arts movement. Some interviews with and essays on Gwendolyn Brooks duplicate this division, recounting her transformative experience at Fisk University, followed by her work with a Chicago teenage gang, the Blackstone Rangers; although William H. Hansell locates three periods in her oeuvre (1987), his essay and other important pieces by George Kent (1987) and Houston Baker (1996) emphasize the 1960s as a crucial hinge for Brooks. She encountered in that conference and, more crucially, in her mentorship of young poets, a new kind of energy and pride in black identity to which Brooks attributes a change in both her life and her writing. In the narrative usually told by anthology headnotes (see, for instance, *The Norton Anthology of Modern Poetry* or *The Harper American Literature*), Brooks moved from poetry in a mix of traditional forms (some European, some African American) to work in open forms, from an integrationist philosophy to black nationalism, from lyrics written for private reading to an oral orientation, drastically reconceiving her audience and intentions. Critics often quote the manifesto from the Appendix to the first *Report*: "My aim, in my next future, is to write poems that will somehow successfully 'call' (see Imamu Baraka's 'SOS') all black people: black people in taverns, black people in alleys, black people in gutters, schools, offices, factories, prisons, the consulate; I wish to reach black people in pulpits, black people in mines, on farms, on thrones; *not* always to 'teach'—I shall wish often to entertain, to illumine. My newish voice will not be an imitation of the contemporary young black voice, which I so admire, but an extending adaption of today's G. B. voice" (1972, 183). Here Brooks seems on the one hand to announce a new orientation: she wishes that her writing might unify a black community. On the other hand, even within this proclamation she signals the continuity between phases of her work: her "newish," not "new," voice will be an "extending adaption" of her current poetry, extending its dependence on apostrophe, adapting that address to a newly configured readership.

Brooks radically marked her commitment to this change in focal audience by cutting her tie to Harper and Row and, after 1971, only publishing at black presses. Some of Brooks's critics ally themselves with one Brooks or the other, arguing either that her early work transcends race or betrays her blackness, that her late work either fails esthetically or finally breaks through its bondage to white forms. The most partisan are often poetic inheritors. Don L. Lee (Haki Madhubuti) naturally favors her post-1967 efforts (1996), while Rita Dove and Marilyn Nelson Waniek lament the detrimental influence of the Black Aesthetic on Brooks's later work (1991). Yet, to draw too dramatic a contrast between the early and later works is to misread them; as Brooks herself insists, although the world around her has changed, "I just continue to write about what confronts me" (1972, 151). In an interview with Claudia Tate, Brooks points out the political nature of many of her early poems, arguing that "in 1945 I was saying what many of the young folks said in the sixties" (1983, 42). D. H. Melham asserts, in fact, that "no facile demarcations exist" in Brooks's canon (1987, 2), supporting recent work by Kathryne V. Lindberg (1996) and Betsy Erkkila (1992). Although she carefully explicates certain transformations in Brooks's work, Erkkila argues that "the simple opposition between early Euro-American and politically incorrect Brooks and later African American and politically correct Brooks breaks down in any careful reading of her work" (201). Not only do continuities exist in her rhetorical poses and her imagery, but in perpetually revising herself Brooks frequently alludes to and incorporates her earlier language in the later poetry, her revisionary poetic in this sense resembling H.D.'s.

One of these subtle shifts in Brooks's use of the lyric is that the maternal rhetorical position Brooks so frequently occupies in her early volumes becomes fused with the more public, sermonic voice that resonates throughout her later poetry. From *Annie Allen* to the "Sermons on the Warpland," however, the voice of the mother and its metaphoric extension into the voice of the minister enables her to investigate whether, or to what extent, the lyric possesses a social function. Her use of apostrophe, finally, takes the tradition of enclosed lyrics from which she emerges—especially the confine-conscious lyrics of previous American women poets, from Emily Dickinson onward—and stretches it, exploiting the lyric's public possibilities. Intriguingly, the poems that manifest this struggle have also been labeled her most "mandarin," suggesting, as Brooke Kenton Horvath notes, a link between stylistic and political resistance (1996, 213, 221).

In a sense, then, Brooks's poetry does move from closed forms and difficult language to an esthetic of openness in structure and style. This chapter begins with the urban confinements and protected elite estates of her first two books, demonstrating how her language patterns correspond to such images of enclosure. However, I subsequently show that this original poetic of enclosure continues to shape Brooks's poems of the late sixties, especially "In the Mecca" and the "Sermons on the Warpland": she depicts positive shelter and negative confinement in these works, and in a parallel manner offers fragments of fixed form and obscure imperatives that simultaneously resist and urge openness. Eventually, Brooks ceases to practice a poetic of enclosure, but this mode describes her poetic practice for much longer than her autobiographies imply.

Urban Zoning

Gwendolyn Brooks's early works show the influence of a range of modernist writers. Much of the poetry of the early twentieth century turns away from pastoral scenes to city geography, reflecting population shifts and the city's links with the extremes of modernity in terms of technology, industry, and cultural life. Brooks borrows simultaneously from Anglo-American high modernism and the Harlem Renaissance in her attempts to represent urban life. In the virtuosically varied *A Street in Bronzeville*, "kitchenette building" echoes "The Love Song of J. Alfred Prufrock" with its comic rhyme ("minute" and "get in it"), fragments of dialogue, and antipoetically polysyllabic diction ("involuntary," "anticipate"); her experiments with form, like the sonnet-ballad in *Annie Allen*, also evoke modernist allusions to and disruptions of received patterns. As Gary Smith points out, Brooks also shares with Eliot an interest in the metaphysical poets, following Donne in some of her variations in sonnet forms (1987, 167–75). On the other hand, Brooks experiments with African American forms and dialects, as in "Queen of the Blues" and "at the hairdresser's." Like Langston Hughes, Brooks attempts to represent, and even speak for, a range of ordinary characters in ordinary urban settings. As Gladys Williams suggests, Brooks also frequently taps into the ballad's dual tradition, English-Scottish and African American (1987, 206). Brooks's links with an African American tradition were forged well before her interest in modernism, through her father's reading aloud and her mother's announcement that "'You are going to be the lady Paul Laurence Dunbar'" (Kent 1990, 1). She was advised to read the high modernists as well as Harlem Renaissance writers when she sent her work to James Weldon Johnson, and she imbibed the period's spare esthetic in her workshops with the imagist-influenced Inez Cunningham Stark.

Brooks read a great deal of Emily Dickinson in junior college, and the influence of this poet illuminates some of Brooks's juvenilia (Kent 1990, 38). She includes a photograph of herself at Emily Dickinson's home in *Report from Part One* with the caption, "I think Emily, after the first shock at my intrusion, would have approved of my natural" (1972, 107): such asides, though minor, do suggest Brooks's continuing admiration for her predecessor. When in "Riders to the Blood-Red Wrath," Brooks announces "I / have sewn my guns inside my burning lips" (1987, 390), she sounds startlingly like Dickinson in her Vesuvian poems, especially "My Life had stood – a Loaded Gun – " (F 764, J 754). Brooks seldom writes pieces as cryptic and compressed as those of the Amherst poet, and their experience and poetic material remain drastically different. Still, in these early works, Brooks's discerning criticism of American culture, her barely bottled anger, and her concern with the narrow spaces of domesticity resemble Dickinson's. Brooks resists categorization as a woman poet, prioritizing race over gender (1972, 199), but she does share with Dickinson and others the "strategy of reticence" Jeanne Kammer locates in many women poets, a tight-lippedness in response both to stereotypes of the sentimental "poetess" and to conventions of feminine propriety (1979, 156). Although Erkkila finds Brooks relatively unconflicted about assuming the voice of the poet, even in her later, more overtly politicized writing Brooks demonstrates careful reserve about some aspects of her personal life.[3]

Nevertheless, Brooks articulates more directly in her poetry than Dickinson, Moore, or H.D. her political and social contexts; her race, class, and time period mean that those circumstances and contexts differ from those of any of the poets I have discussed. Brooks's poetry values enclosure imagery in hard times, as a barely adequate container for rage and chaos, or dreams that must be put aside. Occasionally, her speakers welcome a bit of privacy afforded by an alley, or clothing can function as armor in a hostile world (1987, 362). Elsewhere, confinement remains a negative symptom of poverty and sordidness that Brooks's speakers, like Dickinson's, fantasize about escaping. It can function as a gentle trap, like the responsibility a parent feels to her child, but restricts nonetheless. This is one of the central differences between Brooks on the one hand and H.D. and Moore on the other: Brooks does create a narrative of enclosure and escape, played out both formally and thematically in her writing.

All of Brooks's early books attempt to depict life in Bronzeville, a name given to Chicago's South Side Black Belt by its residents; its boundaries form one of the first circles drawn around Brooks's world. The dreams of her characters are curtailed by racism and sometimes by sexism; Chicago's housing shortage, which frustrated Brooks herself in her attempt to get her family comfortably settled, further limits the Bronzeville denizens to cramped apartments and kitchenettes, commonly with one bath shared between four or five families. Brooks's use of the lyric provides a formal correlative for this sense of confinement: she writes with near-imagist brevity, suggesting rather than elaborating, often within the conventions of a range of literary forms. Her touch is light, her tone often ironic, although she addresses serious subjects, and this contributes to the sense of depth beneath resistant surfaces. Even her novel, *Maud Martha* (reprinted in *Blacks,* 1987), possesses some of these lyric qualities, broken into chapters or vignettes often only a few pages long.

A Street in Bronzeville, her first published collection, contains a set of lyrics subtitled "A Street in Bronzeville," several longer poems, and a wartime sonnet sequence named "Gay Chaps at the Bar." "A Street in Bronzeville" represents or speaks in the voices of various inhabitants of this district in Chicago, ranging from the hopefully dreaming residents of the "kitchenette building" to the dead and buried Madam of "southeast corner" to murderers and preachers; all the poems convey entrapment and congestion, and yet all the characters can enjoy small pleasures, like Matthew Cole remembering "wonderful jokes" in his dirty "stove-heated flat / Over on Lafayette" (1987, 40). Brooks finds a range of formal ways to represent these situations. Sonnets and ballads appear, but Brooks uses a variety of idiosyncratic formal effects to carry other meanings. She stuffs the "crowding darkness" of "the old-marrieds" into long lines, rhymes affectionately coupled like the "old-marrieds" themselves. "kitchenette building" leaves a line or two unrhymed or unsatisfied, like the unfulfilled dreams of its inhabitants, disjunctive between every enclosing rhymed pair. The end-stopped lines of "the ballad of chocolate Mabbie" offer the sonic equivalent of Mabbie's amputated hopes.

"[A] song in the front yard" (1987, 28) contrasts entrapment and freedom through a contrast of rhymed and unrhymed couplets. The speaker of this poem, a girl who has stayed obediently in her neatly tended front yard with the cultivated flowers, obeying curfews, nevertheless longs for a "back yard" life associated with nighttime, sexuality, and "wonderful fun." The backyard, its gate already stolen away, opens into an alley, a tributary to the alluring adult world. This poem, like others in the book, speculates about the benefits of being "bad," here linked with wearing "night-black." The poem feeds off of a series of familiar binaries—day and night, white and black, purity and sexuality—that suggest racial opposition and further bind the trapped girl.

Formally, the backyard resembles, in the first stanza, something that doesn't love a quatrain. It stretches out the length of the third line: "where it's rough and untended and the hungry weed grows." Brooks quickly recuperates it into rhyme, however, by a metrically neater line, "A girl gets sick of a rose," which seems to express boredom by its relative brevity. This poem alternates rhymed couplets with the unrhymed ones in back of them, mimicking the arrangement of front and back yards, until the last stanza, in which rhyme wins out, even as the speaker reasserts her approval of "bad women." Although not obviously about race, this poem plays out the tensions between Brooks's use of "white" forms and her racial identity, inscribed through her interest in forbidden blackness (and even "paint on my face," a way of describing makeup that may intend to evoke her African ancestry).[4]

Brooks also invokes the enclosure of maternity in one of the collection's first poems, "the mother." Ambivalent as this poem remains, Gwendolyn Brooks here chooses a maternal persona, as she will repeatedly in both her work and her life. Brooks became a mother to Henry Blakely Jr. in 1940, before her first book ever saw print; her second child, Nora, was born eleven years later. Biographer George Kent describes how Brooks became a mother to a workshop-full of young African American writers in the late sixties, especially to Don Lee and Walter Bradford (1990, 206). He also notes the maternal pose she takes throughout the various metamorphoses in her writing (250), even choosing to frame the biography with anecdotes about Brooks's mother, Keziah. Brooks has written several books for children, including *Bronzeville Boys and Girls* (1956) and *The Tiger Who Wore White Gloves* (1974), with what D. H. Melham calls a "maternal approach"

(260). According to Betsy Erkkila's reading, Brooks finds in black motherhood an alternative value system, a "morally complex base of social action" (1992, 204): "In fact, Brooks's development from her early years to her more recent years might be read as a progressive unmasking and expansion of the voice and figure of the mother, as Brooks articulates a larger and larger role both for the mother in the black community and for herself as a kind of cultural mother to the political project of black literary and social creation" (1992, 197).

Motherhood, apostrophe, and enclosure begin their entanglement in "the mother." The mother's voice, when Brooks assumes it, often apostrophizes her readers as children, if apostrophe can include "calling" (as Brooks puts it in *Report from Part One*) and advising the living. Such poems characteristically employ the second person and imperatives. In many ways, this voice forces the breaking of enclosures, including the neat box of the poem; it reaches out to create its reader and insists on the relationship between writer and reader as a living one, demanding mutual commitments. Brooks's use of apostrophe also grows out of the African American blues tradition, which itself grew out of the call-and-response patterns within agricultural work groups, first in Africa, then in American slavery. Oral blues forms assume a relationship between performer and audience that is sometimes carried over into literary blues; this interaction occurs both in Brooks's poetry before 1967 and her supposedly new emphasis on the African part of her African American heritage.[5]

Brooks will explore this maternal pose more thoroughly in *Annie Allen*; *A Street in Bronzeville*'s imperatives chiefly occur in Brooks's sonnet sequence in the voice or voices of African American soldier(s), "Gay Chaps at the Bar." Importantly, Brooks leaves Bronzeville in these lyrics, although this epistolary series might address itself to Bronzeville women at home. The sense of constriction associated with Bronzeville, however, remains. First, the form of the sonnet imposes a tight restraint, an economy of language.[6] Second, recurrent images of coffins and sealed containers evoke the situation of the soldiers: angry, but unable to express it; limited to certain kinds of service because of race; powerless to change their dangerous positions. The series' frequent use of the second-person attempts to escape this confinement, but always returns, apparently unable to initiate effective communication. Soldiers and women seem to speak radically different languages, in a gap that only Brooks's impersonations can bridge.

Susan Schweik productively invokes Irigaray's theory of mimicry to explain Brooks's endeavor in the latter series to wear camouflage, "completely violating all home-front taboos against women's literary impersonation of men in uniform" (1991, 110). As Brooks herself says retrospectively, she uses off-rhyme to reflect an off-rhyme situation, as a woman successfully reproducing the conventions of World War II literature, even to the point of mimicking the soldier's fearful misogyny.[7] She dares this partly, as Schweik points out, because her transgressions violate racial conventions more centrally than sexual ones. Further, the "uniform structure" (138) of the sonnet itself offers a costume that Brooks dons, but wears with a difference, pushing its seams into an unfamiliar shape.

One of these sonnets, "looking," actually directs its imperatives to a mother or some woman performing a maternal role. Schweik notes that this woman fails to nourish her lover or son properly, not successfully providing "the word as snack" (127): "You have no word for soldiers to enjoy / The feel of, as an apple, and to chew / With masculine satisfaction" (1987, 67). Over and over again, the sonnets describe a hunger for communication that women cannot satisfy. Women's words seem poor food to men traumatized by war. The sonnet previous to "looking," "my dreams, my works, must wait till after hell," even more insistently concerns hunger, but oddly, the soldier preempts the mother's control over the larder. Here enclosures appear in a thematic as well as in a formal way; the soldier neatly labels and stores his honey and bread, translated only in the title as "dreams" and "works," in "jars and cabinets." This soldier uses a peculiarly housewifely metaphor for his suspended feelings and ambitions; I think this is one place, unremarked by Schweik, in which the author's gender strongly marks itself.

Elsewhere, as in "the white troops had their orders but the Negroes looked like men," enclosures or "box"es occur both as literal coffins and as the imprisoning conceptual frameworks applied to racial identity (Brooks 1987, 70). In "piano after war," the soldier fantasizes about his return home, imagining how a woman unidentified by relationship or even race will heal him by playing music. "Old hungers / Will break their coffins," he hopes, with this image fusing the "jars and cabinets of my will" with the death imagery more broadly implicit in the sequence. The poet's role becomes feminine in contrast to the soldier's, but women and poets make a kind of music that can't encompass the "cry of bitter dead men" (1987, 68). This cry breaks into the protected, feminine-identified "room" of the soldier's daydream the way that "old hungers" burst their latches and lids. The soldier's conclusion that women can't understand (and make art that stands up to) the horrors of war is absolutely undermined, however, by the fact that this sequence, which depicts the identity-shattering effects of war, is created by Brooks's own act of literary transvestitism.

The primary enclosure in this sequence is the sonnet itself, which only uneasily contains Brooks's language. Maria K. Mootry, in fact, identifies the series as "a collage with a modernist aesthetic of indeterminacy, fragmentation, multilocused meaning, and difficulty of interpretation" (2000, 142); highlighting the pun on "iron feet," she links "the tyranny of poetic practice" to "the tyranny of political relations" (146). Brooks's "rhymes" may only have one sound in common, or even only one sound in resemblance; sometimes the full rhymes occur in the wrong places (as in lid and bid, hell and tell, will and till in "my dreams").[8] The frailty of the rhymes emphasizes the fragile balance between the power of language to contain and the exploding force of strong feeling. Enjambment occurs heavily, and a cacophony of voices and vocabularies sounds through the sequence, including "white speech" (64), "raw" mother-speech (67), the cries of bitter dead men (68), religious thees and thous (71–72), and the twisted romantic address of the "love notes" (73–74). These sonnets, however altered, nevertheless manage to function as containers. In the first, title poem, the word "bar" that Schweik rightly identifies as a "word-kernel" with multiple meanings evokes the sonnet as a barred prison (1991, 124). By the second, "still do I keep my look, my identity," the sonnet already resembles a casket; this poem describes the "art" of a dead soldier's body in rigor mortis, itself enclosing the body. By the third poem, the sonnet takes a more familiar and less frightening shape as a jar or cabinet, holding the honey and bread the returning soldiers need for nourishment. Although this food remains inaccessible to the soldiers throughout the sequence, it waits there for them, if they still have the "taste" for it. Food, throughout the series, represents a peacetime language still spoken by women but put away by men, a language both frivolous and nourishing, associated with music and art. Further, with the linkage of coffins and food containers in "piano after war," the preserved food comes to mean the soldiers' sealed-off, dead, prewar selves. Enclosure, in early Brooks, signifies a negative confinement, but does retain pragmatic value.

Admit Me to Our Mutual Estate

With *Annie Allen,* her second book of poetry, Gwendolyn Brooks was the first African American to win the Pulitzer Prize (1950); yet, as Claudia Tate observes, it receives less critical attention than many of

Brooks's other works (1987, 140). It seems less hopeful than *A Street in Bronzeville,* less determinedly political than her subsequent collection, *The Bean Eaters* (1960), and may be the most difficult of Brooks's poetry, dense with wordplay and formal experiment; Don Lee later singles it out as Brooks's work most obviously focused on "poetic style," and therefore at a white audience (1996, 84). More specifically, he laments "an overabundance of the special appeal to the world-runners" (86); Lee accurately notes the racial converse of Redding's remark that certain poems, by their manner of address, construct a readership that excludes him.

While this collection, a series detailing the life of its title character, plies a more cryptic style than other early Brooks, in the last third of this book Brooks makes an important move toward increased openness in the sense of accessibility to a wide audience. She explicitly identifies the voice of the poet with the voice of the mother, in this case a mother of imperiled and lost progeny. *Annie Allen,* in fact, narrates this move toward the mature, mother's voice, a voice (in her poetic world) of leadership and authority.[9] The volume consists of three sections, "Notes from the Childhood and the Girlhood," "The Anniad" and its appendix, and "The Womanhood." The first section shows the literal narrowness of Annie's life as well as the cramping of her will and imagination by her mother; the discipline of form demonstrated by Brooks duplicates the discipline of meek and obedient femininity imposed on Annie. "The Anniad" offers the mock-epic of Annie's failed marriage. In "The Womanhood," Brooks "writes beyond the ending" of heterosexual romance and announces the need for a new direction, which perhaps Brooks only fully finds twenty years later (DuPlessis 1985). Throughout the volume, however, Brooks practices a poetic of formal closure and stylistic complexity; her imagery sometimes echoes the urban confinements of her first volume and sometimes delineates the elite worlds of estates and private cars excluding Annie.

All of the work from the first phase of Brooks's career creates an uneasy dialogue with Anglo-American poetic tradition; *Annie Allen* grapples with some of its most powerful exemplars. "Notes from the Childhood and the Girlhood" consists mainly of light lyrics, especially in ballad stanzas, to set up Annie's expectations for a happy ending through marriage. Brooks writes none of these poems in the second person, except for the last piece in the sequence, "my own sweet good," Annie's quoted address to her future lover. "The Anniad" bows to the epic as it encompasses both a world war and the war between Annie and her husband, or Annie's fantasies and reality;

"Appendix to the Anniad" searches further and ends up with "the sonnet-ballad," a love-lament, to tell the story of the failed marriage. In both of these subsections, body and appendix, Brooks addresses the reader: "The Anniad" begins, "Think of sweet and chocolate" (1987, 99) and ends with parallel imperatives including "Think of tweaked and twenty-four" (109). Many of the sonnets and ballads in the last third of the book, "The Womanhood," direct love not at husbands or lovers but at children, and the whole volume ends on the seriousness of blank verse, addressing a deaf tradition personified as a group of resistant white men and finally asserting Annie's alienation from it and its forms. The collection continuously searches among the Anglo-American traditions of poetic expression for a form that will both hold what Annie's life has been and direct her in her maturity. Annie concludes that there are no "timely godmothers to guide us," that she can expect no admittance to any exclusively enclosed estate, but that she must innovate her own way forward into an open landscape.

The collection begins with Annie's birth, in humble lowercase, into the restricted world already familiar from Brooks's first book, in a poem called "the birth in a narrow room" (1987, 83). The "scanty plot of ground" infant Annie finds to play in implicitly contrasts with Wordsworth's sonnet "Nuns fret not at their convent's narrow room." In Wordsworth's poem, the tightly bound sonnet becomes a place to go for "pastime" when one has "felt the weight of too much liberty"; Annie, of course, does not doom *herself* to this small space, and instead will come to find it "pinchy." Annie's "narrow room" seems overstuffed, and the poem formally imitates this overflow, exceeding the sonnet by a couplet. Even the bees that "murmur by the hour in foxglove bells" in Wordsworth "buzz by in private cars" in Brooks, as if they only wish to sightsee from a distance in Bronzeville.

Often the Anglo-American tradition, as Brooks constructs it, means the major poems of the male English Romantics. In their influence, Brooks follows Harlem Renaissance writers like Claude McKay and Countee Cullen, whose poetries were strongly marked by Wordsworth, Shelley, and Keats. In any case, *Annie Allen* refers richly to these writers. This particular poem of hopeless constriction makes further allusions to the idealized enclosures of other Romantic poets than Wordsworth: doing Stevens's jar one better, Brooks turns Keats's Grecian urn into "old peach cans and old jelly jars," a sticky debris of empty containers, a much less glorifying metaphor for poetry. Art has been divested of its sweetness and saved in a corner in the hope that someone will find a practical use for it. Coleridge's enclosing "bower" will not appear until "the ballad of late Annie," but other of its conventions appear here. The bees in Coleridge's "A Lime Tree Bower, my Prison," exist to fertilize, to make the womb or formal space of the poem bear fruit. Here, in Brooks's poem, the "bugs" might not even be pollinating bees but flies around lifeless remains, as in Dickinson's famous poem (and in this volume particularly Brooks speaks with the indirections usually attributed to Dickinson—incomplete syntax, grammatical substitutions).

Still, even if the peaches have vanished, this poem does bear a kind of fruit: a too-good china child keeps haplessly spilling china cherries, foreshadowing Annie's bad romantic choices. Further, Annie herself equals the fruit, the poem-child; the series makes this clear by so often calling her "sweet." Brooks literalizes this common metaphor for writing (harvest or childbirth) by identifying the poetic product with the child. For Brooks, the identities of mother and poet do not necessarily compete. She uses Coleridge's metaphor with little mark of conflict, although she deglamorizes it considerably.

The parents of "Sweet Annie" have settled for less, and try to teach Annie to do the same, to be thankful even for her lacks and famines, as in "Maxie Allen" (1987, 84). The word "pinch," with its connotations of hunger and violence, appears multiply in the first section of the volume to describe the smallness of the lives and places. The only way out for Annie is spelled out by her own mother in "the ballad of late Annie" (1987, 90): "'Get a broom to whish the doors / Or get a man to marry.'" She may either stay in the house that her mother controls, obeying her orders, or escape through marriage. As Tate observes, the "late" of the title refers to Annie's oversleeping, her "blush-brown" ripeness (fruitlike in her "bower"), and suggests that Annie is already dead (1987, 146). The collection contains its fair share of dead bodies and dead flowers, as if to equate, especially in this section, enclosed life with coffined death.

"Notes from the Childhood and the Girlhood" ends with "promise so golden and gay" (1987, 95) ill fulfilled in "The Anniad." The marriage-plot Annie looks forward to for liberation and some kind of happy ending, a narrative implicit in these sonnets and ballad forms, fails to deliver. "The Anniad," a long poem in fully rhymed seven-line stanzas, delivers Annie from this state of expectation, "All her harvest buttoned in" (99), through marriage to a "man of tan" (100) who "leads her to a lowly room" (101) and then goes off to war, comes home and begins an affair with "a maple banshee" (104), falls ill and is nursed by Annie, and abandons her again. Brooks links the title to

The Iliad and *The Aeneid*; like the classical epics, her poem treats war and loss, although this time from a woman's perspective (Annie a version of abandoned Penelope or Dido). The collection shifts to another set of conventions, from love lyrics to a heroic form, in an attempt to better represent Annie's experience. Since the central war seems to be a marriage, "The Anniad" becomes a mock-heroic poem, with its ordinary heroine who finds that marriage, her fairy-tale destiny, does not in fact satisfy all or any of her dreams. In this collection, marriage also does not end her tale. Rachel Blau DuPlessis's book *Writing Beyond the Ending* (which discusses some of Brooks's work but not *Annie Allen*) sets out some of the ways women writers defeat the marriage plot; although "The Anniad," through its positioning and through its use of Annie's name, takes centrality in this anti-epic of Annie's life, a third of the book yet remains.

"The Womanhood" handles Annie's maturity, in a web of lyrics that subdivides and reproduces in a complex structure. It begins with a five-sonnet sequence entitled "the children of the poor," which seems to follow from the line in "The Anniad" indicating abandoned Annie's strategy: "Then incline to children-dear!" (1987, 107). A mother whose poverty prevents her from adequately caring for her children speaks through the poems, most of which are Brooks's hybrid Petrarchan-Shakespearean sonnets, taking confusing turns, ending in couplets that do not offer resolutions; their tone is "introspective and elegiac," except in the fourth poem (Gary Smith 1987, 174). The fourth poem, with its militant imperatives and tidy ninth-line volta, stands out oddly, almost as a sudden explosion. The sequence resolves, however, with a return to more cryptic and contained language.

The first, "People who have no children can be hard," contrasts the lives of the childless and of parents (115). People who have no children "attain a mail of ice and insolence"; they can be epic heroes, "perish purely," leading lives uncompromised by responsibility to vulnerable others. To have children means to live in a "throttling dark"; the group of parents included in the poem's "we" has an ear for the helplessness and "unridiculous / Lost softness" of children and are trapped and even cursed by this feeling of responsibility. The same helplessness, however, softens the parents' imprisonment, "and makes a sugar of / The malocclusions, the inconditions of love." Further, the *abba* scheme of the octave literalizes the enclosing "mail" of the childless; the sestet ends in three couplets, or dependent pairings, what Brooks will much later call "the rhymes of Leaning" (1987, 450). Brooks uses one of the poetic forms most associated with love, and one of the most constraining forms, to demonstrate how love sweetly binds the options of the lover.

The lover, however, belongs to "we others," or perhaps "we mothers." Again, motherhood suggests enclosure; rather than the mother's body enclosing the fetus, however, the mother herself is gently bound by her love for the child. Brooks demonstrates maternal enclosure in a distinctly different manner from H.D. or Moore in their poems about motherhood, in which the poets acquire maternal protection so that they may produce literary offspring. Dickinson, Moore, and H.D. write mainly (although not entirely) from the perspective of children, vulnerable and needing armor; Brooks writes more truly from the perspective of the mother. In the last poem in the "Appendix to the Anniad," Annie asks her mother, "What can I use an empty heart-cup for." Here, in "The Womanhood," she begins the transformation of Annie from a disappointed girl into a voice of strength, whose authority derives from the fact of her motherhood.

The poem-children metaphor continues, although now Annie becomes the author rather than the authored, the poem reproducing her into "little halves" (116). In the first sonnet of "the children of the poor," the children seem most literal; in the second, the image extends itself to Brooks's metaphorical children. "What shall I give my children? who are poor" compares the speaker to a sculptor. Her "children" beg her "for a brisk contour, / Crying that they are . . . graven by a hand / Less than angelic, admirable or sure" (116). Brooks clearly discusses art, evaluating her own poems as impoverished, although surely even before her Pulitzer they had not been "adjudged the least-wise of the land." The source of their weakness, she seems to feel, lies not in her lack of technical expertise—she knows this volume will be judged formally dazzling—but in not having found her best material. "My hand is stuffed with mode, design, device," she writes, "But I lack access to my proper stone." Here Brooks preempts the later criticisms of those like Don Lee, who find *Annie Allen* expert but wanting. In part this resembles a pose of humility taken by American women poets back to Anne Bradstreet to defuse the subversive charge of their ambitions, but in part, I think, this marks Brooks's real dissatisfaction with her work. Brooks speaks here from her "womanhood," like Annie Allen, needing to "Wizard a track through our own screaming weed" (140), but not having found full voice and clear direction.

Brooks begins to innovate such a voice in the third poem, "And shall I prime my children, pray, to pray?" which satirizes the role religion plays in rounding out the needs of these children (117). Religion ultimately serves only as a bandage around the eyes, a conspirator in imprisonment. The poet confidently ventriloquizes the minister: "Children, confine your light in jellied rules; / Resemble graves." Even stained glass windows become enclosures, confining light in their colored shapes. Presumably, religion threatens to choke the imagination not only out of real children, but out of poems, confining and coloring whatever light the poet might have to shed.

Interestingly, the imperative voice, which will characterize so much of Brooks's writing, first appears in this third poem. Through taking on in mockery the authority of the church, the poet gives the orders "confine," "resemble," "be," "learn." However, as a mother might represent the voice of religion within a family, the roles of mother and minister fuse in the poem; for instance, the mother-minister will "sew up belief / If that should tear." This sonnet offers a negative version of a conjunction that will recur more empoweringly in Brooks's poetry later on. Both the mother and minister speak with authority, addressing "children," giving direction or leadership in the imperative tense.

"First fight. Then fiddle. Ply the slipping string," the fourth poem in the sequence, finally assumes this strong style while simultaneously expressing what seem to be Annie's own values: the anger that had been disciplined in Annie like all her hair tamed down in "The Anniad" becomes explicit in this most commanding poem (118). Brooks writes lovingly of the need to make music, but, she insists, one needs "first to civilize a space / Wherein to play your violin with grace." Brooks strikes a new note here, articulating a much more militant response to the injustices that fill the previous pages, and this poem more than the others looks forward to Brooks's later interest in black nationalism. She "pinches" the word "civilization" from the white, Western culture that would claim it, turning it around by insisting that Euro-American culture, in fact, needs to be civilized. Then, one may "muzzle the note / With hurting love; the music that they wrote / Bewitch, bewilder." These sound like directions to John Coltrane, who bewildered the melodies that the dominant culture produced, doing loving damage to an existing tradition; they also might describe what Brooks does in this revisionary volume. Brooks, however, already fiddles away (fiddling in both senses, making music and altering an already existing lyric tradition), perhaps feeling that she has already fought her war in "The Anniad."

The last poem of this sequence steps completely back from this forthrightness, turning in on itself with a complicated syntax, "charming the rainbow radiance into tightness / And into a remarkable politeness / That is not kind and does not want to be" (119). This sonnet begins "When my dears die," and seems to kill Annie's poem-children off early, itself making them "accept the university of death." Gone are the imperatives, the direct short sentences; Brooks describes the poem-children with a most civil and unthreatening phrase, as having exercised a "mild repartee." Whatever Brooks's reasons for retrenchment, this poem marks a little defeat and contributes to the darkness of the whole collection. Brooks continues to struggle with and within the sonnet for years; she does some of her best work in the form, testing its walls as she explores the containing pressures of her poetic world. Possibly because it combines an esthetic of enclosure with a history of pushing outward in second-person connections, she returns to its strict patterns repeatedly.

Apostrophe offers a crucial tool for such pathfinding, especially in the prescient final poem of this volume. Untitled, it apostrophizes, in a form suggesting blank verse, "Men of careful turns, haters of forks in the road," demanding that they "Admit me to our mutual estate" (139). This voice, distinctly not maternal, does employ the second-person address and imperatives often associated with that pose. Brooks, as a poet, only barely still in the persona of Annie Allen, knocks on the doors of the Anglo-American tradition, demanding to be admitted to its "high" company. She genders her alienation first, comparing her previous relationship to this tradition to a woman loving but fearing a husband who seems alternately brutal and indifferent. Next, Brooks notes the racial component of her ostracization, as these men who hate change respond that "prejudice is native" and "ineradicable," but that she should be satisfied with their new "politeness" (140). Brooks refers not only to a black woman's relationship to "civilization" but to her place in the literary world, as she makes clear by the use of the resonant word "line" to describe her confinement within other people's assessment of her worth: "For the line is there. / And has a meaning . . . the line is / Long and electric" (140). Here Brooks herself calls her use of Anglo-American forms a bondage in politeness; the line, the unit of poetry, itself represents a kind of electric fence.

Annie rejects such enclosure, and Brooks likewise seems to repudiate the limited conception of the brief, expressive, well-wrought lyric she has inherited. She moves from first-person singular to a plural "we" and suddenly seems to turn to a new audience: "Rise. / Let us combine. There are no magics or elves / Or timely godmothers to guide us. We are lost, must / Wizard a track through our own screaming weed" (140). The ending of "men of careful turns" so clearly expresses the necessity of innovation that one might expect Brooks's next volume to strike out in an entirely new direction, past the fence and through weedy unmapped land, with its newly defined army. As Henry Taylor asserts, "If there are sharp divisions in Brooks's career, one of them comes at this point" (1996, 266). However, Brooks spoke her subversions obliquely enough through forms familiarly safe enough to a white audience that apparently her disgust was not visible, or at least not threatening. Brooks's next work in poetry, *The Bean Eaters*, does make some movement in a new direction, and she hoped her novel would reach a larger audience. Nevertheless, *Annie Allen*'s apostrophic gestures support Brooks's own implication that her 1967 "change" is not so utter as it may at first seem.

Kinswomen!

In *Annie Allen,* Brooks both employs and critiques a poetic of enclosure. *In the Mecca,* Brooks's 1968 volume of poetry succeeding *The Bean Eaters* and *Selected Poems* (1963), expresses Brooks's increasing distance from the Anglo-American lyric as a reference point. In it, Brooks continues to move in the more "social" direction she pursues in *The Bean Eaters.* For the most part, however, she leaves behind (or at least reframes) her work in sonnets and ballads, and certain changes in her voice indicate her reach for a new audience and reconception of what her writing can do. *In the Mecca* contains the title poem, Brooks's longest poem to date, and "After Mecca," a set of lyrics exploring, among other subjects, violence and Chicago gang life, including most famously "Boy Breaking Glass" and "The Blackstone Rangers." The volume ends with Brooks's first two "Sermon[s] on the Warpland," not her first experiments with a ministerial voice, but her most important; the third "Sermon" will appear in *Riot* (1969). While imagery of enclosure persists through "In the Mecca," Brooks manipulates it to imply a new openness in her style and form.

The actual Mecca, the primary enclosure of this volume, was built in Chicago's South Side in 1891 and was intended to be a luxurious "multi-family dwelling for the wealthy" (Kenny J. Williams 1987, 60). Rather quickly, by the turn of the century, Chicago's wealthy began to move northward, and the building became "an overcrowded tenement for thousands of dispossessed blacks," estimated to have housed from three thousand to nine thousand people. It was razed in 1952, so Brooks's story in "In the Mecca" of Mrs. Sallie Smith looking for her lost daughter is necessarily retrospective.[10] Brooks herself worked for a quack doctor in the Mecca for a few months around 1937. Her subject remains the crampedness of Bronzeville, although the lyric vignettes of her first book have been fused into one poem of very large scope, and she describes poverty more graphically. Also, Brooks writes more judgmentally, articulating a sometimes sympathetic, sometimes critical attitude toward this beehive of a world.

For "In the Mecca," Brooks creates an interactive storyteller's voice. Her opening resembles a once-upon-a-time, only more biblical and sermonic: "Now the way of the Mecca was on this wise" (1987, 406). She builds up suspense so that her readers participate in Mrs. Sallie's anxiety and invites amusement and anger as she guides us through the Mecca, depicting its human diversity. She directs readers to "Sit where the light corrupts your face," as if wanting to see her audience and its reactions (407); instead of sheltering off-stage in the dark, readers are participants, sharing the spotlight. She names her readers, or some of them, female with her plea, "(Kinswomen!/ Kinswomen!)," hoping to arouse rage for Ida, Prophet Williams's wife, who died "in self-defense" and "alone" (408). She requests that readers "Please pity Briggs," one of Mrs. Sallie's sons, who loses his carefreeness early trying to navigate among dangerous gangs.

Brooks suffuses the poem with authorial presence, inserts the speaker's feelings just as she invokes the readers', and also advises and questions the poem's own characters. After Pepita's family registers her disappearance, the narrator declares, "My heart begins to race. / I fear the end of Peace" (416). "Peace" rings ironically—the "peace"ful domesticity we have just observed in Mrs. Sallie's apartment resembles nothing of the sort; the Smiths share a bleak, undecorated home in which the hungry children's worries concern sex and violence. The speaker also calls as if over the mother's shoulder to the children: "Children, what she has brought you is hock of ham" (410). By the end of the poem, the storyteller truly speaks in apostrophe, addressing the child the mother has been unable to protect, much as the speaker addresses aborted children in "the mother": "How many care, Pepita?" (427) and "these little care, Pepita" (429).

"[T]he mother" is not the only earlier poem Brooks invokes in her all-encompassing "In the Mecca." "Aunt Dill" resembles "the Empty Woman" and the "people" of "people who have no children can be hard"—prosperous but childless, she treats the loss of Pepita callously (432); Mrs. Sallie's plain cheap cooking and her children's lean lack of "chub and chocolate" (414) recall all the failures of women to nourish in "Gay Chaps at the Bar"; this long poem even makes room for "the ballad of Edie Barrow," whose white lover deserts her to marry a woman of his own race, in an opposite version of "The Ballad of Pearl May Lee" (425). "In the Mecca" pulls in all the themes and types from Brooks's earlier work, even some of the forms, encloses them in this one extended poem about a monstrously large building, itself an enclosure around a courtyard, and thus seems to cap the first project of Brooks's career, to write Bronzeville. The Mecca Building, a part of Bronzeville, stands in synecdochally for the entirety. Brooks creates a written work that feels oral, that finds as many ways as possible to include the reader in its community.

"In the Mecca" also bears resemblance to Walt Whitman's "Song of Myself" and attempts a similar scope: the Mecca building serves as a cross-section of a black nation. As Brooks states in her proposal for the poem in *Report from Part One,* "To touch every note in the life of this block-long block-wide building would be to capsulize the gist of black humanity in general. . . . Writing tools are to include random rhyme, off-rhyme, a long-swinging free verse, blank verse, prose verse. The couplet, the sonnet, the ballad . . . It is to be Leisurely and massive. A long wandering tale. It is to have Characters that grow and surprise. Rich humor, horror. Mastery of 'style.' Subtle wit. Social width" (1972, 190). The size of the work, its attempt to include all of black humanity, its biblical echoes, its swinging line, and particularly that capitalized word "Leisure" all point to Whitman as a precursor for this new voice. Further, Brooks's outward reach to animate and connect with her audience resembles a move Whitman makes frequently and sensually, even across time, as in "Crossing Brooklyn Ferry." Brooks is not the only contemporary poet to call up Whitman: Amiri Baraka, one of the people to whom this poem is dedicated, brought Whitman into the Black Arts movement through his association with the Beats, and Whitman's relatively open poetic represents a natural choice for anyone resisting academic or formal strains in poetry, as well as the poetic of enclosure this book describes.

"In the Mecca," for all its continuities with the first three books and with a white American tradition, bears the marks of Brooks's professed change of heart and of the new Black Arts movement. As I mentioned, this poem expresses anger more forthrightly and more graphically depicts its characters' sexuality and the violence of its world: Brooks employs tropes of presence and judgment to convey openness, not closure, in style and content. The free verse, likewise, only alludes to formal enclosures when, for instance, its ballad stanzas (which invoke both Anglo- and African American tradition) mark miscegenation, or a fairy tale of interracial love that cannot be sustained. Brooks also opens this poem to competing ideas about how to mend the intolerable situation the Mecca embodies; the voice for gradual change "grates" just as badly as Amos's suggestion that America, personified as a white woman, be raped and beaten in punishment for her racism (424–25). This last suggestion, chillingly, mirrors what happens to Pepita; such a plan imbedded in a poem deploring violence against a little girl can only seem monstrous.

"In the Mecca" offers examples for how African American poetry might respond to social crisis, reflecting the public role Brooks increasingly intends for her poetry. Brooks critiques what Gayl Jones calls "monochromatic" race poetry (1987, 201) through the character of Alfred, who first worships white writers like Shakespeare and Joyce and then writes poetry celebrating the abstraction of the "Black Woman" while unconcerned about the violent fate of the real Pepita. Alfred seems redeemed by the end of the poem, hit by "an essential sanity, black and electric," perhaps ready to write a new poetry "that is Construction" (433). Importantly, however, "In the Mecca" ends with a fragment of Pepita's own poetry (a couplet), yet unschooled that "black is not beloved," predicated on a sensual joy in the world: "'I touch'—she said once—'petals of a rose. / A silky feeling through me goes!'" (433). The last line of the poem describes Pepita's "chopped chirpings oddly rising," a poetry cut short by her violent death.[11]

Brooks provides little information about Pepita, other than that she's a "smart girl," as worried Mrs. Sallie keeps reassuring herself. Her name manifests a clash of opposites: "Pepita" sounds Hispanic, diminutive, and feminine, while "Smith" connotes England and brawny male labor. If poets apostrophize their muses, Brooks's muse is a dead black girl, for whom race and gender are not prisons, who has the power to hold generously wide "the A and P's fly-open door" (433). The poet-mother or, later, poet-preacher, finds inspiration in her children and speaks to advise or energize them as a sonneteer writes to seduce his lady. This muse becomes not only an unreachable love object, but also a part of Brooks herself, the innocent daughter who gets left behind at the gates of romance in "the ballad of chocolate Mabbie" and *Annie Allen*. Pepita's poem echoes pieces among Brooks's own juvenilia, the "two-line verses" Keziah Brooks discovered with amazement that seven-year-old Gwendolyn was writing (Kent 1989, 1). Perhaps, also, this poem's resonances with the myth of Demeter and Persephone mitigate her death; Brooks's poetry both sacrifices and

resurrects Pepita (Erkkila 1992, 214–15). In any case, Brooks character-
izes Pepita as a muse of openness. Suggestively, though, while this idea
mobilizes Brooks's long poem, its paradoxically diminutive embodiment
inspires chiefly through absence.

"Little addresses to black people, that's all"

In "and shall I prime my children, pray, to pray," from *Annie Allen*,
Brooks experiments with the voice of the preacher or the spiritual
guide, in an imperative mode of address that strongly resembles the
tone of her advising mothers. Brooks fully realizes this mode in her
"Sermons on the Warpland." Erkkila notes how "Brooks addresses the
black community as a kind of female preacher, a role that would have
been denied to her in the more traditional structures of the black
church" (1992, 220). Like the mother, the preacher stands taller than
her less-powerful listeners and dispenses guidance. Although this
hortatory voice grows out of Brooks's maternal pose, it reaches more
widely, acknowledging the public role poetry can exercise, the multi-
plicity of potential readers, the world context and not only the inti-
mate indoor spaces in which poetry is often composed and read.
Sermons are primarily oral and public. Despite Brooks's consequent
widening of the lyric's introspective space, however, on the level of
language these poems remain private, even enclosed, and intensely lit-
erary; they also depend significantly on images of confinement that
hark back to her first volume.

Brooks published two "Sermons on the Warpland" at the end of *In
the Mecca*, and one in her next book of poetry, *Riot*. Brooks works her
way into this powerful voice in stages, always apparently ambivalent;
in the first sermon she encloses her preaching in quotation marks, in
the second she pronounces without mediation, and in the third she
steps back from sermonizing directly, although judgments about the
rioting she depicts remain implicit. Within the series, the title accu-
mulates many different resonances. First, as R. Baxter Miller notes,
Brooks alludes to the Sermon on the Mount (1996, 150). Her alternate
geography also suggests the "warped land" or even the "Waste Land"
of a racist and riot-torn America; it refers, especially in the first poem,
to the "war planned" by black nationalists against white America.

In the first and shortest "sermon," Brooks sets off the homily in
quotation marks, distinctly marking its voice as constructed rather
than personally expressive. Brooks may engineer this distance partly

to avoid, with characteristic modesty, the presumption of divine inspiration. However, the "Single Sermon" is delivered by a chorus of "several strengths," suggesting that the poet functions as a medium through which many people speak; the sermon then becomes a people addressing itself, minimizing Brooks's literary authority. This poem emphasizes mediation through this chorus and through the quotation marks, but such intercession occurs implicitly in all of Brooks's sermons: while the mother speaks for herself, the preacher always serves as a conduit for higher forces. Brooks's shift to a mediating sermonic voice suggests her new role as spokesperson, if an ambivalent one, in the Black Arts movement.

"The Sermon on the Warpland" avoids traditional poetic form, instead organizing itself around the imperative and inspiring rhetoric of the pulpit. "Prepare to meet / (sisters, brothers) the brash and terrible weather," the poem demands; "Build now your Church" (1987, 451–52). Although Brooks employs vocative sentences, however, the poem also contains a metaphoric and intensely alliterative, randomly rhyming language that counteracts its apparent purposes. The sound-play pleases the ear, but some phrases do not possess any clearly assignable meaning. The second "Sermon on the Warpland" amplifies this effect by giving orders that make no immediate sense. Brooks does not tell her flock to march, to pray, to fight; she demands that they read, think, and interact with her language so that they themselves bear responsibility for interpreting her imperatives. The goal her sermon states, the "health" that will be achieved, involves "the heralding of the clear obscure" (451); this oxymoron declares the rightful place of the difficult, or even the irrational, in any poetry, including the poetry of the pulpit (and, here, of the oracle).

Lyric brevity and compression, figured in images of enclosure, perform a positive function in the first poem. The future, the sermon declares, germinates in "doublepod," containing "seeds for the coming hell and health together" (451). Progress becomes organic, the word "hell" breaking out of its pod, swelling or maturing into "health," the full-grown flower. This blossoming out of stasis requires the building of a new church, "never with brick nor Corten nor with granite," but "with lithe love" (452). Again, Brooks invokes paradox as her ideal: this building will resemble a church, will shelter and enclose, but it will exist as an imaginative, not a physical, structure. Its cement will correspond to the bonds between people.

In "The Second Sermon on the Warpland," slightly longer and written in four numbered parts, Brooks drops the distancing quotations and therefore seems to address her community directly. Her imperatives are metaphorical: "Live! / and have your blooming in the noise of the whirlwind" (453); "Define and / medicate the whirlwind" (455); "Conduct your blooming in the noise and whip of the whirlwind" (456). The most difficult series of directives occurs in the second section of this quartet:

> Salve salvage in the spin.
> Endorse the splendor splashes;
> stylize the flawed utility;
> prop a malign or failing light—
> but know the whirlwind is our commonwealth. (454)

Brooks contructs a public pose, meaning to inspire, but this is no populist poetry; this passage sounds less like oratory and more like an excerpt from an avant-garde literary journal. Her diction again mimics growth and blooming as she repeats "salve" more largely in "salvage," echoing the movement from "hell" to "health." As Brooks continues to argue, there exists no "easy" way to "straddle the whirlwind" that is the chaotic world of 1968; apparently a colloquial voice won't do it any better than the "sweetest sonnet" (454). She orders each reader to do his or her own "defining," rather than providing clear directives herself.

In the fourth and last section of the "Second Sermon," Brooks resurrects the speaker of "Big Bessie throws her son into the street" (400) at the end of *Selected Poems*. In the earlier piece, Big Bessie produces large but relatively lucid orders: "Be precise," "Hunt out your own or make your own alone," "Go down the street" (400). Her inclusion reinforces the connection between these two kinds of voices, the maternal and the ministerial. In the "Second Sermon,"

> Big Bessie's feet hurt like nobody's business,
> but she stands—bigly—under the unruly scrutiny, stands
> in the wild weed.
> In the wild weed
> she is a citizen,
> and is a moment of highest quality; admirable. (456)

Erkkila argues that Brooks "represent[s] herself in the figure of Big Bessie who moves out of the house" into a public sphere (1992, 221); certainly the presence of a strong maternal figure here emphasizes the continuity between all of Brooks's rhetorical positions. The "wild weed" imagery comprises another thread that binds Brooks's work back to *A Street in Bronzeville*: from "a song in the front yard" to "men of careful turns" to this "whirlwind"/ "wild weed" scenery, uncultivated land means free and uncharted space where black women can define their own identities. Elsewhere, Brooks speaks affectionately of dandelions, flowers that can grow and delight the eye where nothing else will (1987, 144). Her summons to "live and go out" (455) demands abandoning enclosures and prim front yards, a recapitulation of her decision back at the end of *Annie Allen* to "wizard a track through our own screaming weed."

"The Third Sermon on the Warpland" also revisits Brooks's earlier poetry, but eliminates Bessie and abandons its confident, if obscure, imperatives. This poem, reacting to the 1968 street disturbances in Chicago after Dr. Martin Luther King Jr.'s assassination (Kent 1990, 236), instead includes different black male voices: "The Black Philosopher," twelve-year-old "Yancey," the Blackstone Rangers. Erkkila argues that, from *In the Mecca* on, Brooks becomes gradually silenced by the male-identified Black Power movement, citing Brooks's decreased poetic production and increased address to and emphasis on black masculinity in her poetry (1992, 218–19). While Brooks does not cease to wield apostrophe, this poem does enact a relative stifling of the mother and of Brooks's own authority to guide African American response to racism.

In the middle of the theft and violence and sirens, a maternal figure surfaces, this time apparently a casualty rather than a tired but strong "citizen."

> A woman is dead.
> Motherwoman.
> She lies among the boxes
> (that held the haughty hat, the Polish sausages)
> in newish, thorough, firm virginity
> as rich as fudge is if you've had five pieces.
> Not again shall she
> partake of steak
> on Christmas mornings, nor of nighttime
> chicken and wine at Val Gray Ward's
> nor say
> of Mr. Beetley, Exit Jones, Junk Smith
> nor neat New-baby Williams (man-to-many)
> "He treat me right."
>
> That was a gut gal. (476)

This virgin mother resembles Pepita of "In the Mecca," who dies sac-rificially, yielding up her body and voice to "the war planned." Brooks honors her with a scrap of elegy in the middle of this poem full of angry men. The "Third Sermon" does not represent the death of maternal power or the sermonic voice in Brooks, but it does register the tension between the importance of women's voices and the loyalty to Black Power that threatens Brooks's later poetry.

Kent characterizes this poem as utilizing "the ordinary speech, loose rhythms, and communal reference points that could communi-cate to a mass audience" (1990, 237). The third sermon seems far more likely than the others to achieve Brooks's stated goal of appealing to a wide readership, as the above passage demonstrates. Even here, how-ever, as Kent notes, Brooks can quickly "leave directness for the metaphorical"; he feels "that in such passages she is in territory that some of the younger writers, with their freer use of street language, would handle more effectively. Thus Gwendolyn's old style invaded the new one she was attempting to create" (1990, 237). I see these ser-mons not as failures to communicate at the level Brooks professed to be targeting, but as continuations of her esthetic of complexity and deliberate indirection.

Brooks's old poetry does "invade" the new in an allusion to "Gay Chaps at the Bar" in the "Third Sermon." The labeled jars and cabinets in which the soldier preserves "my dreams, my work" become, in the later poem, the larder of the "keeper":

> The Black Philosopher says
> "Our chains are in the keep of the keeper
> in a labeled cabinet
> on the second shelf by the cookies,
> the sonatas, the arabesques . . .
> There's a rattle, sometimes.
> You do not hear it who mind only
> cookies and crunch them. . . ." (472)

The keeper conceals those constraining chains, themselves enclosures, in another enclosed space, something like the back of the mind of the dominant white culture. The chains share their space with sweets like sonnets/sonatas, "snacks" that distract their enjoyers from the omi-nous rattling of irons. The black soldier in Brooks's early sequence about World War II deposits his peacetime aspirations himself, although the war certainly constrains his options, but Brooks's black philosopher has no ability to unlock these containers, except through violence. Both, however, address an audience that does not properly understand the direness of the situation. Brooks models "Gay Chaps" on soldiers' letters to the uncomprehending women back home; this latter speech might be directed to those resisting or disapproving of the explosive anger of Chicago rioters, implicitly including Brooks herself. In this last "Sermon," Brooks gives much direct voice to opinions she seems to disagree with.

Brooks's most recent work revises her early conception of the lyric, conceiving it negatively as a fixed, boxed-in, static, dead form; she also modifies the strategy of indirection that, ironically, characterizes her sermons and constitutes a link to her original poetic of enclosure. She intends to write occasional poetry, speaking to immediate needs with specific purposes. Similarly, the distinction between public and private upon which the lyric often rests—itself, by post-Romantic convention, private and claiming timelessness, in contrast to public and historical forms like the epic, the novel, and drama—finally collapses for Brooks. Although her poems continue to depend structurally on apostrophe, linking the latest productions with so many of the earliest, the directives emerge more plainly: the suggestively titled *Beckonings* (1975b), for example, illustrates this through the inspirational pieces "A Black Wedding Song" and "Boys. Black. *a preachment*." As the voices of the mother and the preacher fuse, public and private worlds and their separate discourses become indistinguishable; the play between openness and enclosure no longer fuels her work.

Elizabeth Bishop's Inscrutable Houses

I had not then connected the themes of outsider-
hood and marginality in [Bishop's] work, as well
as its encodings and obscurities, with a lesbian
identity. I was looking for a clear female tradition;
the tradition I was discovering was diffuse, elu-
sive, often cryptic.

Adrienne Rich, 1986

Adrienne Rich had been to see Elizabeth in
Boston and had attempted to persuade her to be
more forthcoming about her sexual orientation.
Elizabeth did not regard the enterprise with favor.
After Adrienne's visit, I remember her describ-
ing her new domesticities at Lewis Wharf. "You
know what I want, Richard? I want closets, clos-
ets, and more closets!"

Gary Fountain, 1994

Elizabeth Bishop's poetic of enclosure, like Dickinson's, opposes an
outsider's status to a powerful idea of home, producing many depic-
tions of unstable, endangered houses. Her implicit characterization of
the lyric as container depends on this domestic imagery and on the
relative restraint of her language.[1] However, in Bishop a closed esthetic
meets confessionalism's imperatives to disclosure: as a result, her

poems may openly indicate secrecy, performing silence. The open secret of Bishop's lesbianism complicates the issue, since her lyric may function as a closet. I introduce this chapter with a general discussion of these figures, closet and home, as they appear in Bishop, and briefly address how she might participate in a tradition of American women poets, despite her strong ambivalence about such categorization. In three subsequent sections, I analyze the interaction of images and strategies of enclosure in specific poems, clustered around domesticity, sexuality, and representations of female influence.

In *Epistemology of the Closet*, Eve Sedgwick discusses at length the relationship of the closet, metaphorically a state of silence about "a concealed trouble" (according to the *Oxford English Dictionary*) or, more pertinently in this case, about one's homosexual identity, to the larger culture. She notes that the closet represents both an internal space and a marginal one (1990, 56), and comments that "'closetedness' itself is a performance initiated as such by the speech act of a silence" (3). Although Sedgwick's book focuses on male sexual definition within the works of male prose writers, her comments illuminate the contradictory status of Bishop's coded poems about homosexuality.

Silence becomes a speech act in that it represents the alternative to speech, not only the ground from which speech emerges but a choice against speech, or within its interstices. If Bishop had fully chosen silence and the closet, we would possess none of her poetry (there exists no total poetic of enclosure); instead she opted for a silence within speech, in that her poems find various ways of deflecting attention from questions of sexual definition. Why they should attend to these questions remains, of course, a thorny question. Many readers don't apply the categories of fiction and nonfiction as definitively to poetry the way such genres are held, at least in the average undergraduate curriculum, to define prose; contemporary readers understand poetry as self-expression, true in feeling although perhaps not in exact detail, and one therefore expects poetry especially from after World War II to give voice to some aspects of a writer's own experience. As Lee Edelman and others have observed, Bishop showed particular persistence in making claims such as "that really happened" about specific poems (1993, 91). How, then, could a poetry so attentive to the realities of Bishop's life not take account at least in small, mundane ways of her sexual identity, never mind in poems of larger self-definition like "In the Waiting Room," or in the genre of the love poem?

In fact, Bishop strongly marks her poems by her assertions of and resistances to sexual definition, and her work contains at least a few poems specifically describing the experience of being gay. Every such piece, however, distances itself in some way either from its potential status as self-expression or from a plain-speaking declaration of subject matter, usually both. Although many people close to Bishop, and presumably many people who were not, knew Bishop as a lesbian, she never wanted that label attached to her public identity or to her poetry. The relationship of Bishop the poet to her readers is mediated by the closet.

Bishop's reticence on this subject reflects a personality that eschewed direct expression of many emotions in writing and in person; while her poems, for instance, so often build to feeling-charged epiphanies, she couches such transcendent moments in description, deliberately inexplicit although infused with psychological import ("Rainbow, rainbow, rainbow! / And I let the fish go"). Bishop's specific "silence" on the issue of her sexual orientation, however, became more and more significant as other writers around her became deliberately open. Richard Howard's funny anecdote about Bishop's visit with Adrienne Rich, quoted from Gary Fountain's collection as an epigraph to this chapter, demonstrates both Bishop's awareness of the closet as metaphor and her conscious choice of this silence. Bishop's stance, as it emerges through her poetry, towards open sexual definition is that the very nature of language renders it impossible. Bishop did not intend her poems as self-expressive speech, for one thing, although she often intended them to resemble it. Further, binary terms such as private/public and secrecy/openness define one another interdependently, as the presence of closets (as coded language, in Bishop) serves to indicate the existence of a secret.

Increasingly, critics including Lorrie Goldensohn (1992), Victoria Harrison (1993), Jeredith Merrin (1993), Susan McCabe (1994), Marilyn May Lombardi (1995), and Margaret Dickie (1997) suggest the relevance of sexuality to Bishop's poetry. Scholars have less commonly remarked, however, the figure of the closet than the figure of the house. Many have commented on her work's sometimes obsessive concern with home in relationship to the nomadic lifestyle she began in her early childhood. More literally than that other New England poet, Emily Dickinson, Bishop "never had a mother" (or a secure address): Gertrude Bishop was institutionalized for insanity when her daughter was five and the two never met again; the poet's father died during her infancy. The young Bishop's life was further unsettled by a childhood series of displacements; she was shuttled among relatives, summer camps, and schools until old enough to arrange for her own constant travel. For many years she re-created her first motherland of Nova Scotia, where her maternal relatives lived, in her happy residency in Brazil with Lota de Macedo Soares; that union and the security it provided for the poet also, however, eventually fractured and finally collapsed when Soares committed suicide. As Bishop constantly struggled to find a settled place to live and to sustain the relationships that made those places livable, it is no wonder that house, home, and country became central, if sometimes alienating, rickety, or lightning-struck subjects for her poetry and stories.

Helen Vendler, in her commentary on Bishop's *Questions of Travel* (1965), illuminates not only Bishop's abiding appreciation of domesticity, but her balancing interest in strangeness, in the exotic or unfamiliar (1980). The latter impulse, in fact, disturbs the peace in the many houses Bishop depicts. Further, this tension recurs in Bishop's very practice of the lyric poem not as a confession, as in the workof many of her contemporaries, but as a performance of the tension between confession and concealment, expansiveness and silence, the nesting of a familiar form and the subversion or unsettling of it. Bishop's lyric resembles an "inscrutable house" (1979, 124):[2] in its manipulation of the conventions of personal expression, its apparent disinterest in experiment and periodic use of virtuoso forms including the sestina or sonnet, a most familiar place; and in its obvious fissures and disembodied voices, a most unnerving one.[3]

Bishop, then, employs a poetic of enclosure, like other American women poets before her. Her lyric houses intend to conceal and protect, even while they mimic a self-segregation into an apparently trivial, feminine mode. Simultaneously, however, Bishop expresses ambivalence about and tries to undermine the sealed and private manner she inherits. Part of the need to disrupt her own lyric structures must stem from her literary contexts, including the political thirties in which she attended Vassar and developed many of her ideas about poetry, as well as the esthetic of personal expression that gained steam in the fifties and dominated the poetic scene until her death. As a sometimes-but-not-quite-confessional poet, working in correspondence and mutual admiration with Robert Lowell, Bishop must have used a poetic of enclosure with a sense of disjunction, especially aware of each poem's negotiation between opposing conventions of impersonal restraint and candid self-expression.

Another part, though, of Bishop's desire to unsettle this poetic even as she employs it is her attitude towards its previous practitioners. Bishop stakes out a difficult place as a woman poet, both self-consciously affiliating herself with the most-praised line of descent among American women poets and asserting she wants nothing to do with such a category. As a mostly willing protégé of Marianne Moore and yet as a writer who adamantly refused to be, as she perceived it, ghettoized into women's poetry anthologies, she fits no easy slot in a tradition of American women exercising such a poetic.[4] Her attitude towards Dickinson's poetry and letters reflects the same contradiction: she states in a review that she is "embarrassed" by this ancestor, while finding much to admire in her work (1951). Indeed, the pulls between speech and silence, shelter and escape that shape her poetry also characterize the poetries of Dickinson, Moore, H.D. and Brooks, and stem from the same sources. Bishop felt, according to Frank Bidart, that she would have produced more writing and shown more "directness and ambition" if she had been a man (Fountain 1994, 327); pressures to modesty, to reticence, that have something to do with personality, something to do with the period, and something to do with gender exerted great force on her poetic voice and on her attitude toward publishing and writing, even while her ambition and talent urged her work onward.

Finally, also like some of these women poets, Bishop's relationship to the lyric poem resembles her relationship to the closet. The biographical fact of Bishop's lesbianism or, by alternate accounts, her bisexuality most informs her poetic of enclosure: Bishop's lyric poetry repeatedly articulates one particular confession by silence. In this strategy she not only resembles previous women poets but gay male poets including John Ashbery who, as John Shoptaw makes clear, employs a "misrepresentative poetics" not precisely as a code for, but certainly in response to, his own homosexuality (1994, 4). Bishop playfully tropes on inversion, thirdness, queerness, and gaiety or gayness, as Merrin observes (1993), all the while avoiding direct reference to homosexuality. Bishop's need for a coded language resembles Dickinson's or H.D.'s, but, more than these earlier poets, like Brooks although for different reasons, Bishop strains her poetic of restraint towards an increased openness through hints, jokes, and allegory. Her boxes remain just slightly unhinged.

Housewrecks

Bishop's poetry, perhaps most densely in *Questions of Travel*, depicts many houses in jeopardy. "Jeronimo's House," for example, though a "love-nest" and comfortably domesticated, looks "abandoned," is "perishable" and fragile as a wasp's nest, and serves as a "shelter from / the hurricane," implying a hostile world without (34). In "Electrical Storm" the house in question becomes "really struck" by lightning; here the endangered dwelling implicitly stands in Petropolis (Rio's summer retreat, where Bishop lived for many years with Lota de Macedo Soares), the two women rising together from bed at dawn to find themselves isolated by fused wiring and a dead telephone (100). Although the poem does not propose a reason for the damage, the dawn seems "unsympathetic" and the storm as "personal and spiteful as a neighbor's child"; an insinuation of directed harassment hovers like the whiff of saltpeter after the lightning.

Placed next in the same volume, "Song for the Rainy Season" renders Macedo Soares's half-drowned house as a sanctuary, hidden from outside eyes but open to the mildews and silverfish of the natural world. In this indirect love poem, most of the stanzas depict a thrilling intimacy between the house and its environment. The speaker renders minute and affectionate observations, and Bishop displaces the sensual, bodily closeness of the house's residents onto the scene itself, with its "rib cage" of ferns and "warm breath" of mildew, the "cling"-ing and "holding" of moisture around the building (101–02). Paradoxically, the apparent failure of the house to shelter, its permeability to mold and invasive wildlife, make it a "maculate, cherished" home (102). All this secret vitality, however, will be killed or driven away when the sun reemerges and the house becomes again publicly visible; joy may occur temporarily and only in a "private cloud" of mist and rainfall (101). Further, Bishop hints at the inevitable collapse of this world early on, in the owls' prey on "the fat frogs that, / shrilling for love, / clamber and mount" (101); the demise of these comic lovers anticipates the threat to the human ones. The suggestion in both "Electrical Storm" and "Song for the Rainy Season" is that something about Bishop's household, arguably the fact that it is centered around a lesbian couple, makes it especially vulnerable.

Other poems juxtapose contrasting kinds of houses, and often the outdoor or natural world seems ultimately more homelike than any more conventional residence. "The Prodigal," depicted as an alcoholic, is exiled from home to a pigsty, which nevertheless appeals to him, the animals "safe and companionable as in the Ark" (71). Bishop's "Squatter's Children" prefer "rooms of falling rain," an outdoor "mansion" also compared to an ark, to their house from which calls their "Mother's voice, ugly as sin" (95). Likewise, "The Riverman" finds enchanted rooms within the river, where he finds freedom in his hiddenness and recognition for his gifts. In these poems the protagonists discover parts of themselves unwelcome in the buildings supposed to be their homes and locate more accepting, alternative spaces in nature. For Bishop, the sense of familiarity, comfort, and safety that one attaches to a beloved residence can emerge from unlikely places. Even a dirty "Filling Station" gradually transforms under her hand (by the impulses of its residents, of course, but also by the act of the speaker's mind in gradually noticing domestic details) into a haven, inspiring the poem's final, hopeful reassurance, "Somebody loves us all" (128). Again, the alternative house, often isolated from human society, ultimately proves superior in hospitality.

In many of these poems Bishop foregrounds the lyric itself as a fragile and/or enchanted house, a structure under stress from opposing forces of familiarity and strangeness. "Sestina," for example, in its very title highlights the predictability of the form rather than the newness of the content. The scene the actual poem offers, a child in her grandmother's kitchen drawing pictures of houses, domesticates the piece further, and Bishop limits its vocabulary in excess of the form's stringent requirements, suggesting a childlike voice or perspective and grounding even the sound of the language in the ordinary.

Lorrie Goldensohn rightly remarks that Bishop often uses traditional poetic forms to contain her most troubling, autobiographical, even confessional poems (consider "One Art") (1992, 59). Indeed, "Sestina" depicts a scene that should be utterly cozy—tea, a bustling grandmother, a stove-heated kitchen sheltering them from the autumn rain—as disturbed by some grief never named. Why does the grandmother repress tears? What has happened? Where are the child's parents? Who is the man she draws by her house? Without some knowledge of Bishop's personal history (and a presumption that the poem is autobiographical), a reader can only hazard that there has occurred some tragedy involving the missing parents around which the obsessive form circles but the nature of which it never reveals. "Sestina" resembles the anxiously "rigid . . . inscrutable house[s]" the child keeps drawing, attempting to force a calm, containing image of shelter onto a crisis, which nevertheless cannot prevent the tears that keep erupting wherever the grandmother or grandchild look (1979, 123–24).

"Sestina" contrasts the predictability of seasonal and diurnal cycles ("*I know what I know*, says the almanac," clever and consoling with its jokes and advice) with an unnamed but strongly felt disruption of this domestic idyll. Its physical houses seem rock-stable compared to many of the others in Bishop's writing but remain too rigid and containing. While the house in "Song for the Rainy Season," in many ways a parallel work, appears both protected and open, inscrutable to unfriendly eyes but otherwise permeable and secretly lively, "Sestina" depicts closed houses (also beset by rain) without mouseholes, its dwellers keeping secrets even from one another. Bishop maps an everyday setting over hidden tears, and only total control— the smugness of an almanac, rigid symbolism of a child's drawing, or formality of a sestina—can prevent the entire scene's dissolution.

While these poems so often express ambivalence about the sheltering powers of houses, or even about the desirability of some kinds of shelter (as in "Sestina," in which a front of domestic ordinariness comes to feel tragic), the frequency of this imagery emphasizes its attraction for Bishop. Further, as often as a house falls into danger from within or without, it serves a focus of desire, unattainable or only briefly so. The "I" of "The End of March," for instance, braves an icy and inhospitable beach sustained by a fantasy of reaching a particular house, and the life she might live there:

> I wanted to get as far as my proto-dream-house,
> my crypto-dream-house, that crooked box
> set up on pilings, shingled green,
> a sort of artichoke of a house, but greener
> (boiled with bicarbonate of soda?),
> protected from spring tides by a palisade
> of—are they railroad ties?
> (Many things about this house are dubious.)
> I'd like to retire there and do *nothing*,
> or nothing much, forever, in two bare rooms . . .
>   But—impossible.
> And that day the wind was much too cold
> even to get that far,
> and of course the house was boarded up. (179-80)

Beyond its crookedness, pilings, and vulnerability to the tides, this house appears so unstable it does not seem really to exist. Uncertainty, even unreachability seem to inspire the walker with longing. If it is too cold to get that far, does she? Is she merely guessing that it is boarded up? Are the greenness, the railroad ties, then remembered or fantasized details? In what sense does this constitute a dream-house—is it ideal, imaginary, and/or a site for night and day-dreaming? "There must be a stove, there *is* a chimney," she insists, as if willing the house or at least its appliances into existence, even as Bishop fractures her description with question marks, and she herself accuses the house of "dubious"ness.

Bishop's dream house looks always, like the Fazenda Samambaia in Brazil (as she depicts it), a little imperfect and unorthodox, showing the strains of its relationship with the wildness around it, in fact threatening a certain if temporally distant collapse. The "End of March" house appears bare, falling down, suspect in construction, hazardously situated. Each dream house, however, briefly creates a satisfying unity between its resident and that wildness, a moment when that tension between familiarity and strangeness becomes a perfect balance of forces. The dazzling natural description in "Song for the Rainy Season" represents a momentarily happy coexistence between a northern poet and Brazilian flora and fauna; an epiphanic wash of sunshine closes "The End of March." Likewise, each poem flirts with but does not satisfy regular structural patterns: "Song for the Rainy Season," in six ten-line stanzas, is haunted with rhyme, although often slant and never predictably organized; in "End of March," rhymes become internal and the symmetry of the action (walking up the beach, walking back, reencountering certain details of the landscape) contradicts the conversational disorder of the verse.

"Crusoe in England," a houseless poem, nonetheless offers one of Bishop's most poignant and wryly funny meditations on the idea of home. An allegorical autobiography (as others have observed), it tells in great detail of Crusoe's long and bitter experience of singleness, alluding to his joining forces with Friday in a bare and inarticulately emotional short verse paragraph. Instead of enclosing dream houses, Bishop depicts isolating islands and fifty-two (one a week) miniature volcanoes, that symbol since Dickinson of potentially explosive female anger. Crusoe's singleness sounds full of self-pity:

> What's wrong with self-pity, anyway?
> With my legs dangling down familiarly

over a crater's edge, I told myself
"Pity should begin at home." So the more
pity I felt, the more I felt at home. (163)

Self-deprecating humor aside, the larger part of "Crusoe in England" demonstrates the speaker's struggle to create a feeling of belonging in a barren and alienating environment. He most fears that he will have to live on an endless procession of such islands, "for ages, registering their flora, / Their fauna, their geography" (165). As appealing as Bishop's poetry of description can be, it springs from the kind of traveling without settling that horrifies Crusoe.

Aside from begetting descriptive catalogues, this Crusoe entertains himself by creating music and "home-brew," an alcoholic beverage that distracts him from feeling homeless (Bishop herself suffered from intermittent drinking problems) (164). Drunken and dancing, Crusoe quips, "Home-made, home-made! But aren't we all?" (164). He harks back to, without in this poem ever describing, some original home where his identity first (and apparently irrevocably) formed. His pun recalls Bishop's feeling that she inherited her alcoholism and, she feared, a tendency toward mental illness from her family.

The suddenness and brevity of Crusoe's account of Friday in contrast to the expansiveness of the previous descriptions, as well as his repeated admiration of Friday's "pretty body," suggest a homosexual love between the two that becomes a mirror image of Bishop's own great love affair with Lota de Macedo Soares (165–66). Crusoe implies that Friday's arrival offered relief from the long loneliness, and the poem ends on an elegiac note: "—And Friday, my dear Friday, died of measles / seventeen years ago come March" (Macedo Soares committed suicide in September 1967, four years before the poem was first printed) (166). Now England, the motherland that he had once mourned, no longer feels homelike either; the scenery, the room around him, seems meaningless, its furnishings devoid of the emotional value their island counterparts had possessed. Home, apparently, arises chiefly from relationships, or else it only appears homelike in nostalgia.

"The Moose" likewise depicts home as always falling behind the "lone traveller" into the mists (170). Its protagonist leaves a Nova Scotia farm as evening and fog descend, heading toward Boston; the poem offers sharp and close-to-the-ground perspective, depicting a landscape with which Bishop must have been utterly intimate. Relaxing into a dream, she hallucinates or transforms a conversation in the back of the bus into the distant murmur of her grandparents talking in "Eternity" (a Dickinsonian capital) as they once chatted in their own bed at night. That this conversation seems to descend from some afterlife indicates the disappearance of the real home the grandparents made, as the farm that once housed it recedes through the motion of the bus; home can only be evoked in dreams. Another representative of domesticity then jolts this vision out of existence: a moose on the road, "homely as a house / (or, safe as houses)" (173).

Ironically for Bishop, whose allergies to pets probably often triggered her severe asthma, the presence of animals in her life or poetry often signals a positive feeling of homelike security; peaceful coexistence with them indicates that tenuous harmony with the outdoor world the right kind of home should create. In "Song for the Rainy Season," the interpenetration between inside and outside in the form of animal invasion defines that idyllic period. In "The Moose," this towering female animal crosses a similar kind of border as the one between indoors and outdoors when she moves from the not so "impenetrable wood" into the road, making contact with the human world by sniffing the hood of the bus (172). The moose is, however, far from tame, although "a man's voice assures us / [she is] 'Perfectly harmless. . . .'" (173). Our protagonist recognizes the moose as "grand, otherworldly" (173), and the joy she inspires seems distinct from the earlier dreamy comfort associated with the grandparents' voices; also, when Bishop calls the moose "safe as houses," one cannot but remember how unsafe all her other poetic houses seem to be. (Even the ghostly grandparents discuss distinctly uncozy things, like death, sickness, drink, insanity.)

Without being reducible to a symbol and while maintaining the distinct "other"ness of its own subjectivity, the moose represents both an extension of and an alternative to the kind of home the protagonist has left behind; the moose, in fact, by the end of the poem only lingers in hindsight, her scent lingering intermingled with the human smell of gasoline. Her femaleness (Bishop did see a cow moose on such a trip, but borrows the hood-sniffing moment from another story about a bull moose, and could have chosen either for her poem [Millier 1993, 182–83]) and her connection in the poem with moonlight (the moon often a marker of lesbian content or at least a symbol of female power in Bishop's poetry) may gesture toward the kind of woman-centered home Bishop repeatedly enjoyed and lost, in Nova Scotia, Key West, and Brazil. Or, perhaps, the moose offers the even more ephemeral experience of "home" conjured by lyric epiphanies, in which strangeness and domesticity can briefly coexist. The moose represents both the homely and the otherworldly, two realms linked briefly by simile, and as such constitutes a key representative of Bishop's ambivalent relationship to the house as enclosure.

That World Inverted

Poems including "Insomnia," "The Man-Moth," and "Sonnet," as some have noted, offer lightly coded explorations of the experience of homosexuality as Bishop saw it. She deploys terms for homosexuality including "inverted," "queer," "gay" and variations on thirdness throughout her poetry, but so that they are not visible to unwilling or hostile readers; their presence offers a code key to many of Bishop's more obscure poems. More idiosyncratically, the presence of the moon becomes a similar clue; perhaps because of its associations with Diana (goddess of unmarried maidens), darkness (closets, silence, and alternate or secret worlds), and femininity, it often shines to signal a lesbian subtext.

"Insomnia," too dense a poem not to be quoted in its entirety, presents the clearest exercise of these tropes:

> The moon in the bureau mirror
> looks out a million miles
> (and perhaps with pride, at herself,
> but she never, never smiles)
> far and away beyond sleep, or
> perhaps she's a daytime sleeper.
>
> By the Universe deserted,
> *she*'d tell it to go to hell,
> and she'd find a body of water,
> or a mirror, on which to dwell.
> So wrap care up in a cobweb
> And drop it down the well
>
> into that world inverted
> where left is always right,
> where shadows are really the body,
> where we stay awake all night,
> where the heavens are shallow as the sea
> is now deep, and you love me. (70)

Bishop describes this "world inverted," into which the feminine moon escapes when deserted (by men?), as a place where one dwells on one's mirror image, or, perhaps, on the face of someone who resembles one-self in sex. As insomnia keeps one awake during hours of sleep, reversing normal human cycles, this love poem offers a mirror world in which "normalcy" or heterosexuality becomes askew in a wonder-ful way. (Millier quotes Moore, without specific reference, calling "Insomnia" "a cheap love poem," in what must have been a fit of anx-iety or an appalling lapse of taste on Moore's part [1993, 230]).

Dickinson's influence radiates through much of Bishop's poetry, but the latter poet borrows particularly heavily here. "Insomnia" recalls some of Dickinson's most recurrent imagery, but especially of her depictions of late-night composition in a silent household; "I watched the Moon around the House" (F 593, J 629) depicting the ris-ing moon as a bodiless woman escaping convention and restriction; and of her several spooky and cryptic well poems, including "This Chasm, Sweet, opon [*sic*] my life" (F 1061, J 858). Dickinson becomes a particularly fertile source for Bishop in this incantatory poem, far from the precise, polysyllabic description Bishop learned from Moore.

Importantly, however, while "Insomnia" offers a chance at escape, from Bishop's most celebrated poetic mode as well as a depicted escape into the "world inverted," it suggests many constrictions. For instance, this lyric is brief for Bishop, its three stanzas heavily rhyming, although not regularly (the last two lines do couple in rhyme, providing a much more satisfying sense of closure than Bishop will usually consent to provide). Moreover, imagery of confinement permeates the piece: a bureau mirror frames the transgressive image of the moon gazing at her own likeness, and a well contains the world inverted. The lat-ter presents a genital image of enclosure, suggesting a world of femi-nine interiority, but it also provides a correlative for the codedness of Bishop's language. Finally, the bureau mirror certainly connotes a fet-tering domesticity, and perhaps synecdochally, as Marilyn Lombardi suggests, larger "social structures" (1995, 61).

Bishop's early, surrealist-influenced "The Man-Moth" offers another allegory of homosexual experience, although a less obvious and less positive one. The title character, who was inspired by a newspaper misprint of "mammoth," leads an underground life, circling endlessly backwards through the subway system, and occasionally journeying out and attempting to climb to the moon. "The Man-Moth" depicts a strange, black-and-white superhero, his shadow billowing like a cape as he scales the skyscrapers; he dwells in Bishop's eeriest, most fantas-tic world. Not surprisingly, this poem has engendered many different readings. Anne Stevenson, implicitly with Bishop's encouragement, called it a fable of urban experience (Bishop disliked living in New York) (1996, 82), and other critics have noted suggestions of suicide, madness, and alcoholism in the Man-Moth's attraction to the poisonous third rail, his allusion to inherited "disease," and his sly drinking of his own tear (15). No interpretation can account for the poem as fully, however, as to read it as a bizarrely encrypted account of Bishop's "other" life, apart from her then professional identity of aspiring poet and Moore protégée ("The Man-Moth" was first published in 1936).[5]

The density of Bishop's punning constitutes one clue. The Man-Moth's whole world is one of "inversion," night, the unconscious, and backwards movement. He sees the moon not as a light upon a dark ground but as a gap in the darkness:

> He thinks the moon is a small hole at the top of the sky,
> proving the sky quite useless for protection . . .
>
> he climbs fearfully, thinking that this time he will manage
> to push his small head through that round clean opening
> and be forced through, as from a tube, in black scrolls on the light. (14)

The "opening" of the moon resembles a birth canal, and the Man-Moth desires to be born again through it into another, inverted world, or even to "come out," his identity written in scrolls for all to see. In the decadent tradition of Dorian Gray and Jekyll and Hyde, the Man-Moth also possesses a double, the Man of the first stanza, who controls his own shadow into a dark circle pinned down by his feet, thus reigning in any unruly, secret, double life. The Man never looks up but only feels the moon's "queer light on his hands, neither warm nor cold, / of a temperature impossible to record in thermometers" (14). Despite his refusal to see, the Man's world manifests an uncanny "queer"ness of which the moon again becomes an emblem.

Bishop further obscures her subject through the sex of her central character, who seems more distant from Bishop herself because of his maleness (this poem deals with "misprints" in more ways than one). She does direct the reader, however, to pay very close attention. The Man-Moth returns after his failed moon expedition to his secret underground life, where he rides the subway trains, "dream[s] recurrent dreams," and has to keep his hands in his pockets to "muffle" his own desire to grasp the third rail (the "third sex" is a nineteenth-century term, like "inversion," attached to some theories of homosexual difference) (15). In the last stanza, when he lets slip a tear, we are told,

"Slyly he palms it, and if you're not paying attention / he'll swallow it. However, if you watch, he'll hand it over, / cool as from underground springs and pure enough to drink" (15). While this image certainly does evoke Bishop's relationship to alcohol and the surrealist penchant for its briefly transformative, mind-altering effects, the tear also momentarily externalizes the Man-Moth's "underground" self. Only through our close regard of it, our attentiveness to this poem's language, can we make the necessary connections and receive the codes.

"The Man-Moth" stands as one of the best examples of how Bishop handles the lyric poem as a closet. "The Man-Moth" says nothing directly about the tenor of its extended conceit, and the very fantastic attributes of the poem, the fancifulness of its world—even its footnote, which refers to the poem's whimsical conception inspired by a misprint—distract us from the possibility of reading this poem in a coherent way. Nevertheless, Bishop wrote and published this piece; Bishop presents a description, however cryptic, and perhaps not even based closely on her own, of the experience of leading an underground life, of regarding one's sexuality "as a disease / [one] has inherited the susceptibility to," and of making "fearful" and unsuccessful attempts to emerge into the light (14–15). "The Man-Moth" performs the speech act of silence.

Although Bishop couldn't have planned it this way (Bishop died suddenly of a ruptured cerebral aneurysm), the last poem she published depicts escape from these kinds of restrictions. More strikingly, her last word, which refers to the experience of sudden freedom, is "gay," as if Bishop were coming out of the closet to her readers after all. Once again, Bishop chooses a traditional form for this dangerous fantasy, although this time the poem-as-closet cannot wholly contain its subject matter.

"Sonnet" consists of fourteen lines and its subject matter is limitation, but there its resemblance to the traditional form ends. Bishop, a great admirer and strict critic of poetic technique, produces this sonnet in too-short lines, and with rhymes that slant or stray so anarchically that pairing up rhyme words involves much guesswork; certain rhymes cross even from octave to sestet. Bishop, in fact, reverses octave and sestet, as Joanne Feit Diehl observes, "a rhetorical shift that mirrors Bishop's play of trope" (1990, 110). As in "Sestina," the title of the piece puts primary stress on its formal characteristics, and therefore in this case on the poem's transgression of those rules. Accenting its own betrayal of regular verse measure, the poem describes tools of physical measure—the spirit-level that tests the plane of an object, a compass for direction, thermometer for temperature—then breaks them. As the thermometer cracks, its mercury, "freed," "run[s] away"; the "rainbow-bird" once trapped in the angled edge of the mirror glass (the mirror that once confined the now-empty moon of "Insomnia") now flies "wherever / it feels like, gay!" (192).

"Sonnet" primarily concerns the escape from strictures, and the closet constitutes one of those enclosures, if not by any means the only one. The emphatic placement of the final word, separated by a comma from the rest of the sentence and brought forward sonically and visually by the exclamation point, offers one indicator that gayness, rather than gaiety, constitutes the subject of the poem. The imagery of a divided, doubled self and the description of indecision also echo "The Man-Moth," as the empty mirror may allude to "Insomnia" and other of Bishop's implicitly homosexual poems employing this trope (such as "The Gentleman of Shallott," another precariously divided self). Predicated and informed by a world that encloses, labels, and measures, "Sonnet" becomes Bishop's most anti-enclosure poem, imagining a pursuit of pleasure that knows no pressures other than desire.

The Family Voice

A final contradiction of Bishop's work, like her equivocal attraction to certain houses or her coded airing of issues of sexual definition, remains her deep identification with and simultaneous resistance to membership in a line of American women poets, as mentioned before. Although Bishop deplored attempts to characterize her as a "woman poet," she forged the strongest of links between herself and the premiere "woman poet" of the previous generation, Marianne Moore. Extensive work has been done by many researchers including Lynn Keller (1983, 1987), David Kalstone (1989), Jeredith Merrin (1990), David Bromwich (1990), Lorrie Goldensohn (1992), Betsy Erkkila (1992), and Joanne Feit Diehl (1993) on the relationship between the two and the influence of the older poet upon her protégée, especially in the form of advice that Bishop often appreciated but sometimes repudiated firmly. Bishop learned a great deal from Moore not only about poetic craft but about how to negotiate one's position in relationship to the literary powers, and how to succeed in the world of publication, grants, and prizes on one's own terms, self-protectively; Diehl rightly attributes to Moore an "uncanny ability to disarm various forms of masculine aggression" (1993, 18).

Diehl also reveals how Bishop expresses her rebellions against and ambivalence about her mentor, especially in her memoir "Efforts of Affection": Bishop's fond and admiring prose portrait of Moore, like her poetic "Invitation to Miss Marianne Moore," nevertheless repeatedly notes Moore's tendencies to be overly controlling and even judgmental, personally and poetically. Their conflict over Bishop's "Roosters," which Moore and her mother undertook to rewrite, remains famous and much discussed, and Bishop remarks that Moore even liked to advise the younger writer when to visit the bathroom (1984, 131). Further, rightly or wrongly, Bishop repeatedly differentiates herself in the memoir from what she sees as Moore's "overfastidious"ness, especially regarding sexuality and bodily functions: "I remember her worrying about the fate of a mutual friend whose sexual tastes had always seemed quite obvious to me: 'What are we going to do about X. . . ? Why, sometimes I think he might even be in the clutches of a *sodomite*. . . !' One could almost smell the brimstone" (1984, 130). Some readers, accepting as fact the lens on Moore that Bishop provides, assume from this passage that Moore condemned homosexuality and was unaware of Bishop's sexual orientation. No evidence to the contrary has surfaced, but still I find this supposition unlikely. Moore knew Bishop for a very long time and wrote warm letters to Louise Crane, one of Bishop's companions; given Moore's intelligence and powers of observation, it would require an extraordinary naïveté to suppress at least some suspicions about Bishop's "sexual tastes." Further, Moore maintained a fairly close connection with Bryher, H.D.'s lifelong companion; she interacted with Bryher and H.D. as a couple and, again, must have guessed or known the status of that relationship, all the while valuing their friendship deeply. The conversation Bishop recounts may be a fictional decoy to her readers; alternatively, it suggests Moore joking, perhaps in the presence of her mother. Moore also may have regarded same-sex relations between women in a different light than male homosexuality. While reserve and deadpan humor (including sexual jokes) contribute to Moore's character, Moore was not intolerant, especially of private lives kept private.

Beyond their personal and poetic conflicts and Bishop's reasonable need to distinguish herself from Moore, the concerns of their poems themselves overlap, as Bishop herself admits: "We are profoundly different, I think—but a good deal of her subject matter, her insistence on accuracy, and her way of observing, I'm sure did influence me" (1976 letter to Lynn Keller, quoted in Goldensohn 1992, 142). Although Moore shows far more reserve on the page than Bishop, both use precise descriptive detail as a vehicle, even sometimes as a mask, for other kinds of discussion; both strike an attitude of antipoetic modesty to disarm potential criticism, placating with stereotypically feminine decorum even as they ambush. These qualities have won both poets praise and criticism alternately, as literary tastes cycle. That said, Bishop's poetry speaks more dramatically and more colloquially than Moore's, responding in these and other ways to the increasingly personal, antimodernist esthetic of her own contemporaries. Bishop's written response to Moore's "prudery" deliberately highlights her own modernity. There exists much basis for contrast (if also comparison) between the two writers.

Critics less often recognize Emily Dickinson as a source of influence on Bishop, perhaps because Bishop's Dickinsonian poems do not display those famous, Moore-influenced trademarks of naturalistic description and prosaic, level tone, and are often less popular.[6] In a 1956 letter to Robert Lowell, Bishop expresses a mixture of attraction to and repulsion from Dickinson's work: "Did I really make snide remarks about Emily Dickinson? I like, or at least admire, her a great deal more now—probably because of that good new edition, really. I spent another stretch absorbed in that, and think (along with Randall [Jarrell]) that she's about the best we have. However—she does set one's teeth on edge a lot of the time, don't you think?" (1994, 333). Such comments do testify that Bishop has read Dickinson repeatedly and carefully, and scrutinized Johnson's edition before completing the pieces discussed below; I find her visceral revulsion as telling as the praise in communicating Dickinson's power as a precursor. However, the best evidence of influence lies in the poems themselves. Dickinson, although exercising a reticence related to Moore's, employs a style almost antithetical to that of the modernist poet, and thus provides an alternate model for Bishop's less-anthologized, intensely lyric poetry including "Insomnia," "The Shampoo," "Song for the Rainy Season," "Sonnet," and other pieces. Bishop mined Dickinson's work for its strangeness, its capacity, shared by nursery rhymes (which also resound in much of Bishop's writing), to disconcert and comfort simultaneously. Bishop's elliptic, incantatory love poetry resembles no one's as much as Dickinson's. In fact, following Moore in choosing to review an edition of Dickinson's letters, Bishop portrays Dickinson's writing as centrally concerning love ("Love from Emily"). Bishop found Dickinson to be a fertile source of imagery as well as an admired practitioner of the coded love poem, employing the earlier poet's famous volcanoes, for instance, as a shared emblem of the threat of repressed feeling.

Moore and Dickinson represent two poles for Bishop, two important examples of how to write great poetry self-protectively; it is not surprising that Bishop would have looked to them as the two most lauded American women poets preceding her. As Merrin persuasively insists (1990), Bishop followed other models as well: she herself often cited George Herbert as her favorite poet, and she possessed deep knowledge of his work. Travisano correctly emphasizes the mutual influences among Bishop, Lowell, Berryman, and Jarrell (1999). However, Dickinson and Moore had greater impact on how Bishop negotiated the tensions between public and private in her use of the lyric. Bishop's telling silences and her use of certain enclosures including houses, volcanoes, and animal shells make the most sense in the context Moore and Dickinson provide.

Where Bishop alludes to either poet, she often wrangles with this lineage. "The Armadillo" and "In the Waiting Room" engage in this struggle quietly, while addressing other subjects and directing reader attention elsewhere. I read these poems playfully, aware that they do not take such self-positioning as their main subjects; I do not mean to contradict other interpretations as much to open another field of meaning in which these poems register. Both pieces do illustrate Bishop's pervasive attitudes towards her potential place in a tradition of American women poets.

"The Armadillo," dedicated to Robert Lowell, is often juxtaposed to his poem "Skunk Hour," with its complementary subtitle. Although that pairing remains a fruitful one, "The Armadillo" also merits consideration in relation to Moore's "The Pangolin" and, to a lesser degree, Dickinson's "You've seen Balloons set—Hav'nt You?" (F 730, J 700).[7] Bishop's poem offers both a tribute and an ambivalent description of the effects of tribute, and the two contradictory voices the poem employs, while sparring about the social cost of estheticism, also articulate her difficult relationship to her poetic precursors.

The "frail, illegal fire balloons" sent up to celebrate St. John's Day in Rio and the title animal itself constitute the chief enclosures of "The Armadillo" (103). Each becomes an icon of the lyric poem. The balloons seem delicate, apparently living although man-made, compared to hearts or "egg[s] of fire"; objects of beauty, they paradoxically can turn dangerous and ignite the landscape. The armadillo truly lives but seems hard and defensive, reflective of light rather than translucent, his silhouette resembling a "weak mailed fist" as he emerges a survivor from the destruction. With these two images Bishop holds Dickinson and Moore's lyric strategies against each other.

"The Armadillo" indicts Robert Lowell's penchant to estheticize personal suffering: hence the heartlike transparency of the fire balloons, resembling confessional poems in their exposed beauty but risking results catastrophic to domestic happiness (embodied in the ravaged owl's nest and the baby rabbit dislodged from its burrow). At some level, however, Bishop must also have had Dickinson's ill-fated balloons in mind. In "You've seen Balloons set," Dickinson also depicts the "flare and falter" of a balloon, exquisitely beautiful, that, crashing into a tree, "Tears open her imperial Veins – / And tumbles in the Sea – ." In the vein image Dickinson, like Bishop, sees the red light that keeps the balloon aloft as circulating blood that eventually spills; Dickinson's poem emphasizes the transcendent loveliness of her "Gilded Creature," whose disastrous plunge becomes merely a titillating spectacle for the vulgar crowd and "Clerks in Counting Rooms." Dickinson's tragic balloon, in fact, resembles the fallen women populating nineteenth-century literature, who ambitiously soar and then fatally stumble; the balloon's breath and "Liquid Feet" (a prosodic pun common in Dickinson) imply its connection to the lyric poem's attempts at transcendence.

"The Armadillo" thrills with its predecessor poem at the balloons' display. When Dickinson turns, however, to mark the reactions of unimaginative crowds, siding with fallen beauty, Bishop lowers her gaze still further to count the natural costs of this man-made exhibition. In a sense, "The Armadillo" qualifies as another of Bishop's poems about endangered houses; she seems both to protest the damage and to admire the agents of harm ("egg"like, the balloons might be presumed to engender as well as destroy). Further, the spectacular, wayward fire balloons resemble Dickinson's poems; from Bishop's point of view, the Amherst poet both threw open possibilities for later women poets and closed them, as her legend (the childish, virginal recluse) dominated later poetry by women in unwelcome ways.

The image that survives the wreckage of Dickinson's lyric strongly resembles one of Moore's emblems for her own lyric practice. Moore's "The Pangolin" offers a celebration of that armored animal's "unpugnacious" hardiness and grace, and his "power to defy" all efforts to unroll him. He becomes, by the end of the poem, not only one of Moore's most modestly heroic animals but a model for her own poetry, likewise "made graceful by adversities." Bishop's armadillo becomes the American version of Moore's African animal, also deflective of attempts to read him or her (Bishop does not assign her animal a sex), and also a solitary survivor. Bishop names the poem after the armadillo to show that the piece tells his or her story, a tale of the "adversities" that make a virtue of impenetrable shells. The title also indicates where Bishop's ultimate allegiance in poetic style lies.

Bishop asserts her own esthetic as differentiated even from Moore's, however, when the last stanza's change of fonts indicates the shift to a new voice. "*Too pretty, dreamlike mimicry!*", "The Armadillo" protests, objecting to the skill and control of Bishop's own description, tellingly called a "mimicry," perhaps of Moore's style. As reserved as Bishop can seem, where Moore exercises moral commentary, Bishop tends to record feeling, inserting herself more interactively into her own landscapes. Here, as Moore never does with the pangolin, Bishop speaks the armadillo's anger, although not with great explicitness, just as she emotionally responds to other animals in "The Moose," "The Fish," and "Pink Dog."

The waiting room itself must constitute Bishop's most famous enclosure, as the title image of another of her most canonized and analyzed poems. As in "The Armadillo," its allusions to Moore and Dickinson, although fainter and less this time to specific poems, mark its concern with how Bishop fits in with and stands apart from "the family voice" or the poetic of enclosure practiced by previous poets. "In the Waiting Room" depicts a panicked slippage between Bishop's own work and the potentially overpowering voices of literary "relatives" and neighbors, deploying a familial metaphor for literary influence that emphasizes the idea of inheritance.

"In the Waiting Room" sets itself retrospectively; although published only three years before the poet's death, in *Geography III* (1976), it seems to recount an event from nearly sixty years before, in Bishop's girlhood. Again like "The Armadillo," it asserts how it ought to be read, this time not in relation to another poem or poet but as a significant fragment of autobiography. "In the Waiting Room" participates in certain tropes of confessional poetry in order to secure its status as a real memory: Bishop strongly identifies the speaker's voice with her own through the name "Elizabeth," and she recounts narratively and with much specific historical detail (place names, dates) a childhood trauma, her dizzying plunge into some new world, whether adulthood, womanhood, modernity, and/or poetry (Bishop leaves adequate room, as usual, for multiple readings). Some of the most persuasive arguments concerning "In the Waiting Room" assert that the poem's crisis is centered on the little girl's awakening to gender identity; the terrifying state of womanhood, characterized by timidity, deformity, and awful legacies, seems to await the poem's protagonist.

By building on the readings of Lee Edelman, Brett Millier, and the numerous others who investigate this suggestive poem, and by drawing out the poem's allusions to Moore and Dickinson, I argue that this poem of initiation and inheritance also represents a statement of Bishop's relationship to the poetic of enclosure that pervades so much of American poetry by women. "In the Waiting Room" tells of the deep conflict that Bishop felt about her membership in this tradition, the paradoxically "ambivalent oneness" Costello finds in the poem (1991, 123). Because the poem's speaker passionately resists this kinship (she depicts influence as familial), images of women in the poem seem overwhelmingly negative, fractured by distress into body parts such as breasts, necks, knees, hands, and threatening to subsume the reluctant child's identity. The voice of "Elizabeth," for instance, becomes joined and confused with her aunt Consuelo's when the older relative cries out in pain from "inside," and she veers between identifying herself as a separate individual—"you are an *I*, / you are an *Elizabeth*"—and as "one of *them*" (160). The poem's speaker is not at all happy to hear the "family voice" in her own.

The child's anxious uncertainty about her relationship to the women around her resonates with Bishop's wavering between affiliating and distancing herself from other women poets. Aunt Consuelo, who has been carefully identified in essay after essay as Bishop's own aunt Florence, exerts a dominance over the child that resembles Marianne Moore's over Bishop. The frightening blur of voices represents the struggle of one poet to disengage her poetic voice from that of her mentor. In her panic she feels herself sliding beneath a black wave, invoking the imagery of Moore's "The Fish," a poem, perhaps importantly, written at about the time that Bishop's poem tells us repeatedly that it is set, during World War I (one of the poem's images of strife). The Elizabeth of "In the Waiting Room" also reads *National Geographic*, one of Moore's sources for the kind of natural detail that is the very texture of the older poet's work. Overwhelmed by the photographs, the speaker tries to contain them by emphasizing "the yellow margins, the date"; Bishop attempts to contain Moore's poetry safely within her own work (159).

Bishop's powerful predecessors, however, will not stay enclosed. "In the Waiting Room"'s allusion to Dickinson lurks in the volcano she finds in that issue of *National Geographic* (the article "The Valley of Ten Thousand Smokes" constitutes the only one of those pictures actually in that number of the magazine[8]). It, too, at first apparently dead and full of ashes, erupts into Bishop's poem, "spilling over / in rivulets of fire" (159). The volcano spews interiority outward, mixing public and private, gesturing to each poet's central concern with insides and out-sides; later, the poem will even pun on the phrase "inside-out," trans-forming it, as Susan McCabe notes, into "Outside, / in" (1994, 223). Bishop's struggle here with Dickinson and Moore becomes almost Bloomian, a life-or-death wrestle for control of her voice.

Towards the end of the poem Bishop asks:

> What similarities—
> boots, hands, the family voice
> I felt in my throat, or even
> the *National Geographic*
> and those awful hanging breasts—
> held us all together
> or made us all just one?
> How—I didn't know any
> word for it—how "unlikely". . . (161)

Bishop's alter ego never escapes the waiting room, as even the poetry of her full maturity has not lost all echoes of "the family voice." "Unlikely" as it may seem for a poet so resolutely opposed to projects like mine, set as she was against the label "woman poet," this imagery, this closeted reserve of language, does indeed join her with Dickinson, Moore, and others as a practitioner of a poetic of enclosure.

Rita Dove
The House Expands

More than any other poet included in this study, Rita Dove recognizes and explicitly describes the centrality of enclosure imagery to her own work and to lyric poetry generally (1995a). Her lectures, interviews, and essays reveal both her passionate reading and her professorial knowledge of tradition; unsurprisingly, then, her poetry also exhibits intense connections and contrasts with the writers treated in this book. In particular, her literary bonds with the two mid-century poets, Elizabeth Bishop and Gwendolyn Brooks, reveal two central aspects of Dove's own poetic of enclosure: her preoccupations with domestic space and with maternity as a figure for influence. Dove depicts both houses and maternal enclosure with significant ambivalence, and, correspondingly, practices a version of lyric poetry that precariously balances the enabling and limiting qualities of formal confinement.

Like Bishop, Dove places tensions between home and travel at the center of her work. Also like Bishop, Dove figures the lyric poem as an unstable house and resists the assumptions about personal expression that shape so much late twentieth-century lyric practice. Gwendolyn Brooks's racially inflected urban constrictions, on the other hand, strongly differ from Dove's midwestern houses, and the younger black poet criticizes the Black Arts perspective that Brooks fervently adopts mid-career. Nevertheless, Dove's parallel use of the same tropes of

enclosure mark a concealed engagement with this powerful predeces-
sor, the most distinguished and canonized African American woman
poet of the century. This influence becomes particularly clear in the
sonnet cycle *Mother Love* (1995b), in which Dove omits Brooks from
her references to key literary foremothers and yet employs the lyric
form Brooks most masterfully manipulates in her early work.

139

This last chapter begins by situating Dove in the tradition my
study describes, exploring some of her affiliations with an inherited
poetic of enclosure and outlining the characteristics of Dove's own
enclosed lyric. I then discuss Dove's suburban homes in *The Yellow
House on the Corner* (1980) and a later piece, "In the Old Neighbor-
hood," delineating her modifications to this defining image for so many
women poets. I conclude with a treatment of maternal enclosure and
influence in *Mother Love*. Through the poems of Rita Dove, my con-
clusion draws together two recurrent features of the poetic of enclo-
sure: deliberate correlations of femininity, domesticity, and the lyric
genre; and images of enclosure as markers of a female line in American
poetry. A full treatment of the influence of the poetic of enclosure on
contemporary poetry by American women remains beyond the scope
of my study, but I hope this chapter suggests its persistent relevance
even in poetry that seems at least as open as it does confined.

Responding to *Mother Love,* Alison Booth writes that "in 1995, Dove
can claim a large family without fanfare" (1996, 125). Indeed, Dove's
publications in varied genres testify to the wide range of poetry that
she's considered carefully, as befits the first poet in this study to sup-
port herself primarily through university teaching. Her lectures
as poet laureate (1993–94), gathered with an autobiographical essay
in *The Poet's World* (1995a), refer to a roster of female poets, includ-
ing Sexton, Plath, Clifton, Bishop, Moore, Kumin, Rich, Cisneros,
Lorde, Atwood, Rukeyser, and H.D., among others. Further justifying
Jeredith Merrin's insistence on the inseparability of literary influ-
ences, though, she cites a comparable number of male writers, from
Shakespeare, Donne, Shelley, and Keats to twentieth-century figures
such as Roethke, Berryman, Langston Hughes, Williams, Stevens,
Merwin, Heaney, Rilke, and Lorca (1990). Conscious of her public mis-
sion as laureate, she may have framed these allusions with deliberate
attention to diversity: her pantheon includes not only women and

men but Europeans and Americans, gay and straight writers, and a spectrum of ethnic and racial backgrounds.

The references in *The Poet's World* encompass whole poems by certain writers and passing allusions to others; the names indicate the scope of her reading as a practicing poet and teacher and not necessarily the writers whose precedents have most shaped her own esthetics. As previous chapters indicate, nor do I accept a poet's proffered list of influences as defining her most urgent poetic engagements: Moore's citations of male prose writers, for instance, do not preclude the textual echoes of Dickinson I identify. In Moore's case, too, a conscious dislike of Whitman may inform some poems more significantly than her admiration for other authors. Dove praises many writers, sometimes ardently and sometimes with careful tact, but an impulse to inclusion, as above, or the interests of a given interviewer may affect whom she names and the nature of her comments. "I feel accompanied by earlier generations," Dove told Helen Vendler in 1990, naming Rilke, Walcott, Morrison, and Heine (491); Dove likes, admires, alludes to, and feels sustained by these writers. At Malin Pereira's prompting, in contrast, she describes her reading of H.D. "in very small dosages; otherwise I'd start sounding like her" (1999, 204); Dove "wanted to forget" H.D. entirely during the composition of *Mother Love,* lest she imitate the modernist's approach to myth (205). All these writers potentially inform Dove's literary practice. However, which experience, accompaniment or conscious avoidance, signals greater influence?

In the same interview, Dove does speak of reading H.D. with fondness. She limits her study of the earlier author only because "I love her poetic work. It's so much itself, if that makes any sense, and it's so very musical in its insistent phrasing" (Pereira 1999, 204). Dove's praises, however, decrease in coherence, although the contemporary poet can generally describe her own life and work with great articulateness: "What I admire about her is the way she could take the outrageous circumstance of her life sometimes and write a poem or a sequence which was absolutely beautiful; I thought she could do that and it was not self-indulgent, it was not really confessional in any sense, and I'm glad I don't have that situation in my life" (205). Dove appears to sympathize with H.D.'s guarded early lyric, her imagist encoding of autobiography into gorgeous, impersonal fragments. The ambiguous last phrase, however, suggests two meanings. Perhaps Dove contrasts her own success and stability to the modernist's sufferings as a bisexual exile composing those poems, during miscarriage, marital failure, and the personal and public losses of World War I. On the other hand, or even simultaneously, Dove may express pleasure that she need not compose such coded poetry: her "situation" does not require the same evasions.

Pereira raises the subject of H.D. in response to Dove's various cita-
tions of H.D.'s prose in *The Poet's World* and *Mother Love*. In fact, such epigraphs and, even more crucially, echoes within the poems them-
selves indicate more truly than deliberate statements which sources haunt a writer's imagination the most instrumentally. By this register, images and strategies of enclosure as practiced by many of the poets in this study have exerted a significant force on Dove's version of the lyric. She herself observes the prevalence of confined imagery in her work, noting her "poetic consciousness of occupied space . . . All of my books but one bear titles concerned with matters of definable space" (1995a, 15). Her lecture "Stepping Out: The Poet in the World" discusses how she and other poets situate their poems in houses and rooms, noting particularly the gender and racial associations with the kitchen and back door. She judges that "the female or ethnic artist who eschews the kitchen completely also denies the positive anima of this spiritual domicile—its privacy and intimacy" (1995a, 32). How-
ever, Dove emphasizes one particular suburban locale as a recurrent site in her own work: "I realized that quite a number of my poems take place in backyards. . . . My backyard emerges as a place for confronta-
tion. All the required elements of a psychic landscape—comfort and loss, suffocation and risk—come together in the struggle of enclosure versus exposure" (19–21). Dove correlates confined space with the lyric poem even as her lectures question, and even mock, the navel-gazing inwardness of some contemporary pieces.[1]

The epigraph to this book's introduction begins with a quote from the same collection: "Each poem has its house of sound, its own geo-
graphical reverberations" (18). While Dove remarks the prevalence of enclosure imagery in the twentieth-century lyric, and her own depend-
ence on house and yard imagery links her clearly with the poets treated here, she hints more sparely at stylistic correspondences to thematic enclosures. *The Poet's World* values the lyric's shelter, as her frequent allusions to Gaston Bachelard's rapturous *The Poetic of Space* (1964) testify, but also insists on the necessary interpenetration of art and a larger world. As Patricia Wallace argues, "Dove is preoccupied with history, less frequently personal history . . . than American history and history more generally" (1993, 12). As for Brooks, race inflects Dove's approach to the enclosed lyric: while her remark about kitchens links gender and race, suggesting that a black female

poet may experience an intensified relation to certain domestic spaces, Dove experiences public obligations similar to those that direct Brooks's apostrophes. Dove explains to Pereira, "There is a pressure, not just from the Black Arts movement, but from one's whole life, to be a credit to the race" (1999, 197); her 1991 essay with Waniek defines African American poetry partly through its "sense of mission" (220). Dove's ambiguous remark on H.D.'s "situation" highlights the same ambivalence about the coded lyric versus the poem as public instrument. The conscientious laureate, therefore, poses recurrent questions in her poems that are central to this study: What do "closed" and "open" mean in twentieth-century poetry? How can a poet value enclosure and yet grapple with history and power? What even constitutes inside and outside for the lyric, and what relationship should these spaces possess to one another?

Every poet featured in this book demonstrates that her persistent interest in enclosure mandates a related consciousness of exposure, openness, escape, freedom—however the given poet or piece constructs the opposition. Dickinson, Moore, H.D., Brooks, and Bishop all construe reserve, compression, and/or fixed forms as enabling, at least for parts of their careers; some link constraint irrevocably with mortality and/or language itself. Simultaneously, however, all challenge lyric tradition by disrupting received forms, creating multivocal or discontinuous lyric subjects, or meddling with the devices of privacy and inwardness, and some of them thereby intend to combat other cultural inheritances as well. An interest in accessibility, politics, free verse, or any other connotation of openness, then, does not preclude Dove's participation in the tradition I've indicated. In fact, Dove recognizes the inward lyric's potential to educate the prejudiced by conveying the complex humanity of alien subjects (Mullaney 1998, 33).

Formally, much contemporary poetry "opens" the lyric far more radically than Dove does, by incorporating nonpoetic discourses, for instance, or through typographical experiment that disrupts the familiar boxlike shape of the printed poem.[2] Dove's relatively prompt professional success, in fact, suggests her mainstream appeal to publishers, university professors, and prize committees. Even though Dove celebrates the radical turns in Rich's career (Erickson 1999, 90) and describes her own struggles "to escape the trap of the 'workshop poem'" (1995a, 87), even though she resists categorization in any literary school, and even though her work offers unexpected difficulties and ambiguities, Dove's version of the lyric does not prioritize

challenging her audience's generic expectations. She may write in mul-
tiple genres (nonfiction prose, short stories, the novel, and drama as
well as individual lyrics and poetic sequences[3]), but she identifies her-
self first as a poet (Mullaney 1988, 87) and writes poems in the most
recognizable modes of her era. For example, although relatively few
of Dove's poems might qualify as personal lyrics, legitimate reasons
exist for Dove's inclusion in interview collections such as *The Post-
Confessionals* (Ingersoll, Kitchen, Rubin 1989). Poets including Anne
Sexton helped open the way for Dove's frankness about sexuality and
the female body. Even when Dove creates poetic narratives in mark-
edly fictive voices, as she does in each volume but most famously in
Thomas and Beulah (1986), she employs the conventions of authentic-
ity developed by confessional poets, and for the most part prioritizes
expressivity over language play.

Dove's training as a musician (she studied the cello and continues
to play the viola da gamba) might suggest strong formal attention to
the lyric's music: in fact, she composes primarily in a free verse that
often alludes to, but never completely obeys, received lyric shapes.
Musical terminology (for instance, the title of *Grace Notes* [1989]) and
attention to sound constitute the chief artifacts of this education in
her lyric practice. Nevertheless, her poems remain lyric according to
the definition I've applied: musical reference; allusions to a solitary,
expressive speaker even when that speaker does not resemble Dove;
brevity; and a concern with the traditions of the genre. Further,
despite the pressures towards the personal lyric defining confession-
alism and the socially utile lyric prescribed by Black Arts, Dove tends
to exert unusual reticence, exaggerating lyric privacy into the esthetic
of reserve I've elsewhere identified. Her poems do employ autobiogra-
phy, but Dove emphasizes the mediated, shaped, even inaccessible
quality of personal experience translated into poetry; she also omits
key referents, as do Dickinson and H.D., and distances herself from
verisimilitude through surreal and magical elements.

Critics have responded to this reticence in various ways. While an
important early essay by Arnold Rampersad praises Dove's first vol-
umes profusely, he finds her "too reserved" and urges her toward a
more public role "as a poetic reformer, one with great potential as a
leader" (1986, 59, 53). Helen Vendler, however, while reluctantly con-
ceding the roles of race and gender in a poet's work, praises her for
the same impersonal intelligence. Defining lyrics as "poems of self-
definition"—a problematic formula—Vendler notes "Dove's continued

watchful distance from pure lyric" (1995, 63, 75). Even though their agendas differ, both scholars present reserve as a defining trait of Dove's poetic efforts. Dove may express some skepticism about the enclosed lyric, but her practice still engages enclosure not only in image but in stylistic and formal strategies.

Stranded Galleons

In *Mother Love*, Rita Dove writes mainly from two perspectives: she becomes Demeter, outraged and grieved by what she alternately characterizes as her daughter's abduction or defection from the family; she also speaks as Persephone, a traveling daughter who, for better or worse, has broken with home irrevocably, but must visit it repeatedly. In fact, a great deal of Dove's writing concerns homecoming: she interrogates ideas of home repeatedly, while equally concerned with the impossibility of ever actually arriving there.[4] The suburban homes Dove sometimes depicts are "inscrutable houses" (to use Elizabeth Bishop's term): objects of interest, critique, and some desire that resist complete understanding. Dove's perspective on house, home, and even country is that of a dispassionate, even alienated observer. Further, her practice of the lyric in relation to Anglo-American poetic tradition reproduces the same tension between comfortable familiarity and foreignness; Dove's poetry, while striving toward accessibility and eschewing the experimentality that characterizes the avant-garde, resists that accessibility in flashes of uncanniness. In "Geometry," "Ö," and "In the Old Neighborhood," the former two poems from the beginning of her career and the latter a production of subsequent poetic success, Dove employs an unsettled and unsettling house as an explicit figure for the lyric and her own ambivalent habitation of it. Finally, she resembles Demeter struggling to keep the past intact far less than the dispossessed or runaway Persephone.

Dove's book-length premiere, *The Yellow House on the Corner*, grants title space to this significant image even while emphasizing its liminal location. The volume includes the red house of "Small Town," which seems paradoxically to represent the fissure of a marriage (SP 8);[5] the stucco house of "Night Watch," sheltering and isolating a privileged speaker from "the shanties in the mountains" (19); and the manor or "The House Slave," so dramatically different from nearby slave quarters (29). In each case, Dove depicts the guilty alienation of an inhabitant from the house. Also in each instance, the poem attends to the necessary relation between inside and outside, observing suffering that occurs beyond the house's protection even as the speaker remains on its grounds. Through such poems, Dove identifies the house, and by association the lyric poem, as a space of privilege that anxiously registers its own luxuries.

These elliptical pieces range from thirteen to twenty lines, organized into unrhymed stanzas. An even more compressed poem, "Geometry" (SP 17), consists of three unrhymed triplets, the lines unmetered but evoking a rough blank verse in their ten- to thirteen-syllable lengths; it imagines architectural mayhem, the house unmaking itself to exhilarating effect. On this occasion, the speaker, perhaps an adolescent doing homework, "prove[s] a theorem and the house expands": an intellectual achievement disrupts the house's stability so that "the ceiling floats away with a sigh," the walls become transparent, and the windows flap off like butterflies "to some point true and unproven." The last image amplifies the play between enclosure and release by suggesting liberation from a cocoon, that necessary but temporary shelter; it implies the speaker's own maturation as a natural deliverance from houses, as she stands "out in the open" at last. The visual structure of three triplets, each stanza and the poem itself therefore a container, emphasizes productive containment rather than release; interestingly, though, the enjambed inner stanza contrasts with the end-stopped lines of the first and third, as if to evoke freedom within constraint. This poem, like the others, is enabled by its own enclosures, and yet it celebrates openness, the transcendence of suburban cocoons through an adventurous act of the intelligence.

In "Ö," which closes this first volume, the actual yellow house on the corner of the book's title is dislodged from its stable centrality by an encounter with an alien language and the new knowledge associated with that language; it subsequently threatens to "[take] off over the marshland" (SP 64). This poem, like "Geometry," conveys Dove's abiding interest in the idea of home, an interest balanced by her opposing commitment to what she calls "serious travel." Dove has defined "serious travel" to an interviewer as "trying to understand a place and not just passing through, taking pictures" (Taleb-Khyar 1991, 351); it also implies a seriousness about travel, a commitment to searching out new ways of seeing that one can import back to one's own world.

Dove's early poetry rarely cites race as the, or even a, cause or her sense of displacement, although she is an African American woman with Cherokee and Blackfoot ancestors in a racist society. Instead, Dove presents herself more generally as a student of the unfamiliar. For instance, as her partly autobiographical novel *Through the Ivory*

Gate (1992) observes, Dove's study of the German language and subsequent Fulbright in Germany were not obvious courses for an African American woman in the 1970s to pursue: her trip abroad became one of the many ways Dove deliberately embarked on an unexpected path. It contributed to the defamiliarized perspective her poems assume: to Dove's eyes, even Akron constitutes a foreign country, an unreal place impossibly isolated from the rest of the world.

Despite this literary investment in strangeness, Dove's reputation places her in the poetic mainstream; as poet laureate, surely a mainstream position within American letters, she declared her goal to make poetry more accessible to more people (*Current Biography* 1994, 12). As plainly as her poems often speak, however, they contain a tension between the homely and the strange, something Dove herself recognizes when she tells interviewers that intuition is her ordering principle (Rubin and Kitchen 1989, 162), accuses herself of overly cryptic language, or describes her resistance to strong poetic closure (Walsh 1994, 147). Dove has said that she tries to write in the very early morning, in a time of eerie clarity and disorienting stillness: a surreality results in some of her poetic landscape that reflects this angle of vision and strengthens her poetry's resolve not to offer perfect coherence (or predictability).

Dove's poetry of the middle American suburbs is typically surreal, challenging their inhabitants' calm sense of normalcy with the rich illogic of dreams. Dove generates this illogic partly through the instability of her pronouns. In "Ö," the "we" near the center of the poem designates a stubbornly self-sufficient family, complete in itself, and, it imagines, securely anchored in the unchangeable present moment. The first-person plural pronoun signifies Dove's identification with this mentality, even as within the same poem her shift to the first-person singular indicates an ambivalent detachment. The strong presence of a second-person address further unsettles the poem: its first line speaks an imperative that seems primarily to instruct the reader, but also includes the speaker herself and members of this dislocated neighborhood. The poem ends with an even more ambiguous use of the second person: "You start out with one thing, end / up with another, and nothing's / like it used to be, not even the future." The speaker could be addressing any of the same three parties, but this time seems to emphasize internal monologue, an uncertain speaker musing to herself.

The poem tells us that its title syllable means "island" in Swedish; the typographical symbol even looks like an island, emphasizing the smug isolation of the dwellers in the yellow house. The letter "o," although here given that disorienting umlaut, visually and aurally evokes other meanings. As a magic circle of protection, it further islands the suburban family and probably also the "I" of the poem, also an alienated figure. As the sound of surprise in English, it marks the intrusion of something startling or unfamiliar, such as a Swedish word or the speaker's own critical perspective. It also signals the poetic figure of apostrophe, the reach from a poem's inside to some outer, absent or inanimate person or force, such as the illuminating foreignness of Swedish, which in the poem's imagery becomes the wind that will dislodge the stranded house or ship. The sound "o" simultaneously signifies surprise, a call to change, the protection of the status quo, and an impetus toward movement in this heartland neighborhood.

The yellow house on the corner becomes a "galleon stranded in flowers" because it cannot sustain its illusion of fixed inevitability after the introduction of an outsider's critical perspective: Akron housing developments don't seem quite so utterly normal after one has known other kinds of worlds. Mere language, according to Dove, can introduce a new and estranged mode of vision. The fact that the house becomes a galleon—not just any ship, but a large Spanish warship or trader from the fifteenth or sixteenth century, even a relic of European colonization of the Americas—magnifies the transformation that occurs in the poem. Dove suddenly reveals the house suddenly as not just an icon of the present but as a consequence of a particular past; the grounded vessel becomes a lodging for explorers who have stopped moving, perhaps temporarily. Perhaps as a warship, but certainly as a craft avoiding "the misted shoals," it is also endangered, not the secure refuge one might otherwise expect.

For this speaker, the domestic aspect of the American dream suddenly becomes visible not only as one choice in a world of possible "futures," but as a choice beset by threatening forces. Dove's poetry of home potentially functions as a feminist critique of the suburban home as institution, engaging the history of the house as a figure in other poetry by American women. Her handling of the image particularly suggests the poetries of Emily Dickinson and Elizabeth Bishop, who also write of house and home from insider and outsider positions, and also use the house as a metaphor not only for the lyric but for tradition and descent in the literary sense. Dove participates with these and other American women poets in her ambivalent relation to the house as prison, shelter, and feminine institution. Dove's poetry of home reacts against the stereotypical position of women within houses, identified with that refuge but not owning the structures themselves; it also reveals how she places herself within a larger lyric tradition, inhabiting an inherited mode with critical resistance.

After the Pulitzer Prize–winning *Thomas and Beulah*, Dove's perceived place within that tradition began to strengthen. "In the Old Neighborhood," another poem focused on the same kind of suburban house (possibly the same house), ends the introduction to her *Selected Poems*, which appeared in 1993 as a result of that increased status. In this poem, a longer piece that stretches lyric brevity while invoking lyric tropes, Dove revisits her childhood home to serve as matron of honor in a sister's wedding; the speaker juxtaposes home as a site of instability and violence against memories of her first engagement with literature within its walls.[6] The title may respond to Rampersad's hope that Dove will return "to some place closer to her old neighborhood" (1986, 69), an implicit wish for increased commitment on Dove's part to African American writers and readers. Instead, Dove conveys complex and ambivalent allegiances.

Dove depicts other domestic spaces subsidiary to the parents' house, but all the homes within the poem seem threatened or threatening. Her sister's bridal apartment, in the first verse paragraph, has been invaded by raccoons, which Dove depicts as both violent and sexual: "ferocious and faggy, licking / their black-gloved paws" (SP xxii). The speaker recalls weeping for fear in a backyard tent, apparently a particularly precarious and vulnerable shelter even in its proximity to the chief edifice of the poem, the family home itself. She associates this conventional suburban house with annual tragedies, such as the songless bird who gets caught in the attic fan in a scene that Dove describes unflinchingly, or the "pebbly toad / the lawn mower had shuffled / into liver canapes" (xxv). Even the roses the father tends in the garden are "mutants" and function as images of domesticity in jeopardy. One of his new breeds evokes "bruised petticoats," Victorian femininity here linked with violence; the other resembles a "sudden teacup / blazing empty, its rim / a drunken red smear," an image of lipsticked impropriety or even of female sexual abandon (xxii).

The speaker views her childhood home newly, in this adult homecoming, as shifting and surreal. She accompanies the most intense moment of disorientation with nostalgic longing, occurring in parentheses in the center of the poem:

(Let me go back to the white rock
on the black lawn, the number
stenciled in negative light.
Let me return to the shadow
of a house moored in the moonlight,
gables pitched bright above
the extinguished grass,

and stalk the hushed perimeter,
roses closed around their scent,
azaleas dissembling behind the garage
and the bugeyed pansies
leaning over, inquisitive,
in their picketed beds.

What are these, I'll ask, stooping
to lift the pale leaves, and these?
Weeds, my father mutters
from his pillow. *All weeds.*) (SP xxiv–xxv)

Even ordinary backyard flowers become estranged voyeurs, as Dove
views this suburban home skeptically, from the outside, at night, as if
in a dream. As in "Ö," the fact that the house is "moored" like a ship
suggests its potential mobility, and the poem displaces a pervasive
sense of danger, as in "Ö" onto a roaring leaf-blower, onto plants that
lie, spy, and grow out of control. Here Dove takes a familiar experi-
ence—the adult homecoming that reveals one's parents as eccentric,
perhaps boring, and one's self as still trapped in childish relation to
them—and heightens it to the point of unreality. The fact that this
parenthetical section suggests a photographic negative foregrounds
race as a factor in the speaker's estranged viewpoint: Dove is black
while the stereotypical inhabitant of that American photograph (the
child in the suburban backyard) is not.[7]

The speaker of "In the Old Neighborhood" stands apart from
the other members of her household, and especially from her mother,
in even more blatant ways. Although she serves as the matron of
honor in the wedding at hand, she seems detached from the prepa-
rations. While her sister struggles to domesticate that "bridal apart-
ment" gone wild, the speaker's mother engages in conventional
maternal tasks: generating a "sudsbath / of worries" (xxii), cooking,
and planning the wedding flowers. The speaker retreats from such
duties, at least until the end of the poem, by reading "far past / my

mother's calling" (xxiii). The adult immerses herself in a newspaper; the remembered child reads every book in the house to the point of contrition for her neglect of other responsibilities, presumably domestic chores. The house offers shelter for this activity even as its caretaker and chief representative, the mother, curbs the young speaker's reading with her summons, or as the house itself kills the starling in the attic fan, "a bird with no song" (implicitly an image of a stifled poet) (xxv).

Dove represents books as an alternate kind of nurture in "In the Old Neighborhood"—specifically, she links them with snacking, a solitary and vaguely illicit kind of consumption. She identifies each book with a particular food: *Romeo and Juliet* with sardines, *The Iliad* with stuffed green olives, comic books with candy. The poem yokes the vice of snacking with the vice of reading, both activities that set the speaker apart from the world of the "old," and implicitly the outgrown, neighborhood.

None of the books the speaker remembers reading contain lyric poetry (nor, in answer to Rampersad, does Dove name African American writers here). The figure of the songless bird does imply an investment in the lyric, however, and the poem's own epigraph places "In the Old Neighborhood" not only within an Anglo-American poetic tradition but specifically within a family of American women poets. However, Adrienne Rich's "Shooting Script," which Dove quotes in that key position, qualifies as a long lyric or even a series of lyrics that by its very title reaches across genres; if this poem represents any "tradition," it designates a somewhat transgressive one. Further, the quote itself, the last line of "Shooting Script," concerns leaving one's past behind.

This seems to be the project of "In the Old Neighborhood": to eat one last meal at home, and then to leave it behind. Even a serious traveler, however, does not abandon home so easily. The poem, in fact, ends on a note of complicity with conventional domesticity: the speaker answers her mother's call, assumes her role as matron of honor and firstborn daughter, nodding *"yes"* and doing her chores as she "had been taught to do" (xxv–xxvi). Dove seems to choose Rich as a literary mother in preference over that actual arranger of tea roses in the kitchen, and the lyric as a home over that precarious suburban institution, until the poem's ambiguous ending, which places her exactly where her family would have her.

Singing in Chains

Nor has Dove's most recent poetry left this site: her poetic fascination with houses and the relationships they embody, especially that between mother and daughter, connects her first poems with her mature productions, and all her work with the lyric poetry of American women before her. Before *Grace Notes* (1989), which contains a group of poems depicting a mother's relationship to a small daughter, little of Dove's work directly explored the subject of mother and daughters. *Mother Love*, however, tells the story of Demeter and Persephone from both perspectives (with the voice of Hades, the abductor, occasionally interrupting), telescoping between classical myth and photographs on milk cartons, the clichés of contemporary child abduction. At the figurative heart of the volume is the lake over the abduction site, now encircled by a racetrack; the poems themselves orbit a dark center, invested in understanding, though never reaching, what the track encloses. Likewise, Dove's 1995 volume never resolves the opposing pressures or the painful rifts in perspective that characterize the particular mother-daughter relationship it depicts, but offers a deeply interesting engagement with that gap from all sides at once. Further, its network of allusions makes visible some of Dove's own literary mothers. The collection participates in a problematic but persistent metaphor for literary influence: nurturing and, simultaneously, smothering kinship.

Dove highlights the competition between mother-daughter and romantic love by basing all the poems in *Mother Love* on the sonnet. In her introduction to the volume, "An Intact World," Dove remarks on the tension between order and freedom, sealedness and violation, that characterizes the form: "I like how the sonnet comforts even while its prim borders (but what a pretty fence!) are stultifying; one is constantly bumping up against Order. The Demeter/Persephone cycle of betrayal and regeneration is ideally suited for this form since all three—mother-goddess, daughter-consort and poet—are struggling to sing in their chains" (ML, introduction unnumbered). Dove's very punctuation—"(but what a pretty fence!)" picketed in by parentheses—emphasizes the power of the sonnet to contain and control. However, as the Demeter/Persephone myth offers "a tale of a violated world," Dove violates the sonnet form from the beginning. Each lyric, with the exceptions of "Lost Brilliance" and the seven-sectioned "Persephone in Hell," consists of fourteen lines or is composed of fourteen-line sections; however, rhyme is irregular or absent, line length changes radically, and Dove offers many variations on the sonnet's traditional structure of argument. By invoking the sonnet and then diverging from it so radically, Dove represents the break and the link between mother and daughter: her sonnets preserve mother-daughter love in their "beautiful bubbles," but also reflect permanent damage. Again, Dove sides rather more with movement (even when violent) than with containment, although as Stephen Cushman declares, she finds form enabling: her "fourteeners . . . do not function as chains she sings in spite of but rather as talismans she is able to sing because of" (1996, 133).[8]

Mother Love's attitude towards poetic influence, the literary version of this troubled relationship, also takes multiple sides and also eventually favors the defiant daughter. The familial metaphor for influence (parent to child; sibling to rivalrous sibling; even, implicitly, mentor to student) presumes relationships between poets rather than, as is often the case, between poems; nevertheless, it has been irresistible to many critics and many poets themselves, as this study repeatedly demonstrates. In this collection about mothers and daughters, dedicated to Dove's mother and daughter, Dove overtly acknowledges many other women artists: the acknowledgments cite Helene Cixous and Kadia Molodowsky (via Adrienne Rich); epigraphs invoke Mother Goose, H.D., Jamaica Kinkaid, and Muriel Rukeyser; one poem describes the work of Frida Kahlo. The first and last sections quote male sources, including John Milton—fathers constitute a larger part of the literary genealogy than they do of the series itself—however, mothers (and perhaps sisters) emerge more prominently here. Susan Van Dyne posits a related subtext of literary connection: she remarks that "Dove seems to avoid distinctively racial subjects, attitudes, or idiom more often than she adopts them" (1999, 68), but uses this mother-daughter theme to place Dove in a "specifically African-American tradition of female poets," theorizing that "poems of black motherhood are a central feature of this tradition . . . the figure of the mother is much more consistently valorized as a source of racial pride, endurance, and political resistance" (73).[9]

The H.D. quoted in *Mother Love* makes considerable sense, since H.D.'s revisions of Greek myth support her place in the canon and in classrooms, such as the Iowa workshops where Dove first encountered the modernist's work (Pereira 1999, 204). However, there exists at least one startling omission from all this invocation. Surely, Gwendolyn Brooks's set of five sonnets on motherhood, "the children of the poor," haunts *Mother Love*. Brooks collects these sonnets in *Annie Allen* (1949), a volume concerning a daughter less loved than Dove's Persephone, whose heterosexual romance fails and who comes to define herself as a poet/mother, the two roles inextricably fused as they are in much of Brooks's work. Dove's 1991 history of African American poetry, written with Marilyn Waniek, even quotes this sequence while praising *Annie Allen* as "a *Bildungsroman* in verse" (235–36). Clearly, Dove has read this volume carefully.

153

Although Dove speaks warmly of Brooks in public, she has criticized in writing Brooks's controversial move to a more overtly political poetic. While admiring the older writer's "exquisite, word-intoxicated poems," Dove laments how "her career took a sudden turn in the Sixties and fell under the detrimental influence of younger, more militant poets" (Dove and Waniek 1991, 233–34). Certainly, the styles and settings of both poets reflect their differing backgrounds, and Dove generally avoids Brooks's motherly apostrophes to her race. Critics have forged tentative links between the poets, but only the broadest claims convince: for instance, Rampersad reasonably argues for Dove as "the most disciplined and technically accomplished black poet to arrive since Gwendolyn Brooks began her remarkable career in the nineteen forties" (1986, 53), while Vendler less persuasively juxtaposes Dove's "Nigger Song: An Odyssey" to Brooks's "We Real Cool" (1995, 67). Dove's deliberate distance from the distinguishing trends of Brooks's poetry is brought into relief by the parallel subject matter of *Mother Love*: Persephone shrugs off her fettering mother and never looks back, unless in abstract obsession (as H.D. does to the Lady in *Trilogy*), circling with binoculars around a dark, inaccessible pool.

Dove, in fact, stands in a similar relation to Gwendolyn Brooks as modern poets like H.D. and Marianne Moore do to Emily Dickinson. Dickinson was not the first American woman poet, nor even the first successful one, but she stood directly in the light for the female modernists: her work anticipated and influenced modern poetry, although modernists rarely overtly acknowledged it (while Sappho, another woman poet of the lyric fragment but temporally and geographically distant, received a share of the credit). Dove's poetry emerges not only from a poetic of enclosure and, more largely, from the history of the Western lyric; it is engages in an African American tradition, as Van Dyne asserts, although sometimes by means of resistance. Like Dickinson among all American women poets, Brooks is not the first African American woman poet, but she looms largest. Perhaps because Brooks's poetic voice concerns maternity more than Dickinson's, her presence imposes more powerfully: after all, Brooks's imperatives to her race, sons and "daughters of the dusk," include Dove in their mandates.

Commenting on a poem she composed as an undergraduate, "Upon Meeting Don L. Lee, In a Dream" (SP 12), Dove tells an interviewer, "I *was* terrified that I'd be suffocated before I began, that I would be pulled into the whole net of whether this was black enough, or whether I was denigrating my own people" (Pereira 1999, 197). Dove, however, has exercised relative silence on Brooks's example, to what extent it has enabled her own practice or engendered a deliberate resistance (even a terror of suffocation, to paraphrase her vivid language). The lack of overt gestures of indebtedness, however, may only signify the inescapability of Brooks's influence. In *Mother Love*, a sense of this African American line emerges primarily in images of blackness displaced from race: a landscape charred by Hades's eruption, Persephone's chic black clothes, the "water black and still" that fills that gap in the earth where daughters disappear (75).

As Van Dyne observes, the volume begins with a matricide in "Heroes" (ML 3–4): "this poet's raid on her mother's garden violates the genealogy of recovery and indebtedness that, according to Alice Walker's definition of literary tradition, links black womanist artists to their foremothers" (1999, 82). Reading *Mother Love* as a whole, however, produces a more ambiguous picture. While Dove's loose interpretation of the sonnet form contrasts sharply with Brooks's displays of craft, her disrespect of conventions might seem to follow an imperative from the fourth sonnet of "the children of the poor" to "Bewitch, bewilder" the "music that they wrote." Dove also emphasizes the vulnerability created by maternal love, as does Brooks in that sequence, and a mother's inability to protect her children from a harsh world.

The title poem of *Mother Love,* a double sonnet, expresses Dove's double attitudes towards influence by defining what it calls the "attitude of mothering" in terms of its most basic contradiction. The nurturing, self-sacrificing mother of the first stanza yields to the second stanza's bad mother or witch, who cures a baby on a spit, killing him to preserve him. This resembles how H.D., in a coded way, wrote of her own mother (and implicitly the whole nineteenth century) in her early poetry: sheltered gardens ultimately spoil the fruit, for what begins as nurture and order ends in suffocation. Despite the fairy-tale gruesomeness of "Mother Love," Dove ultimately sympathizes with Demeter more than that; the poem, after all, is written in the first person, and Demeter mildly apologizes for her deranged grief: "Oh, I know it / looked damning" (ML 17). In fact, according the original myth, a devastated Demeter means to save Metaneira's son Demophoön from old age and death. Nevertheless, Demeter's mothering seems too powerful for the child's health. The contradictions of poetic influence are similar: to utter an acceptance of mother-love destroys the child; unless Persephone really does leave home, her relationship with the mother will have no public consequences, just as a younger poet can only honor her influences by transforming them.

Dove investigates these paradoxes from multiple perspectives and with considerable humor. For instance, a subsequent poem, "Persephone in Hell," offers the daughter's point of view: hell is Paris, introduced through a descent into "stone chasms," and Persephone is "not quite twenty" (ML 23), experimenting with a new sexuality and a new language, bored with her mother's worry, charmed to drink Chartreuse with Satan at the Centre Pompidou. Dove suddenly inverts tale of abduction and grief into a narrative of adolescent struggle for independence. Dove offers up the myth as a metaphor for the standard conflict between a mother's protectiveness and a teenaged daughter's desire for danger. From this perspective, Persephone disappears because she is growing up and wants to cast off her daughterly identity for adult freedom; she is not raped away from innocence but chooses a new life, a lover naturally replacing her mother in her allegiance. The volume's chief thematic enclosure is both hell and Paris, a site with contradictory resonances, to say the least.

In the central section of the volume, these two perspectives confront one another, and neither mother nor daughter is innocent of distortion. In "The Bistro Styx" (ML 40–42), Demeter meets Persephone for dinner in a stylish Parisian restaurant. Persephone has indeed become the Queen of the Dead, artistically thin and chicly dressed in charcoal gray. Demeter inwardly addresses her as "my blighted child" and abhors the sordid life Persephone has taken up with a painter. Despairingly, she watches her beloved daughter hungrily devour the food that will bind her forever to the underworld (a nourishment she has chosen in opposition to her mother's cooking). Further, Persephone's dessert evokes the forbidden fruit that initiates Eve's sexual awakening and, subsequently, turns her out of the garden (another safe but lost enclosure):

> Nothing seemed to fill
>
> her up: She swallowed, sliced into a pear,
> speared each tear-shaped lavaliere
> and popped the dripping mess into her pretty mouth.
> Nowhere the bright tufted fields, weighted

vines and sun poured down out of the south.
"But are you happy?" Fearing, I whispered it
quickly. "What? You know, Mother"—

she bit into the starry rose of a fig—
"one really should try the fruit here."
I've lost her, I thought, and called for the bill.

"The Bistro Styx" both indicts and sympathizes with each charac-
ter. The mother conveys a comically intense sense of doom and the
daughter behaves with hopeless pretension, smug in her mastery of
this world so different from home. However, Persephone may justifi-
ably resent this judgmental mother, and Demeter's real sense of loss
deepens through her righteous feminist ire that Persephone should
consent to be "a cliché and, what's worse, // an anachronism, the brood-
ing artist's demimonde" (40). Ultimately, however, Dove's sympathy tilts
toward the wayward daughter. To be a daughter, she notes, means to
be "the one who comes and goes" (ML 62), and all Dove's writing has
been enchanted with such travel; Persephone's enthusiasm for adven-
ture remains more attractive than Demeter's greedy love. Further, the
pilgrimage to the ruins that closes the collection emphasizes the success
and endurance of Persephone's romantic alliance: its first-person plural
includes not mother and daughter (what might seem like the obvious
way to conclude this volume), but daughter and husband.

Dove ends *Mother Love* by gesturing both toward the indelibil-
ity of influence and the blocked bridge between familial and poetic
generations:

Only Earth—wild
mother we can never leave (even now
we've leaned against her, heads bowed
against the heat)—knows
no story's ever finished; it just goes
on, unnoticed in the dark that's all
around us: blazed stones, the ground closed. (ML 77)

Since in this sonnet cycle, "Her Island," the last line of each poem
becomes the first line of the next, the entire sequence begins and ends
with formal and thematic closure, encircling the lyrics through the
device of repetition and describing the mystery contained in the most
familiar tales and relationships.

Dove continues these concerns in her subsequent collection, *On
the Bus with Rosa Parks* (1999). This volume displays, among other

preoccupations, her persistent interest in "history and the individual" (91), focused here through female icons: not only Rosa Parks, a heroine of the civil rights struggle, but also the Venus of Willendorf and a series of less famous mothers, daughters, sisters, and working women. A mixed-race muse even emerges in "Incarnation in Phoenix," as Raven, the "African Valkyrie" whose name suggests both black lyricism and Native American tricksters, squeezes milk from the speaker's engorged breasts in an image of creativity miraculously, if painfully, unlocked (51–52). Dove compares Raven in her hospital whites to "an envelope issuing smoke": her latest collection, filled with closets, jails, castles, parlors, and various vehicles, frequently joins its strong women to imagery of enclosure and mysterious revelation. Rita Dove cannot represent a diverse field of American women poets, but the generative power of enclosure in her work does signal its continued relevance even in a society significantly altered since Dickinson's era. Dove, in the middle of her career, deliberately joins confinement and release in her compressed lyric. Even as she celebrates a range of liberations, her poetry engages and advances a poetic of enclosure.

Notes

Introduction

1. See Poe (1981). A. Walton Litz has observed in lectures at Princeton University that, in recordings, T. S. Eliot delivers *The Waste Land* in just less than half an hour.

2. I refer to lyric voice as a trope, but for a compelling interrogation of this position, see Kinereth Meyer's article "Speaking and Writing the Lyric 'I'" (1989). Meyer refers to the lyric subject as a meeting ground of speech and trope. He argues that "all lyrics are to some degree both confessional and impersonal; the poet is both present in speech and absent due to the usurpation of writing" (134).

3. See *Lyric Poetry: Beyond New Criticism* (Hošek and Parker 1985) for a range of essays considering subjectivity and voice in the lyric. For instance, Culler's clarifying history of lyric theory (much fuller than my brief comments on lyric definition) notes a general shift from voice as utterance to voice as trope (49). Parker's introduction also discusses "the haunting or inhabiting of an apparently autonomous voice by traces of alien voices or texts" (17).

4. On the other hand, Barbara Herrnstein Smith argues that "it is by virtue of its enclosure that the poem achieves its amplitude and infinitude" (1978, ix); I render a similar point about the interdependence of openness and confinement within the works of these poets.

5. I think particularly of how some gay male writers construct a poetics of the closet; see, for instance, Shoptaw on John Ashbery's "misrepresentations" (1994). Even Whitman, paradigm of openness, values privacy and containment in parts of "Song of Myself," although I'd hardly class that work as

an enclosed lyric; the short works of Hart Crane and James Merrill might provide apter cases.

6. Jack Capps also connects these two poems but argues that Dickinson's revision owes more to Elizabeth Barrett Browning's "A Vision of Poets" (1966, 83). His convincing triangulation of these works further demonstrates the complex and nonlinear nature of influence.

My parenthetical citations refer to two important editions of Dickinson's poems that number each lyric differently: Franklin's (F, 1998) and Johnson's (J, 1960). All extended discussions also use the first line. My transcriptions follow Franklin's in all but one respect: I imitate Dickinson's original lineation, which I often find suggestive. I remain unconvinced by those studies that read Dickinson's variously slanted and differently sized dashes as a complex array of significant marks, and therefore I simply imitate Franklin's one-en dash. Most of the poems I read at length happen not to possess variant words and phrases, but I indicate their existence where relevant.

Chapter 1. Emily Dickinson's Fairer Houses

1. See Capps's *Emily Dickinson's Reading* (1966), Walker's *The Nightingale's Burden: Women Poets and American Culture before 1900* (1982), St. Armand's *Emily Dickinson and Her Culture: The Soul's Society* (1984), Wolosky's *Emily Dickinson: A Voice of War* (1984), Sanchez-Eppler's *Touching Liberty: Abolition, Feminism, and the Politics of the Body* (1993), Petrino's *Emily Dickinson and Her Contemporaries: Women's Verse in America, 1820–1885* (1998), and others.

2. "L" refers to Johnson's *The Letters of Emily Dickinson* (1958).

3. See, for instance, Nancy Woloch's *Women and the American Experience* (114–20). In Dickinson's time, at least in the Northeast, the home was ceasing to be a center for production by all family members. Men started working outside the home to earn the salaries that supported it; women stayed at home, assuming full responsibility for the running of the household and the raising of children. "Home" was beginning to acquire its meaning as "refuge."

4. See Dickinson's letters, especially her comment that "My Mother does not care for thought" (L 261), or Higginson's quoting of Dickinson in the same volume, "I never had a mother" (L 342b). Emily Norcross Dickinson was, nevertheless, relatively well-educated and devoted to her children's development; the latter quote vastly understates her influence on her middle child.

5. See the reminiscences gathered in Jay Leyda's *The Years and Hours of Emily Dickinson* (1960, 478–80).

6. I refer here and elsewhere to the fascicle groupings designated by number in *The Manuscript Books of Emily Dickinson* (Franklin 1981). The year in

parenthesis indicates the fascicle's probable composition date according to Franklin.

7. This "submerged phrase" works on the same principle as the "crypt words" John Shoptaw locates in John Ashbery's poetry. See "Ashbery's Misrepresentative Poetics" in *On the Outside Looking Out: John Ashbery's Poetry* (1994).

8. Fascicle 21 consists of the following poems, according to Franklin:

(F 440, J 609) I – Years had been – from / Home –
(F 441, J 610) You'll find – it when you / try to die –
(F 442, J 611) I see thee better – in the Dark –
(F 443, J 447) Could – I do more – for Thee –
(F 444, J 612) It would have starved a Gnat –
(F 445, J 613) They shut me up in Prose –
(F 446, J 448) This was a Poet –
(F 447, J 614) In falling Timbers buried –
(F 448, J 449) I died for Beauty – but / was scarce
(F 449, J 450) Dreams – are well – but / Waking's better –
(F 450, J 451) The Outer – from the / Inner
(F 172, J 174) At last – to be identified –
(F 451, J 452) The Malay – took the Pearl –
(F 452, J 453) Love – thou art high –
(F 453, J 615) Our journey had advanced –
(F 454, J 616) I rose – because he sank –
(F 455, J 454) It was given to me by / the Gods –

Chapter 2. Marianne Moore: Freedom and Protection

1. Throughout this chapter, the abbreviation *Prose* refers to *The Complete Prose of Marianne Moore,* ed. Willis (1986). I reserve the initials CP for *The Complete Poems of Marianne Moore* (1967); SP refers to *The Selected Poems of Marianne Moore* (1935).

2. Brief suggestions about influential predecessors abound in Moore studies—Emerson and Henry James seem key to many critics—but I list here some of the more extended comparisons of Moore to other poets. Jeredith Merrin treats Bishop's and Moore's relations with male Renaissance and Romantic writers (1990). Keller (1983), Kalstone (1989), Bromwich (1990), Erkkila (1992), and Diehl (1993) consider the cross-influence of Moore and Bishop. Cynthia Hogue compares Dickinson and Moore (1998). Celeste Goodridge analyzes Moore's reviews of male modernists (1989) and Robin Schulze focuses on the "web of friendship" between Moore and Wallace Stevens in a book-length study (1995).

3. See H.D.'s "Marianne Moore" in *Egoist* 3 (1916, 118–19).

4. Moore's elephant, in fact, evokes Kristeva's figure for the relation between the semiotic and the symbolic in Mallarmé: "Indifferent to language, enigmatic and feminine, this space underlying the written is rhythmic, unfettered, irreducible to its intelligible verbal translation; it is musical, anterior to judgement, but restrained by a single guarantee: syntax" (1986, 97). Written language, the symbolic, is the inescapable surface, marked with the "history of power"; the semiotic is the "beautiful unreason" underlying it, inaccessible to—although represented through—language.

5. Moore echoes this directive in a 1936 letter, telling Bishop she'd like "to subterraneously change the observer" (1997, 365).

6. See Cixous (1980).

7. For example, see Moore's interview with Hall (Tomlinson 1969).

8. See Durham on how Moore's poetry inscribes the female body (1989).

9. The most influential treatments of literary influence must be Bloom's (1973, 1975), revised by Gilbert and Gubar (1987). Significant reassessments within Moore studies include Gilmore (1989), Merrin (1990), Erkkila (1992), and Diehl (1993).

10. See Moore's 1919 letter to Ezra Pound (1997, 122–25).

11. Rosenbach Museum and Library (I:02:14).

12. See Schulman (1986, 13–14) and Diehl (1990, 58) for more on the intersections of Moore and Whitman. Gregory locates an allusion to another "Sea-Drift" poem in "In the Days of Prismatic Color" (1996, 173). Bishop records Moore's most quoted repudiation of the nineteenth-century poet: "Elizabeth, don't speak to me about that man!" (1984, 143).

13. For helpful discussions of how "The Paper Nautilus" figures maternity, see Costello (1981), Ostriker (1990a), and Schulze (1995), among others. Gregory provides insightful comments on maternal influence in Moore's work generally (1996, 137–41).

14. Rosenbach Museum and Library (I:03:23).

15. Here I refute Heuving, who contends that this poem "depends on and inscribes the conventional oppositions of internal and external, valuing the former over the latter" (1992, 163).

Chapter 3. H.D.: Smothered in Wool

1. For the text of all poems up to and including *Trilogy* I refer to H.D.'s 1983 *Collected Poems*, abbreviated throughout as CP.

2. The imagist manifesto appeared in *Poetry* in 1913, Pound's ideas mediated by F. S. Flint: "1. Direct treatment of the 'thing,' whether subjective or

objective. 2. To use absolutely no word that does not contribute to the presentation. 3. As regarding rhythm: to compose in sequence of the musical phrase, not in sequence of a metronome" (199). Ezra Pound's "A Few Don'ts by an Imagiste" followed just after, anti-imagistically expounding and repeating the briefer guidelines.

3. See Friedman's *Psyche Reborn,* chapter 3, "Hieroglyphic Voices: The Unconscious and Psychoanalytic Modes of Translation," especially the discussion of imagism and H.D.'s "Oread" (55–59).

4. For example, see *The Pound Era*; Hugh Kenner's imagery in his descriptions of H.D. evokes a dry, sterile, self-destructive woman (174–76), who "dilates" not as a woman should, in childbirth, but "on her preferred imagery of weeds and sandy shores, turn[ing] choruses from Euripides into statements of her own impassioned sterility" (523).

5. Cassandra Laity, on the other hand, demonstrates the key influence of Swinburne on H.D. even from the beginning, arguing that in fact H.D. "did not attempt to disguise her lifelong debt to the romantics" (1990, 110), and was not antagonistic to her literary predecessors the way some of her contemporaries seemed to have been (1990, 125).

6. Since, as Susan Gubar points out, "the shell enclosing the pearl is a common image of female genitals" (204), H.D.'s ecstatically "torn shells" suggest sexual freedom.

7. Less than a month after Perdita was born on March 31, 1919, H.D. placed her in a London nursery. By the summer H.D. was in the Scilly Isles with Bryher. Adalaide Morris compellingly associates H.D.'s "management of motherhood," which seems "at best odd, at worst suspicious or even pernicious," with a Moravian "gift economy" (1990a, 52). Perdita Schaffner's own "Sketch of H.D." illustrates how H.D. did manage her motherhood: she was sometimes affectionate, sometimes inaccessible, and never Perdita's primary caretaker. Schaffner found H.D. "a much better mother" when the two were adults together, "and friends" (1990, 6). H.D. pursued her demanding career with great discipline; she did not find this path compatible with full-time mothering in any conventional sense. Instead, Schaffner's recollections of H.D. evoke H.D.'s memories of her own distant and fascinating father.

8. In her edition of Richard Aldington's letters, Zilboorg describes a closeness between Mrs. Doolittle and her daughter during this period, based on the lack of conflict recorded in the mother's diary (1992, 14). Although H.D.'s fiction is autobiographical, it is fiction, and H.D. had the liberty to exaggerate the tensions that did exist between the two women, or focus disproportionately

on negative rather than positive interactions, to make her point about the characters.

9. See Gavaler (1996).

10. On the importance of maternal imagery to *Trilogy,* also see Gelpi (1990).

Chapter 4. Gwendolyn Brooks: Heralding the Clear Obscure

1. I quote all of Brooks's poetry from *Blacks* (1987).

2. Others have noted the act of will that apostrophe represents. Thomas M. Greene writes that apostrophe, an address to the absent, constitutes one half of an invocation, which also includes "a summons to appear or make its influence felt in the invoker's experience" (1993, 495). Jonathan Culler, likewise, asserts that "to apostrophize is to will" (1981, 139).

3. For example, in *Report from Part One,* after a brief statement about her separation from her husband, Brooks writes, "(That won't be enough for the reader but it is enough for me)" (1972, 58).

4. Female bodies also enclose in this early poetry: "hunchback girl: she thinks of heaven" fantasizes about death as a release from the prison of a crooked body (1987, 27). "hunchback girl" might encode Brooks's early feelings of ostracization as a dark-skinned African American child (more explicitly dramatized in "the ballad of chocolate Mabbie"). Failing to possess light skin or "good grade" hair or prestigious parents, and without the "sass and brass" to succeed among the other dark-skinned children, Brooks, like the hunchback girl, took refuge in "scholarly nonchalance." For both the young poet and the child in the poem, the look of one's body limits one's options.

5. See Sherley Williams's "The Blues Roots of Contemporary Afro-American Poetry" (1979).

6. Bill Mullen juxtaposes Brooks's use of the sonnet in "Gay Chaps" to Claude McKay's (1999, 176).

7. Schweik argues that the "love notes," "more hostile than wistful, unsparingly mimic misogyny" by identifying the female lover with the flag and then punishing it by pulling it down the foxhole, burning it, and subjecting it to gunfire (1991, 136–37).

8. For some of my observations and ideas about this series, and also the three "Sermon(s) on the Warpland," I am indebted to the discussions in John Shoptaw's graduate seminar on contemporary poetry in the fall of 1992 at Princeton University.

9. Treating later poems, Phillip Brian Harper also discusses Brooks's assumption of a maternal role, arguing that she "demonstrates as false the ostensible universality of the condition" (1994, 103).

10. For a more extended discussion of the Mecca building and Chicago's South Side, see Kenny J. Williams's informative "The World of Satin-Legs, Mrs. Sallie, and the Blackstone Rangers: The Restricted Chicago of Gwendolyn Brooks" (1987).

11. Compare "chopped chirpings oddly rising" with Whitman's "Out of the Cradle Endlessly Rocking," another poem linking literary production to loss (and another poem full of "chirpings").

Chapter 5. Elizabeth Bishop's Inscrutable Houses

1. Although there exists no consensus on the issue, many of Bishop's published readers have characterized her poetry as reticent. Some late twentieth-century examples: Travisano describes her "personal reticence and artistic restraint," as well as describing early poems as "fables of enclosure" (1988, 6); in a subsequent study he does fit her work to definitions of confessionalism, but then argues against the usefulness of that term (1999). Goldensohn narrates how Bishop's contained lyric "gradually and significantly enlarged . . . to include the directly personal" (1992, x); Dodd finds that "reticence is a consciously chosen formal element" in Bishop (1992, 125); in a study of difficulty in postmodern poetry, Shetley emphasizes her "consistent strategy of reticence and withholding" (1993, 37); Doreski discusses Bishop's "poetic of reticence" in a book subtitled *The Restraints of Language* (1993, 14); Harrison notes Bishop's "principle of privacy" (1993, 19) even as she remarks the "direct and personal" address of the poems (1); Dickie asserts that Bishop is "more secretive than private" (1997, 7); Shigley suggests that "Bishop's refusal to use direct experience in her poems . . . lures readers into revealing their own prejudices" (1997, 10). Many of these readers posit an authentic self cloaked by rhetoric, which I do not. For example, Lombardi states that "Bishop's poetry, like all narrative, is founded properly and necessarily on secrecy and parable, simultaneously proclaiming and concealing truth," then goes on to assert that recourse to Bishop's private papers "unveil the flesh-and-blood author behind the poetic personae" (1995, 4).

2. I quote Bishop's poetry from *The Complete Poems* (1979), which reprints all her collections.

3. This chapter emphasizes tensions between reticence and confession in Bishop's poetry, merely alluding to formal enclosures in her lyric practice. I believe her persistent use of fixed patterns of meter and rhyme justifies this

description, but would point out that, like the other poets treated in this study, Bishop does challenge lyric definition. Keller, for example, describes Bishop's "strictly regulated poetic forms" (1987, 94), and Travisano refers to her "revisionary versions of closed forms" (1999, 9). Bishop also highlights the constructed nature of the apparently expressive lyric utterance; see Brogan (1993) or Harrison (1993) for more on Bishop's experiments with voice. Also see Colwell on how Bishop uses poetic form as a metaphor for the body (1997, 17).

4. Bishop always refused to be included in women's issues of journals and in single-sex anthologies, on the grounds that categories like "woman poet" diminish rather than illuminate the work. Bishop has been quoted expressing this opinion many times. On November 7, 1971, for instance, she reiterates this to May Swenson, explaining: "—[T]his has nothing to do with the present Women's Lib Movement (although I'm in favor of a lot of that, too, of course). I see no reason for them [collections of "just women"] and I think it is one of the things to be avoided—and *with* "Women's Lib" perhaps even more so. Literature is literature, no matter who produces it. . . . I don't like things compartmentalized like that, and in this case I think it defeats the very purpose it's supposed to be for. I like black & white, yellow & red, young & old, rich & poor, and male & female, all mixed up, socially—and I see no reason for segregating them, for any reason at all, artistically, either" (1994, 549).

5. For my reading of "The Man-Moth," and indeed for many of the ideas expressed in this chapter, I am indebted to the exciting discussions that occurred in an undergraduate seminar I taught at Washington and Lee University entitled "Major American Women Poets" (spring 1995). I would especially like to thank Jeanne Dillon and Babli Sinha for their illuminating seminar papers on Bishop, and Jeanne Dillon for her subsequent thesis on inversion in Bishop's work.

6. However, Joanne Feit Diehl finds connections between Dickinson and Bishop (1990, 1993); see also Keller and Miller, who link the poets through strategies of indirection (1984).

7. I was inspired to discuss these poems in conjunction by a lecture of John Shoptaw's on Marianne Moore at Princeton University in the spring of 1991, in which he yoked the figures of the armadillo and the pangolin as armored animals possibly embodying the armored poetics of these poets. In his graduate-level seminar on Emily Dickinson and Walt Whitman, Shoptaw also suggested links between "You've seen Balloons Set" and "The Armadillo."

8. See Edelman (1993). Bishop's factual inaccuracies in this poem, which asserts such strong claims to autobiography, emphasize the constructed nature of poetic confession.

Chapter 6. Rita Dove: The House Expands

1. See Dove's "composite poem of our times," "From My Couch I Rise" (1995a, 34–36). For further discussion of space in Dove's poetry, see Steffen (2001). I regret that the first book-length study of Dove emerged as my own book neared publication and that I could not fully assimilate Steffen's work into this chapter.

2. An earlier version of this chapter contrasted Dove to Susan Howe, a figure often associated with the experiments of language poetry. Howe's canvaslike use of the page, lines collaged at odd angles so as to completely disrupt the conventional reading experience, declares that the lyric can no longer be and never really was an enclosure. Howe rejects the formal enclosure of the lyric in favor of exploring what is variously figured in her work as margin and wilderness; however, the lyric remains her starting point, a center of literary power she wishes to dismantle but still adheres to with some nostalgia. Furthermore, Howe's attraction to the lyrics of Emily Dickinson demonstrates the inevitable relevance of the poetic of enclosure to contemporary American women poets because it remains one of this century's dominant traditions.

3. See Keller's 1997 treatment of Dove's sequence, *Thomas and Beulah*.

4. My entry on Rita Dove in Scribner's *American Writers Supplement IV* briefly suggests, but does not fully explore, this line of inquiry (1996b). Portions of this chapter were also delivered at a 1995 symposium, "Women Poets of the Americas," and others were published in a review of *Mother Love* in *Critical Matrix* (1996a).

5. I quote *The Yellow House on the Corner* and "In the Old Neighborhood" from *Selected Poems* (1993), more readily available than the original volumes it contains, abbreviated throughout as SP. I abbreviate *Mother Love* (1995) as ML.

6. Resonances between the poem and the introduction itself almost mandate a biographical reading; as usual, however, I assume that Dove performs a version of herself here, signaling through various devices both the poem's authentic relation to fact and its constructed nature.

7. Peter Erickson also makes this point in "Rita Dove's Shakespeares" (1999), adding that the raccoons may encode a racial slur and that the black starling who meets a grisly fate represents the precarious position of the African American poet (96–97).

8. Booth modifies this reading slightly, finding that "the sense of encircling, varied but closed form works against progress or escape" (1996, 126). Scott Ward, on the other hand, critiques Dove's free handling of this inherited pattern: "By playing loosely with the form, Dove abandons the psychological appeal of the sonnet; she sacrifices the opportunity to locate herself in and

comment upon the great history of the English sonnet" (1995, 115). In my reading, Dove quite deliberately locates herself *out*side of that particular "great history," although she identifies with other literary traditions.

9. Van Dyne rightly describes a critical preoccupation with blackness, or the lack of it, in Dove's poetry. For some critics and for Dove herself, this problem crystallizes around different attitudes towards the Black Arts movement. Dove and Waniek, while sympathizing with its "rage" transformed into black pride, dismiss the poetry of this period as ineffective "noise" (1991, 243, 255). See also Dove's infamous (and funny) poem, "Upon Meeting Don L. Lee, In a Dream" (SP 12) for Dove's attitudes towards the Black Arts movement in particular, as well as her comments on the latter poem to Pereira (1999, 197). "It's so ass-backwards to say that there is a black way of writing and then there is a white—that's madness," she exclaims in the latter interview (196).

References

Andersen, Charles R. 1960. *Emily Dickinson's Poetry: Stairway of Surprise.* New York: Holt, Rinehart, and Winston.

Bachelard, Gaston. 1964. *The Poetics of Space.* Boston: Beacon.

Baker, Houston. 1996. "From 'The Florescence of Nationalism in the 1960s and 1970s.'" *On Gwendolyn Brooks: Reliant Contemplation.* Ed. Stephen Caldwell Wright. Ann Arbor: Univ. of Michigan Press. 116–23.

Bar-yaacov, Lois. 1988. "The Odd Couple: The Correspondence between Marianne Moore and Ezra Pound, 1918–1939." *Twentieth Century Literature* 34.4: 507–27.

Benfey, Christopher E. G. 1984. *Emily Dickinson and the Problem of Others.* Amherst: Univ. of Massachusetts Press.

Bennett, Paula. 1990. *Emily Dickinson: Woman Poet.* Iowa City: Univ. of Iowa Press.

Bishop, Elizabeth. 1951. "Love from Emily." *New Republic,* August 27.

———. 1979. *The Complete Poems: 1927–1979.* New York: Farrar, Straus, Giroux.

———. 1984. *The Collected Prose.* Ed. Robert Giroux. New York: Farrar, Straus, Giroux.

———. 1994. *One Art.* Ed. Robert Giroux. New York: Farrar, Straus, Giroux.

Bloom, Harold. 1973. *The Anxiety of Influence: A Theory of Poetry.* New York: Oxford Univ. Press.

———. 1975. *A Map of Misreading.* New York: Oxford Univ. Press.

Booth, Alison. 1996. "Abduction and Other Severe Pleasures: Rita Dove's *Mother Love.*" *Callaloo* 19.1: 125–30.

Borroff, Marie. 1979. *Language and the Poet.* Chicago: Univ. of Chicago Press.

Brogan, Jacqueline Vaught. 1993. "Elizabeth Bishop: *Perversity* as Voice." *Elizabeth Bishop: The Geography of Gender.* Ed. Marilyn May Lombardi. Charlottesville: Univ. Press of Virginia. 175–95.

Bromwich, David. 1990. "That Weapon, Self-Protectiveness." *Marianne Moore: The Art of a Modernist.* Ed. Joseph Parisi. Ann Arbor: UMI Research Press.

Brooks, Gwendolyn. 1956. *Bronzeville Boys and Girls.* New York: Harper & Row.

————. 1972. *Report from Part One.* Detroit: Broadside.

————. 1974. *The Tiger Who Wore White Gloves: or, What you are you are.* Chicago: Third World.

————. 1975a. *A Capsule Course in Black Poetry Writing.* Detroit: Broadside.

————. 1975b. *Beckonings.* Detroit: Broadside.

————. 1983. Interview. *Black Women Writers at Work.* By Claudia Tate. New York: Continuum. 39–48.

————. 1987. *Blacks.* Chicago: Third World.

————. 1996. *Report from Part Two.* Chicago: Third World.

Brownstein, Marilyn L. 1990. "Marianne Moore." *The Gender of Modernism: A Critical Anthology.* Ed. Bonnie Kime Scott. Bloomington: Indiana Univ. Press. 323–34.

Buck, Claire. 1991. *H.D. and Freud: Bisexuality and a Feminine Discourse.* New York: St. Martin's Press.

Cameron, Sharon. 1979. *Lyric Time: Dickinson and the Limits of Genre.* Baltimore: Johns Hopkins Univ. Press.

————. 1992. *Choosing Not Choosing: Dickinson's Fascicles.* Chicago: Univ. of Chicago Press.

Capps, Jack. 1966. *Emily Dickinson's Reading: 1836–1886.* Cambridge: Harvard Univ. Press.

Chisholm, Dianne. 1992. *H.D.'s Freudian Poetics: Psychoanalysis in Translation.* Ithaca, NY: Cornell Univ. Press.

Cixous, Hélène. 1980. "Sorties." *New French Feminisms.* Ed. Elaine Marks and Isabelle de Courtivron. Trans. Ann Liddle. New York: Schocken Books. 90–98.

Clark, Suzanne. 1991. *Sentimental Modernism: Women Writers and the Revolution of the Word.* Bloomington: Indiana Univ. Press.

Coffman, Stanley K., Jr. 1951. *Imagism: A Chapter for the History of Modern Poetry*. Norman: Univ. of Oklahoma Press.

Colwell, Anne. 1997. *Inscrutable Houses: Metaphors of the Body in the Poems of Elizabeth Bishop*. Tuscaloosa: Univ. of Alabama Press.

Costello, Bonnie. 1981. *Marianne Moore: Imaginary Possessions*. Cambridge, Mass.: Harvard Univ. Press.

———. 1991. *Elizabeth Bishop: Questions of Mastery*. Cambridge, Mass.: Harvard Univ. Press.

Crumbley, Paul. 1997. *Inflections of the Pen: Dash and Voice in Emily Dickinson*. Lexington: Univ. Press of Kentucky.

Culler, Jonathan. 1975. *Structuralist Poetics: Structuralism, Linguistics, and the Study of Literature*. Ithaca: Cornell Univ. Press.

———. 1981. *The Pursuit of Signs: Semiotics, Literature, Deconstruction*. Ithaca: Cornell Univ. Press.

Current Biography Yearbook: 1994. Ed. Judith Graham. New York: H. W. Wilson. 143–47.

Cushman, Stephen. 1996. "And the Dove Returned." *Callaloo* 19.1: 131–34.

Dickie, Margaret. 1991. *Lyric Contingencies: Emily Dickinson and Wallace Stevens*. Philadelphia: Univ. of Pennsylvania Press.

———. 1997. *Stein, Bishop, & Rich: Lyrics of Love, War, & Place*. Chapel Hill: Univ. of North Carolina Press.

Dickie, Margaret, and Thomas Travisano, ed. 1996. *Gendered Modernisms: American Women Poets and Their Readers*. Philadelphia: Univ. of Pennsylvania Press.

Dickinson, Emily. 1960. *The Complete Poems of Emily Dickinson*. Ed. Thomas H. Johnson. Boston: Little, Brown. 3 vols.

———. 1998. *The Poems of Emily Dickinson: Variorum Edition*. Ed. R. W. Franklin. Cambridge, Mass.: Belknap Press. 3 vols.

Diehl, Joanne Feit. 1981. *Dickinson and the Romantic Imagination*. Princeton: Princeton Univ. Press.

———. 1990. *Women Poets and the American Sublime*. Bloomington: Indiana Univ. Press.

———. 1993. *Elizabeth Bishop and Marianne Moore: The Psychodynamics of Creativity*. Princeton: Princeton Univ. Press.

Diggory, Terence. 1979. "Armored Women, Naked Men: Dickinson, Whitman, and Their Successors." *Shakespeare's Sisters: Feminist Essays on Women Poets*.

Ed. Sandra M. Gilbert and Susan Gubar. Bloomington, Indiana Univ. Press. 135–50.

Dobson, Joanne. 1989. *Dickinson and the Strategies of Reticence: The Woman Writer in Nineteenth-Century America.* Bloomington: Indiana Univ. Press.

Dodd, Elizabeth. 1992. *The Veiled Mirror and the Woman Poet: H.D., Louise Bogan, Elizabeth Bishop, and Louise Glück.* Columbia: Univ. of Missouri Press.

Doreski, C. K. 1993. *Elizabeth Bishop: The Restraints of Language.* New York: Oxford Univ. Press.

Dove, Rita. 1989. *Grace Notes.* New York: Norton.

———. 1992. *Through the Ivory Gate.* New York: Vintage.

———. 1993. *Selected Poems.* New York: Vintage.

———. 1995a. *The Poet's World.* Washington, D.C.: Library of Congress.

———. 1995b. *Mother Love.* New York: Norton.

———. 1999. *On the Bus with Rosa Parks.* New York: Norton.

Dove, Rita, and Marilyn Nelson Waniek. 1991. "A Black Rainbow: Modern Afro-American Poetry." *Poetry after Modernism.* Ed. Robert McDowell. Brownsville, Ore.: Story Line Press. 217–75.

DuPlessis, Rachel Blau. 1985. *Writing Beyond the Ending: Narrative Strategies of Twentieth Century Women Writers.* Bloomington: Indiana Univ. Press.

———. 1986. *H.D.: The Career of That Struggle.* Indianapolis: Univ. of Indiana Press.

———. 1990. "Romantic Thralldom in H.D." *Signets: Reading H.D..* Ed. Susan Stanford Friedman and Rachel Blau DuPlessis. Madison: Univ. of Wisconsin Press. 406–29.

———. 1994. "'Corpses of Poesy': Some Modern Poets and Some Gender Ideologies of Lyric." *Feminist Measures: Soundings in Poetry and Theory.* Ed. Lynn Keller and Cristanne Miller. Ann Arbor: Univ. of Michigan. 69–95.

Durham, Carolyn A. 1989. "Linguistic and Sexual Engendering in Marianne Moore's Poetry." *Engendering the Word: Feminist Essays in Psychosexual Poetics.* Ed. Temma Berg. Chicago: Univ. of Illinois Press. 224–43.

Eberwein, Jane Donahue. 1985. *Dickinson: Strategies of Limitation.* Amherst: Univ. of Massachusetts Press.

———. 1998. "Dickinson's Local, Global, and Cosmic Perspectives." *The Emily Dickinson Handbook.* Ed. Roland Hagenbuchle, Cristanne Miller, and Gudrun Grabher. Amherst: Univ. of Amherst Press.

References

Edelman, Lee. 1993. "The Geography of Gender: Elizabeth Bishop's 'In the Waiting Room.'" *Elizabeth Bishop: The Geography of Gender.* Ed. Marilyn May Lombardi. Charlottesville: Univ. Press of Virginia. 91–107.

Edmunds, Susan. 1994. *Out of Line: History, Psychoanalysis, and Montage in H.D.'s Long Poems.* Stanford: Stanford Univ. Press.

Eliot, T. S. 1960. *Selected Essays.* New York: Harcourt, Brace and World.

Emerson, Ralph Waldo. 1983. *Essays and Lectures.* New York: Library of America.

Erickson, Darlene Williams. 1992. *Illusion Is More Precise Than Precision: The Poetry of Marianne Moore.* Tuscaloosa: Univ. of Alabama Press.

Erickson, Peter. 1999. "Rita Dove's Shakespeares." *Transforming Shakespeare: Contemporary Women's Re-Visions in Literature and Performance.* Ed. Marianne Novy. New York: St. Martin's Press.

Erkkila, Betsy. 1992. *The Wicked Sisters: Women Poets, Literary History and Discord.* New York: Oxford Univ. Press.

Farr, Judith. 1992. *The Passion of Emily Dickinson.* Cambridge: Harvard Univ. Press.

Flint, F. S. 1913. "Imagisme." *Poetry* 1.6: 198–200.

Fountain, Gary. 1994. *Remembering Elizabeth Bishop: An Oral Biography.* Amherst: Univ. of Massachusetts Press.

Franklin, R. W. 1967. *The Editing of Emily Dickinson: A Reconsideration.* Madison: Univ. of Wisconsin Press.

———, ed. 1981. *The Manuscript Books of Emily Dickinson.* 2 vol. Cambridge: Belknap.

Freud, Sigmund. 1953. *A General Introduction to Psychoanalysis.* Trans. Joan Riviere. New York: Pocket Books.

Friar, Kimon, and John Malcolm Brinnin, eds. 1951. *Modern Poetry, British and American.* New York: Appleton-Century-Croft.

Friedman, Susan Stanford. 1981. *Psyche Reborn: The Emergence of H.D.* Bloomington: Indiana Univ. Press.

———. 1983. "'Remembering Shakespeare Always, But Remembering Him Differently: H.D.'s *By Avon River.*" *Sagetrieb* 2.2: 45–70.

———. 1990. *Penelope's Web: Gender, Modernity, H.D.'s Fiction.* Madison: Univ. of Wisconsin Press.

———. 1994. "Craving Stories: Narrative and Lyric in Contemporary Theory and Women's Long Poems." *Feminist Measures: Soundings in Poetry and Theory*. Ed. Lynn Keller and Cristanne Miller. Ann Arbor: Univ. of Michigan. 15–42.

Friedman, Susan Stanford, and Rachel Blau DuPlessis, eds. 1990. *Signets: Reading H.D.* Madison: Univ. of Wisconsin Press.

Frye, Northrop. 1957. *Anatomy of Criticism*. Princeton: Princeton Univ. Press.

Fryer, Judith. 1986. *Felicitous Space: The Imaginative Structures of Edith Wharton and Willa Cather*. Chapel Hill: Univ. of North Carolina Press.

Gage, John T. 1981. *In the Arresting Eye: The Rhetoric of Imagism*. Baton Rouge: Louisiana State Univ. Press.

Garrigue, Jean. 1965. *Marianne Moore*. Minneapolis: Univ. of Minnesota Press.

Gavaler, Christopher. 1996. "I Mend a Break in Time: An Historical Reconstruction of H.D.'s Wunden Eiland in *The Gift* and *Trilogy*." *Sagetrieb* 15.2: 95–120.

Gelpi, Albert. 1990. "Re-Membering the Mother: A Reading of H.D.'s *Trilogy*." *Signets: Reading H.D.* Ed. Susan Stanford Friedman and Rachel Blau DuPlessis. Madison: Univ. of Wisconsin Press.

Gilbert, Sandra M. 1990. "Marianne Moore as Female Female Impersonator." In *Marianne Moore: The Art of a Modernist*. Ed. Joseph Parisi. Ann Arbor: Univ. of Michigan Press. 27–46.

Gilbert, Sandra M., and Susan Gubar. 1979. *The Madwoman in the Attic: The Woman Writer and the Nineteenth-Century Literary Imagination*. New Haven: Yale Univ. Press.

―――. 1987. *No Man's Land: The Place of the Woman Writer in the Twentieth Century. Volume I: The War of the Words*. New Haven: Yale Univ. Press.

Gilmore, Leigh. 1989. "The Gaze of the Other Woman: Beholding and Begetting in Dickinson, Moore, and Rich." *Engendering the Word: Feminist Essays in Psychosexual Poetics*. Ed. Temma Berg. Chicago: Univ. of Illinois Press. 81–102.

Goldensohn, Lorrie. 1992. *Elizabeth Bishop: The Biography of a Poetry*. New York: Columbia Univ. Press.

Golding, Alan. 1991. "'Openness,' 'Closure,' and Recent American Poetry." *Arizona Quarterly* 47.2 : 77–91.

Goodridge, Celeste. 1989. *Hints and Disguises: Marianne Moore and Her Contemporaries*. Iowa City: Univ. of Iowa Press.

Greene, Thomas A. 1993. "Poetry as Invocation." *New Literary History* 24.3: 495–517.

Gregory, Eileen. 1997a. *H.D. and Hellenism: Classic Lines*. Cambridge: Cambridge Univ. Press.

———. 1997b (revised). "H.D.'s Volume of Dickinson's Poems; and, a Note on Candor and Iniquity." *The H.D. Newsletter* 3.1: 44–46.

Gregory, Elizabeth. 1996. *Quotation and Modern American Poetry: "Imaginary Gardens with Real Toads."* Houston: Rice Univ. Press.

Gubar, Susan. 1979. "The Echoing Spell of H.D.'s *Trilogy*." *Shakespeare's Sisters: Feminist Essays on Women Poets*. Ed. Sandra M. Gilbert and Susan Gubar. Bloomington: Indiana Univ. Press.

Guest, Barbara. 1984. *Herself Defined: The Poet H.D. and Her World*. Garden City: Doubleday.

Hall, Donald. 1969. "The Art of Poetry: Marianne Moore. An Interview." In *Marianne Moore: A Critical Collection*. Ed. Charles Tomlinson. Englewood Cliffs: Prentice Hall. 20–45.

———. *The Cage and the Animal*. New York: Western Publishing Company, 1970.

Hansell, William H. 1987. "The Poet-Militant and Foreshadowings of a Black Mystique: Poems in the Second Period of Gwendolyn Brooks." *A Life Distilled: Gwendolyn Brooks, Her Poetry and Fiction*. Ed. Maria K. Mootry and Gary Smith. Chicago: Univ. of Illinois Press. 30–46.

Harper, Phillip Brian. 1994. *Framing the Margins: The Social Logic of Postmodern Culture*. New York: Oxford Univ. Press.

Harrison, Victoria. 1993. *Elizabeth Bishop's Poetics of Intimacy*. New York: Cambridge Univ. Press.

H.D. 1916. "Marianne Moore." *Egoist* 3: 118–19.

———. 1961. *Helen in Egypt*. New York: New Directions.

———. 1972. *Hermetic Definition*. New York: New Directions.

———. 1974. *Tribute to Freud*. New York: New Directions.

———. 1979. *End to Torment: A Memoir of Ezra Pound*. New York: New Directions.

———. 1983. *Collected Poems 1912–1944*. Ed. Louis L. Martz. New York: New Directions.

———. 1992. *Paint It Today*. Ed. Cassandra Laity. New York: New York Univ. Press.

———. 1998. *The Gift*. Ed. Jane Augustine. Gainesville: Univ. Press of Florida.

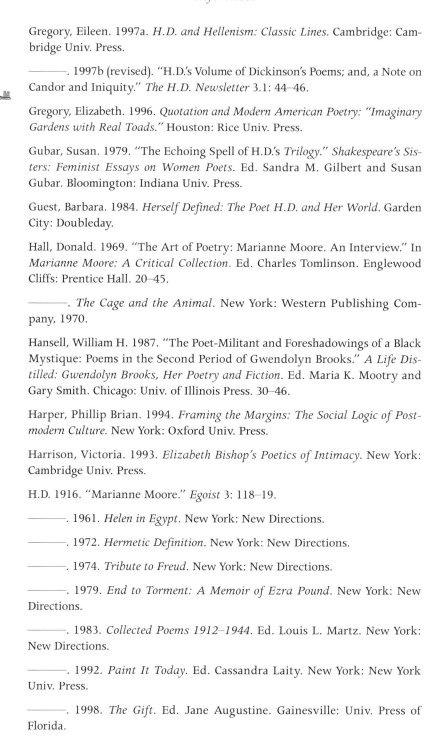

Heuving, Jeanne. 1992. *Omissions Are Not Accidents: Gender in the Art of Marianne Moore*. Detroit: Wayne State Univ. Press.

Hogue, Cynthia. 1995. *Scheming Women: Poetry, Privilege, and the Politics of Subjectivity*. Albany: State Univ. of New York Press.

————. 1998. "'The Plucked String': Emily Dickinson, Marianne Moore and the Poetics of Select Defects." *The Emily Dickinson Journal* 7.1: 89–109.

Hollander, John. 1990. "Observations on Moore's Syllabic Schemes." *Marianne Moore: The Art of a Modernist*. Ed. Joseph Parisi. Ann Arbor: UMI Research Press. 83–104.

Hollenberg, Donna Krolik. 1991. *H.D.: The Poetics of Childbirth and Creativity*. Boston: Northeastern Univ. Press.

————. 1997. *Between History and Poetry: The Letters of H.D. and Norman Holmes Pearson*. Iowa City: Univ. of Iowa Press.

Holley, Margaret. 1987. *The Poetry of Marianne Moore: A Study in Voice and Value*. Cambridge: Harvard Univ. Press.

Homans, Margaret. 1980. *Women Writers and Poetic Identity: Dorothy Wordsworth, Emily Bronte, and Emily Dickinson*. Princeton: Princeton Univ. Press.

Horvath, Brooke Kenton. 1996. "The Satisfactions of What's Difficult in Gwendolyn Brooks's Poetry." *On Gwendolyn Brooks: Reliant Contemplation*. Ed. Stephen Caldwell Wright. Ann Arbor: Univ. of Michigan Press. 213–22.

Hošek, Chaviva, and Patricia Parker, eds. 1985. *Lyric Poetry: Beyond New Criticism*. Ithaca, N.Y.: Cornell Univ. Press.

Howe, Susan. 1985. *My Emily Dickinson*. Berkeley: North Atlantic Books.

Ingersoll, Earl G., Judith Kitchen, and Stan Sanvel Rubin, eds. 1989. *The Post-Confessionals: Conversations with American Poets of the Eighties*. Rutherford, N.J.: Fairleigh Dickinson Univ. Press.

Jarrell, Randall. 1969. "Her Shield." *Marianne Moore: A Critical Collection*. Ed. Charles Tomlinson. Englewood Cliffs: Prentice Hall. 114–24.

Johnson, Barbara. 1987. "Apostrophe, Animation, Abortion." *A World of Difference*. Baltimore: Johns Hopkins Univ. Press. 184–222.

Johnson, Thomas H., ed. 1955. *The Poems of Emily Dickinson*. 3 vol. Cambridge: Belknap.

————, ed. 1958. *The Letters of Emily Dickinson*. 3 vol. Cambridge: Harvard Univ. Press.

Jones, A. R. 1965. "Imagism: A Unity of Gesture." *American Poetry*. Ed. Irvin Ehrenpreis. New York: St. Martin's. 115–63.

Jones, Gayl. 1987. "Community and Voice: Gwendolyn Brooks's 'In the Mecca.'" *A Life Distilled: Gwendolyn Brooks, Her Poetry and Fiction.* Ed. Maria K. Mootry and Gary Smith. Chicago: Univ. of Illinois Press. 193–204.

Joyce, Elisabeth W. 1998. *Cultural Critique and Abstraction: Marianne Moore and the Avant-Garde.* Lewisburg, Pa.: Bucknell Univ. Press.

Juhasz, Suzanne. 1978. *Naked and Fiery Forms: Modern American Poetry by Women, a New Tradition.* New York: Octagon.

———. 1983. *The Undiscovered Continent: Emily Dickinson and the Space of Mind.* Bloomington: Indiana Univ. Press.

Juhasz, Suzanne, Cristanne Miller, and Martha Nell Smith. 1993. *Comic Power in Emily Dickinson.* Austin: Univ. of Texas Press.

Kalstone, David. 1989. *Becoming a Poet: Elizabeth Bishop with Marianne Moore and Robert Lowell.* New York: Farrar Strauss Giroux.

Kammer, Jeanne. 1979. "The Art of Silence and the Forms of Women's Poetry." *Shakespeare's Sisters: Feminist Essays on Women Poets.* Ed. Sandra M. Gilbert and Susan Gubar. Bloomington: Indiana Univ. Press.

Kauffmann, Michael. 1997. "Gendering Modernism: H.D., Imagism, and Masculinist Aesthetics." *Unmanning Modernism: Gendered Re-Readings.* Ed. Elizabeth Jane Harrison and Shirley Peterson. Knoxville: Univ. of Tennessee Press.

Keller, Karl. 1979. *The Only Kangaroo among the Beauty: Emily Dickinson and America.* Baltimore: Johns Hopkins Univ. Press.

Keller, Lynn. 1983. "Words Worth a Thousand Postcards: The Bishop/Moore Correspondence." *American Literature.* 55:3: 405–29.

———. 1987. *Re-making it New: Contemporary American Poetry and the Modernist Tradition.* New York: Cambridge Univ. Press.

———. 1997. *Forms of Expansion: Recent Long Poems by Women.* Chicago: Univ. of Chicago Press.

Keller, Lynn, and Cristanne Miller. 1984. "Emily Dickinson, Elizabeth Bishop, and the Rewards of Indirection." *New England Quarterly* 57.4: 533–53.

———, ed. 1994. *Feminist Measures: Soundings in Poetry and Theory.* Ann Arbor: Univ. of Michigan Press.

Kenner, Hugh. 1971. *The Pound Era.* Berkeley: Univ. of California Press.

———. 1975. *A Homemade World: The American Modernist Writers.* New York: William Morrow and Company.

Kent, George E. 1987. "Aesthetic Values in the Poetry of Gwendolyn Brooks." *A Life Distilled: Gwendolyn Brooks, Her Poetry and Fiction.* Ed. Maria K. Mootry and Gary Smith. Chicago: Univ. of Illinois Press. 30–46.

———. 1990. *A Life of Gwendolyn Brooks.* Lexington: Univ. Press of Kentucky.

Kinnahan, Linda. 1996. "Experimental Poetics and the Lyric in British Women's Poetry: Geraldine Monk, Wendy Mulford, and Denise Riley." *Contemporary Literature* 37.4: 620–70.

Kloepfer, Deborah Kelly. 1989. *The Unspeakable Mother: Forbidden Discourse in Jean Rhys and H.D.* Ithaca, N.Y.: Cornell Univ. Press.

Kristeva, Julia. 1986. *The Kristeva Reader.* Ed. Toril Moi. New York: Columbia Univ. Press.

Laity, Cassandra. 1990. "H.D.'s Romantic Landscapes: The Sexual Politics of the Garden." *Signets: Reading H.D.* Ed. Susan Stanford Friedman and Rachel Blau DuPlessis. Madison: Univ. of Wisconsin Press. 110–28.

———. 1996. *H.D. and the Victorian Fin de Siècle: Gender, Modernism, Decadence.* Cambridge: Cambridge Univ. Press.

Leavell, Linda. 1995. *Marianne Moore and the Visual Arts: Prismatic Color.* Baton Rouge: Louisiana State Univ. Press.

Lee, Don L. 1996. "Gwendolyn Brooks: Beyond the Wordmaker—The Making of an African Poet." *On Gwendolyn Brooks: Reliant Contemplation.* Ed. Stephen Caldwell Wright. Ann Arbor: Univ. of Michigan Press. 81–96.

Leyda, Jay. 1960. *The Years and Hours of Emily Dickinson.* 2 vol. New Haven: Yale Univ. Press.

Lindberg, Kathryne V. 1996. "Whose Canon? Gwendolyn Brooks: Founder at the 'Margins.'" *Gendered Modernisms: American Women Poets and Their Readers.* Ed. Margaret Dickie and Thomas Travisano. Philadelphia: Univ. of Pennsylvania Press. 283–311.

Lindberg-Seyersted, Brita. 1968. *The Voice of the Poet: Aspects of Style in the Poetry of Emily Dickinson.* Cambridge: Harvard Univ. Press.

Loeffelholz, Mary. 1991. *Dickinson and the Boundaries of Feminist Theory.* Urbana: Univ. of Illinois Press.

Lombardi, Marilyn May. 1995. *The Body and the Song: Elizabeth Bishop's Poetics.* Carbondale: Southern Illinois Univ. Press.

Lowell, Amy. 1984. "Emily Dickinson." *Critical Essays on Emily Dickinson.* Ed. Paul J. Ferlazzo. Boston: G. K. Hall.

Mandel, Charlotte. 1983. "The Redirected Image: Cinematic Dynamics in the Style of H.D." *Literature/Film Quarterly* 11: 36–45.

Martin, Taffy. 1986. *Marianne Moore: Subversive Modernist*. Austin: Univ. of Texas Press.

McCabe, Susan. 1994. *Elizabeth Bishop: Her Poetics of Loss*. University Park: Pennsylvania State Univ. Press.

McNeil, Helen. 1986. *Emily Dickinson*. London and New York: Virago-Pantheon.

Melham, D. H. 1987. *Gwendolyn Brooks: Poetry and the Poetic Voice*. Lexington: Univ. Press of Kentucky.

Merrin, Jeredith. 1990. *An Enabling Humility: Marianne Moore, Elizabeth Bishop, and the Uses of Tradition*. New Brunswick: Rutgers Univ. Press.

———. 1993. "Elizabeth Bishop: Gaiety, Gayness, and Change." *Elizabeth Bishop: The Geography of Gender*. Ed. Marilyn May Lombardi. Charlottesville: Univ. Press of Virginia. 153–72.

Meyer, Kinereth. 1989. "Speaking and Writing the Lyric 'I.'" *Genre* 22: 129–49.

Miller, Cristanne. 1987. *Emily Dickinson: A Poet's Grammar*. Cambridge: Harvard Univ. Press.

———. 1995. *Marianne Moore: Questions of Authority*. Cambridge: Harvard Univ. Press.

Miller, R. Baxter. 1996. "'Define . . . the Whirlwind': Gwendolyn Brooks's Epic Sign for a Generation." *On Gwendolyn Brooks: Reliant Contemplation*. Ed. Stephen Caldwell Wright. Ann Arbor: Univ. of Michigan Press. 81–96.

Miller, Ruth. 1968. *The Poetry of Emily Dickinson*. Middletown, Conn.: Wesleyan Univ. Press.

Millier, Brett C. 1993. *Elizabeth Bishop: Life and the Memory of It*. Berkeley: Univ. of California Press.

Mitchell, W. J. T. 1989. "Space, Ideology, and Literary Representation." *Poetics Today* 10: 91–102.

Molesworth, Charles. 1990. *Marianne Moore: A Literary Life*. New York: Atheneum.

Montefiore, Jan. 1987. *Feminism and Poetry: Language, Experience, Identity in Women's Writing*. New York: Pandora.

Moore, Marianne. 1935. *The Selected Poems of Marianne Moore*. New York: Macmillan.

———. 1967. *The Complete Poems of Marianne Moore.* New York: Macmillan.

———. 1986. *The Complete Prose of Marianne Moore.* Ed. Patricia C. Willis. New York: Viking.

———. 1997. *The Selected Letters of Marianne Moore.* Ed. Bonnie Costello. New York: Knopf.

———. Marianne Moore Collection. Papers. Rosenbach Museum and Library, Philadelphia.

Mootry, Maria K. 1987. "'Down the Whirlwind of Good Rage': An Introduction to Gwendolyn Brooks." *A Life Distilled: Gwendolyn Brooks, Her Poetry and Fiction.* Ed. Mootry and Gary Smith. Chicago: Univ. of Illinois Press. 1–20.

———. 2000. "'The Step of Iron Feet': Creative Practice in the War Sonnets of Melvin B. Tolson and Gwendolyn Brooks." *Reading Race in American Poetry: "An Area of Act."* Ed. Aldon Lynn Nielsen. Chicago: Univ. of Illinois Press. 133–47.

Morris, Adalaide. 1990a. "A Relay of Power and of Peace: H.D. and the Spirit of the Gift." *Signets: Reading H.D..* Ed. Susan Stanford Friedman and Rachel Blau DuPlessis. Madison: Univ. of Wisconsin Press. 52–82.

———. 1990b. "The Concept of Projection: H.D.'s Visionary Powers." *Signets: Reading H.D..* Ed. Susan Stanford Friedman and Rachel Blau DuPlessis. Madison: Univ. of Wisconsin Press. 273–96.

Mossberg, Barbara Antonina Clarke. 1982. *Emily Dickinson: When a Writer Is a Daughter.* Bloomington: Indiana Univ. Press.

Mudge, Jean McClure. 1975. *Emily Dickinson and the Image of Home.* Amherst: Univ. of Massachusetts Press.

Mullaney, Janet Palmer. 1988. "Rita Dove." *Truthtellers of the Times: Interviews with Contemporary Women Poets.* Ann Arbor: Univ. of Michigan Press.

Mullen, Bill. 1999. *Popular Fronts: Chicago and African-American Cultural Politics, 1935–46.* Urbana: Univ. of Illinois Press.

Oberhaus, Dorothy Huff. 1995. *Emily Dickinson's Fascicles: Method and Meaning.* University Park: Pennsylvania State Univ. Press.

Ostriker, Alicia. 1986a. *Stealing the Language: The Emergence of Women's Poetry in America.* Boston: Beacon Press.

———. 1986b. "What Do Women (Poets) Want? H.D. and Marianne Moore as Poetic Ancestresses." *Contemporary Literature* 27: 475–92.

———. 1990a. "Marianne Moore, The Maternal Hero, and American Women's Poetry." In *Marianne Moore: The Art of a Modernist.* Ed. Joseph Parisi. Ann Arbor: UMI Research Press. 49–66.

————. 1990b. "No Rule of Procedure: The Open Poetics of H.D." *Signets: Reading H.D.*. Ed. Susan Stanford Friedman and Rachel Blau DuPlessis. Madison: Univ. of Wisconsin Press. 336–51.

Parisi, Joseph, ed. 1990. *Marianne Moore: The Art of a Modernist*. Ann Arbor: UMI Research Press.

Patmore, Coventry. 1900. *Poems*. London: George Bell and Son. Vol. 1.

Pereira, Malin. 1999. "An Interview with Rita Dove." *Contemporary Literature* 40.2: 183–213.

Perloff, Marjorie G. 1985. *The Dance of the Intellect: Studies in the Poetry of the Pound Tradition*. Cambridge: Cambridge Univ. Press.

Petrino, Elizabeth. 1998. *Emily Dickinson and Her Contemporaries: Women's Verse in America, 1820–1885*. Hanover, N.H.: Univ. Press of New England.

Poe, Edgar Allan. 1981. "The Philosophy of Composition." *The Complete Poems and Stories of Edgar Allan Poe, with Selections from His Critical Writings*. Ed. A. H. Quinn. New York: Knopf.

Pollak, Vivian R. 1984. *Dickinson: The Anxieties of Gender*. Ithaca: Cornell Univ. Press.

Pondrom, Cyrena N. 1990a. "Marianne Moore and H.D.: Female Community and Poetic Achievement." *Marianne Moore: Woman and Poet*. Ed. Patricia C. Willis. Orono, Maine: National Poetry Foundation. 371–402.

————. 1990b. "H.D. and the Origins of Imagism." *Signets: Reading H.D*. Ed. Susan Stanford Friedman and Rachel Blau DuPlessis. Madison: Univ. of Wisconsin Press. 85–109.

Porter, David T. 1981. *Dickinson: The Modern Idiom*. Cambridge: Harvard Univ. Press.

Pound, Ezra. 1954. *Literary Essays of Ezra Pound*. Norfolk, Conn.: New Directions.

Rampersad, Arnold. 1986. "The Poems of Rita Dove." *Callaloo* 9: 52–60.

Ranta, Jerrald. 1988. "Marianne Moore's Sea and the Sentence." *Essays in Literature* 15.2: 245–57.

Redding, J. Saunders. 1996. "Cellini-Like Lyrics." *On Gwendolyn Brooks: Reliant Contemplation*. Ed. Stephen Caldwell Wright. Ann Arbor: Univ. of Michigan Press. 6–7.

Rich, Adrienne. 1986. *Blood, Bread, and Poetry: Selected Prose 1979–1985*. New York: Norton.

Rubin, Stan Sanvel, and Judith Kitchen. 1989. "'The Underside of the Story': A Conversation with Rita Dove." *The Post-Confessionals: Conversations with*

American Poets of the Eighties. Ed. Earl G. Ingersoll, Kitchen, and Rubin. Rutherford, N.J.: Fairleigh Dickinson Univ. Press. 151–66.

Sanchez-Eppler, Karen. 1993. *Touching Liberty: Abolition, Feminism, and the Politics of the Body*. Berkeley: Univ. of California Press.

St. Armand, Barton Levi. 1984. *Emily Dickinson and Her Culture: The Soul's Society*. Cambridge: Cambridge Univ. Press.

Schaffner, Perdita. 1990. "A Sketch of H.D.: The Egyptian Cat." *Signets: Reading H.D.* Ed. Susan Stanford Friedman and Rachel Blau DuPlessis. Madison: Univ. of Wisconsin Press. 3–6.

Schulman, Grace. 1986. *Marianne Moore: The Poetry of Engagement*. Chicago: Univ. of Illinois Press.

Schulze, Robin G. 1995. *The Web of Friendship: Marianne Moore and Wallace Stevens*. Ann Arbor: Univ. of Michigan Press.

Schweik, Susan. 1991. *A Gulf So Deeply Cut: American Women Poets and the Second World War*. Madison: Univ. of Wisconsin Press.

Sedgwick, Eve Kosofsky. 1990. *Epistemology of the Closet*. Berkeley: Univ. of California Press.

Shetley, Vernon. 1993. *After the Death of Poetry: Poet and Audience in Contemporary America*. Durham: Duke Univ. Press.

Shigley, Sally Bishop. 1997. *"Dazzling Dialectics": Elizabeth Bishop's Resonating Feminist Reality*. New York: Peter Lang.

Shoptaw, John. 1994. *On the Outside Looking Out: John Ashbery's Poetry*. Cambridge: Harvard Univ. Press.

Showalter, Elaine. 1977. *A Literature of Their Own: British Women Novelists from Bronte to Lessing*. Princeton: Princeton Univ. Press.

Shurr, William H. 1983. *The Marriage of Emily Dickinson: A Study of the Fascicles*. Lexington: Univ. Press of Kentucky.

Sielke, Sabine. 1997. *Fashioning the Female Subject: The Intertextual Networking of Dickinson, Moore, and Rich*. Ann Arbor: Univ. of Michigan Press.

Slatin, John. 1986. *The Savage's Romance: The Poetry of Marianne Moore*. University Park: Pennsylvania State Univ. Press.

Small, Judy Jo. 1990. *Positive as Sound: Emily Dickinson's Rhyme*. Athens: Univ. of Georgia Press.

Smith, Barbara Herrnstein. 1968. *Poetic Closure: A Study of How Poems End*. Chicago: Univ. of Chicago Press.

———. 1978. *On the Margins of Discourse*. Chicago: Univ. of Chicago Press.

Smith, Gary. 1987. "Gwendolyn Brooks's 'Children of the Poor,' Metaphysical Poetry and the Inconditions of Love." *A Life Distilled: Gwendolyn Brooks, Her Poetry and Fiction*. Ed. Maria K. Mootry and Gary Smith. Chicago: Univ. of Illinois Press. 165–76.

Smith, Martha Nell. 1992. *Rowing in Eden: Rereading Emily Dickinson*. Austin: Univ. of Texas Press.

Spain, Daphne. 1992. *Gendered Spaces*. Chapel Hill: Univ. of North Carolina Press.

Stapleton, Laurence. 1978. *Marianne Moore: The Poet's Advance*. Princeton: Princeton Univ. Press.

Steffen, Therese. 2001. *Crossing Color: Transcultural Space and Place in Rita Dove's Poetry, Fiction, and Drama*. New York: Oxford Univ. Press.

Stevenson, Anne. 1996. *Elizabeth Bishop*. New York: Twayne.

Taleb-Khyar, Mohamed B. 1991. "An Interview with Maryse Conde and Rita Dove." *Callaloo* 14.2: 347–66.

Tate, Claudia. 1987. "Anger So Flat: Gwendolyn Brooks's *Annie Allen*." *A Life Distilled: Gwendolyn Brooks, Her Poetry and Fiction*. Ed. Maria K. Mootry and Gary Smith. Urbana: Univ. of Illinois Press. 140–50.

Taylor, Henry. 1996. "Gwendolyn Brooks: An Essential Sanity." *On Gwendolyn Brooks: Reliant Contemplation*. Ed. Stephen Caldwell Wright. Ann Arbor: Univ. of Michigan Press. 254–75.

Tomlinson, Charles, ed. 1969. *Marianne Moore: A Collection of Critical Essays*. Englewood Cliffs: Prentice-Hall.

Travisano, Thomas J. 1988. *Elizabeth Bishop: Her Artistic Development*. Charlottesville: Univ. of Virginia Press.

———. 1999. *Midcentury Quartet: Bishop, Lowell, Jarrell, Berryman and the Making of a Postmodern Aesthetic*. Charlottesville: Univ. Press of Virginia.

Van Dyne, Susan R. 1999. "Siting the Poet: Rita Dove's Refiguring of Traditions." *Women Poets of the Americas: Toward a Pan-American Gathering*. Ed. Jacqueline Vaught Brogan and Cordelia Chávez Candelaria. Notre Dame, Indiana: Univ. of Notre Dame Press. 68–87.

Vendler, Helen. 1980. *Part of Nature, Part of Us: Modern American Poets*. Cambridge: Harvard Univ. Press.

———. 1990. "An Interview with Rita Dove." *Reading Black, Reading Feminist*. Ed. Henry Louis Gates, Jr. New York: Meridian.

———. 1995. "Rita Dove: Identity Markers." *The Given and the Made: Strategies of Poetic Redefinition*. Cambridge: Harvard Univ. Press. 59–88.

Walker, Cheryl. 1982. *The Nightingale's Burden: Women Poets and American Culture before 1900*. Bloomington: Indiana Univ. Press.

Wallace, Patricia. 1993. "Divided Loyalties: Literal and Literary in the Poetry of Lorna Dee Cervantes, Cathy Song and Rita Dove." *Melus* 18.3: 3–19.

Walsh, William. 1994. "Isn't Reality Magic? An Interview with Rita Dove." *The Kenyon Review* 16.3: 142–52.

Ward, Scott. 1995. "No Vers Is Libre." *Shenandoah* 45.3: 107–19.

Wardrop, Daneen. 1996. *Emily Dickinson's Gothic: Goblin with a Gauge*. Iowa City: Univ. of Iowa Press.

Weisbuch, Robert. 1975. *Emily Dickinson's Poetry*. Chicago: Univ. of Chicago Press.

Wheeler, Lesley. 1996a. "Attitudes of Mothering: A Review of Rita Dove's *Mother Love*." *Critical Matrix* 10.1–2: 106–12.

———. 1996b. "Rita Dove." *American Writers: Supplement IV, Part 1*. Ed. A. Walton Litz and Molly Weigel. New York: Charles Scribner's Sons. 241–58.

Williams, Gladys. 1987. "The Ballads of Gwendolyn Brooks." *A Life Distilled: Gwendolyn Brooks, Her Poetry and Fiction*. Ed. Maria K. Mootry and Gary Smith. Chicago: Univ. of Illinois Press. 205–23.

Williams, Kenny J. 1987. "The World of Satin-Legs, Mrs. Sallie, and the Blackstone Rangers: The Restricted Chicago of Gwendolyn Brooks." *A Life Distilled: Gwendolyn Brooks, Her Poetry and Fiction*. Ed. Maria K. Mootry and Gary Smith. Chicago: Univ. of Illinois Press. 47–70.

Williams, Sherley A. 1979. "The Blues Roots of Contemporary Afro-American Poetry." *Chant of Saints: A Gathering of Afro-American Literature, Art and Scholarship*. Ed. Michael S. Harper and Robert B. Stepto. Chicago: Univ. of Illinois Press.

Willis, Patricia C., ed. 1990. *Marianne Moore: Woman and Poet*. Orono, Maine: National Poetry Foundation.

Wolff, Cynthia Griffin. 1986. *Emily Dickinson*. New York: Knopf.

Woloch, Nancy. 1984. *Women and the American Experience*. New York: Knopf.

Wolosky, Shira. 1984. *Emily Dickinson: A Voice of War*. New Haven: Yale Univ. Press.

Zilboorg, Caroline, ed. 1992. *Richard Aldington and H.D.: The Early Years in Letters*. Bloomington: Indiana Univ. Press.

Index

This book was designed and typeset on a PC computer system using QuarkXpress software. The text is set in Apollo, and display type is set in Bauer Bodoni. This book was designed and typeset by Bill Adams and manufactured by Thomson-Shore, Inc.